Us be goin' to Barnstaple Fair!

Maureen E Wood

GU00587131

First published 2001 by
Edward Gaskell *publishers*
6 Grenville Street
Bideford
Devon
EX39 2EA

© Barnstaple Town Council

isbn 1-898546-50-9

Us be goin' to Barnstaple Fair

Maureen E Wood

Printed and bound by
Lazarus Press
Unit 7 Caddsdown Business Park
Bideford
Devon
EX39 3DX

This book is dedicated to my grandchildren
Natasha, Aimée, Leanne, Samuel and Nathan.

And also

To the memory of my beloved mother
Florence Annie (Anne) Woods
1914-2001

Acknowledgements

My Grateful Thanks to All...

Joanna Andrews – Barnstaple Heritage Centre
Mike Taylor – Barnstaple Town Clerk (1984-2001)
Andy Cooper – The North Devon Journal
Les Franklin – Barnstaple Athenaeum
The Staff of Barnstaple Local Studies and Records Office
Alison Mills & Robin Davey – Museum of North Devon
Liz Taynton – Beaford Archive
William (Bill) Forward – Mayor 1987, 1988, 1997
Heather Clay – Showmen's Guild of Great Britain (Western Sector)
Mary Bellamy – for her kindness regarding her father W.J. Nott's fair information
Mrs L Roberts – for her kind help with carnival information
Malcolm Taylor – Librarian,'The English Folk Dance and Song Society'
Peter Christie – Local Historian
Martin Burridge – Barnstaple Fair Enthusiast

Picture Sources:

W.J. Nott Collection: 14, 18, 20, 22, 45, 48, 51, 52, 57, 58, 59, 60, 71, 72, 73, 77, 78, 79, 80, 81, 82, 83, 84, 85, 86

North Devon Athenaeum Collection: 5, 15, 17, 19, 26, 27, 28, 33, 34, 37, 39, 40, 42, 53, 61, 62, 66

Museum of Barnstaple & North Devon Collection: 1,7,12,25,29,41,42,62,66

L. Roberts Collection: 88,89,90,91,92,93,94,98

Barnstaple Town Council Collection: 2,4,6,7,8,9,11,25

S. Woods: 3,29,35,36,55,56

Dave Fry Collection: 23,67,68,69,74,74A,75

Tom Bartlett Postcard Collection: 16,24,30,50,54

Beaford Archive: 32,47,49,87

Martin Burridge Collection: 63,64,65,76

North Devon Journal: 95,96,97

Knights Collection: 38,43,44

L. French Collection: 13,31

M. Wood Collection: 70

Medina Gallery Collection: 46

R.W. Forward Collection: 21

M. Bellamy Collection: 99

Bob Scarboro: 10

Please Note:

*Museum of Barnstaple & North Devon pictures are part of the North Devon On Disk project, collecting a visual record of North Devon's past.

*Copyright Reserved (C.R.) is found next to pictures for which the photographer and/or copyright holder is either uncertain or unknown. Every effort has been made to ensure the proper credits are duly assigned to every image used. This has been done to the very best of our knowledge at the time of production.

Line Drawings   Watercolours
Claire Blick   W.J. Nott

Cover picture: W.J. Nott's watercolour, 1967 View of Fair

Foreword

Maureen Wood is to be congratulated on the extensive research she has put into producing this book. It is a book that needed to be written, addressing, as it does, the major Civic event in Barnstaple – the Fair Proclamation Ceremony – and the annual visit of the September Fair to the town.

This book helps to remind us in today's environment of constant change, that Barnstaple has one major tradition which has survived over many years. It also shows that Barnstaple Fair has evolved over the years to keep pace with the changing circumstances in the town. The Fair remains an event anticipated with pleasure by young and old. Long may it continue.

M C Taylor
Town Clerk 1984-2001

Preface

I do not profess to be an historian – I can only describe myself as someone who takes an avid interest in the history of the town of Barnstaple, which includes the ancient customs, the townspeople (both famous and infamous) and the "goin's on" associated with it down through the centuries. Barnstaple Great Fair is a subject dear to my heart, and now after many long months of research I feel I have attained at least a modicum of historical knowledge from the project.

I have tried to be correct in all aspects regarding the content of this book, therefore I apologise in advance to my learned superiors for any mistakes I may have made. As with any research, information is only as good as the original source or informant – even I with my basic knowledge discovered errors along the way!

Please note that the dates given for the mayor in office at the time of the fair for that year are not necessarily those at the time of their election.

Some of the book's text is a faithful reproduction of the original charters, records and newspaper reports. It is indicated as such by quotation marks or italics... All 'old' spellings of person and place names, and parlance of the day, have been published as written to preserve the historical 'feel' of the time. Any *Journal* newspaper accounts used have been reproduced by the courtesy of the *North Devon Journal*.

For me, the research and writing journey of *Us be goin' to Barnstaple Fair!* has, at times, been an arduous one. But it has been a voyage in time that I would not have missed, or exchanged for any reason, my ticket to 'the fair'.

Maureen E. Wood.

Contents

Courtesy of Museum of Barnstaple & North Devon
Barnstaple Fair 1876

Barnstaple Fair 1909

Origins & Charters

The word 'Fair' originates from the Latin word 'Feria.' This was a feast to celebrate a saint's day or religious festival and an ideal time to hold a fair, for it was then that most people were free from work to attend. The Fairs were basically huge markets. Merchants travelled great distances to sell their products at these annual events, which lasted for a few days. It was a time when the public could purchase commodities that they were unable to buy in their locality.

People thronged in vast numbers to the Fairs and expected to be entertained with all the fun and fascination that the fair folks could muster — performing animals, acrobats, wrestling, freaks of nature etc. Gradually the entertainment side took over the fairgrounds and by the end of the nineteenth century, buying and selling had almost stopped. Only a few old-style fairs had survived into the early twentieth century, mainly in rural areas such as Barnstaple where annual cattle, sheep and horse fairs continued. These have now been replaced by regular auctions in local livestock markets.

According to English law, all towns had to get the King's permission to hold markets or fairs. But in 1086 William the Conqueror found that only fifty towns had actually done so. He demanded that a charter must be obtained before markets and fairs could be held. The charter strictly stated where and when these could take place, and laid down who could collect tolls, who could check weights, and who was to enforce the law and punish criminals.

Charters were usually granted to churches or influential local people enabling them to profit from organising the markets and fairs. Money was collected by them, from all those who traded at these events. Fairs were especially profitable — they were usually timed to coincide with an important saint's feast day.

After listing these few basic facts, it is now time to link in with our own Barnstaple Great Fair...

The origins of Barnstaple Great Fair lies within the haze of antiquity, but is often quoted as "most probably as old as the town itself." It has been argued that it may reasonably be assumed that King Athelstan granted Barnstaple it's first charter in 930 A.D. (chartered fairs were a well known institution long before 900 A.D.) and as our many learned members of the Borough Authorities of yore have averred — "Tradition must be accepted as fact until disproved."

The following document dated 1154 (the year of the accession of Henry II) is in the possession of the North Devon Athenaeum, and shows the great antiquity of Barnstaple Fair. It is emphasised by the fact that the grant of ten shillings made to the monks of the abbey of the Holy Saviour was to be paid at the annual September Fair of Barnstaple.

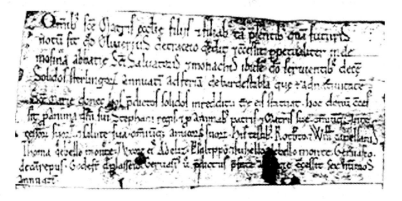

Translation: 'To all the sons and daughters of the Holy Mother Church both present and future, be it known that Oliver de Traceio has given and granted in perpetuity in alms to the Abbey of the Holy Saviour and the monks serving God in that place ten shillings sterling annually at the fair of Bardestabla which is held at the Nativity of the Holy Mary as long as those said shillings belong to him for rent of land. This gift he concedes for the soul of his lord King Stephen and for the souls of his father his mother and all of his ancestors and for the well being of all his friends. Witness ... Robert and William chaplains: Thomas de Bellomonte and his wife Adeliza: Philip and Juel de Bellomonte: Gervase de Camprepus: Godefrey de Plasseio. Gervase also grants the said Abbey sixpence annually.'

According to Thomas Wainwright and his studies of the 'Barnstaple Records' original documents, an inquisition taken at Barnstaple quoted the charter granted in the reign of King Edward the third, the privilege of the Fair as being confirmed and renewed. It states that *"they, their heirs and successors, burgesses of the borough aforesaid, may have one Fair in the borough aforesaid every year, for four days to last — that is to say, on the eve and on the day of the blessed Mary Magdelene, and for two days next following."* The inquisition also mentions the burgesses as saying that *"they enjoy liberties by the charter of the Lord Athelstan, of famous memory, once King of England, and that they choose from amongst themselves, a Mayor."*

In a duplicate copy of the original charter under the great seal dated March 23rd 1444 King Henry VI states: *"We have seen an inspeximus and confirmation of charter of second year of King John,(1200) granting the burgesses of Barnstaple... and to have the customs of London as by the charter of Henry II."*

The grant was endorsed in subsequent charters — Phillip and Mary's (1556) and James I's (1610)

1595. Paid the town clerk for writeing a copie of the new charter and other work, 38s. 8d.

It would appear from these early records that Barum's fair commenced anciently on the 9th of July, the feast of the Nativity of the Blessed Virgin - St. Mary Magdelene. But on the granting of Queen Mary's charter it was changed to September the 8th, and so too it seems, the observance of the nativity of St. Mary itself? It is unclear to me as a mere amateur why this should be. Suffice to say that the very task of trying to un-ravel the intricacies, changes and references to the various charters and such-like, has been for me, a journey into the outer reaches of insanity! However, with 'Gribble' nudging at my elbow, I can only quote his theory — "It was probably done on the granting of Queen Mary's charter, September being considered perhaps a more convenient time than July."

The description of "The ancient privileges belonging to Saint Mary Magdalen's fair at Barum" are of an ancient date, and are as follows:

"1st. It shall continue for four days, viz on the eve and the day of the blessed Mary Magdalen and the two next days following.

2nd. The whole soil of Boutport Street, and the other streets within the said Borough, belongs to the Mayor and Comonaltie of the said Borough during the fair, and until 12 o'clock at noon on the day afterwards.

3rd. The said Mayor and Comonaltie may set and demise the said soil one day before the eve of the said fair, and have the whole profits of the said fair, and the Bailiffs of the said Borough shall collect and receive the same.

4th. Also that they shall there have the Cognizance of Pleas, and a Court of Pie Poudre*, as incident to all fairs."

From the date of September 8th it changed yet again to the date of September 19th. This was probably in the eighteenth century when in accordance with an act of Parliament in 1752, the calendar was revised and eleven days were dropped between the 2nd and 14th of September consequently bringing the 8th to the 19th.

If the 19th of September fell either on a Monday, Tuesday or Wednesday, the Fair continued until Saturday night, and when Thursday or Friday saw it's commencement, it ran on until the Friday of the next week; but only for the first two days (in either case) was its legitimate purpose observed, and the sale and purchase of staple commodities actively carried on.

With the new provisions made in the Barnstaple Market Act of 1852, the time for commencing the fair was better arranged and restriction of duration to three days only. The opening of the fair finally came to rest at the present date of the Wednesday preceding the 20th September, and lasts for four days rather than the three days of a few decades ago.

*The name of 'Court Pie Poudre' has more than one meaning and it is of interest to note the following:
(a) Fairs being held mainly in the summer, the suitors have dusty feet ...
(b) Or because justice is done so speedily, the dust cannot be wiped from the feet before the decision is given.
(c) According to Barrington (Ancient Statute 337) it is from Pied-Pouldreaux, — (a pedlar) — an ancient court, noticed in several of the statutes, held in fairs, for rendering justice to buyers and sellers, and the redress of grievances arising out of them.

1495 — Paid for broken silver for a mace, 6s. 3d.; for making the same, 2s. 8d.

1555 — Paid for two ounces and a quarter of silver to mend the Town Mace 15s.10d. and for mendying the same mace.

Traditions

Many references are made to Barnstaple Fair and the fair related traditions that were part of the annual scene. Although some of the information collected touches on a few centuries ago, in the main, I have decided to feature the nineteenth and twentieth centuries for the purposes of this book.

> 1588. *"The fair this year was kept on Monday the ix September, because there should be no buying and selling Sunday."* — Wyot.

In the early part of the nineteenth century whichever day the 19th of September fell upon (except if it should fall on a Sunday) that was the day the fair was proclaimed.

Traditionally this started with the first day allocated for the Cattle and Sheep Fair, the second for the Horse Fair and the permitted days following for the Pleasure Fair. Buying and selling of staple commodities would go on for the duration of the fair, purchases of walnuts from Somerset, fairing of gingerbread and highly delectable confectionery etc. were high on everyone's list. During this time, other events surrounded the occasion and became part of the customary celebrations. These usually started with the 'Fair Stag Hunt,' then attendance was the rule for the genteel 'Fair Ball' the following day. The traditional 'Hospitalities' of the tradesmen of the town would be sought after and the famous 'Barnstaple Fair Ale!' Ringing matches were arranged between Barnstaple bell-ringers and those of surrounding villages; the joyous pealing of the church bells could be heard all over the town and the fair. Wrestling matches took place, much to the disapproval of some of the 'higher classes!' The Horticultural Exhibitions such as the Barnstaple and North Devon Cottage Garden Society were well attended, and special entertainment at the Theatre and Music Hall was at its very best for Barnstaple Fair. Nothing seemed to be forgotten — In accordance with a custom of many years, the Sunday of Fair Week was given to a sermon in the Parish Church in aid of funds for the Blue Coat Schools. His Worship the Mayor and Corporation would be in attendance as an accustomed part of the ceremony.

Of all traditions concerning the fair, something must come first to start off the festivities. This then, is the Proclamation of the opening of Barnstaple Great Fair and the customs associated with it.

In the nineteenth century before the proclamation took place, it was accepted that the Mayor treated the Council and his friends to a few hospitalities in the Guildhall. It was the practice on the first morning of the fair, to assemble in the Council-chamber, which had been converted for the occasion into a banqueting hall. A plentiful supply of spiced ale, toast and cheese was provided of which the guests would be expected to partake freely.

Loyal and patriotic toasts were made — The reigning Monarch, The Town and Trade, Agriculture, and "Success to Barnstaple Fair" among them. (Much the same toasts are used today as are the hospitalities provided. The inclusion of 'fairing' at the familiar twentieth century ceremony, were introduced at a later date. In 1901 mention is made of "a pretty custom in recent years is to hand around a tempting plate of "Barum Fairing" to the ladies.") At the conclusion, the Mayor would invite the corporation, the constables, the mace-bearers etc., the chaplain, the chief magistrate and other gentlemen to accompany him to the High Cross, the South –gate, and the West-gate for the usual reading of the Proclamation performed by the Town Clerk. This however could only take place after the Town Clerk had read the initial proclamation inside the Guildhall, following the various toasts, and the subsequent ancient ritual of the showing of the white glove (the hand of welcome) suspended from the Guildhall window above the entrance.

The following description for the ceremony in the year of 1853 is reproduced here in part, by courtesy of the *North Devon Journal*.

"The Mayor (William Avery) commenced by calling the Council together at half-past eleven o'clock, in the Guildhall, to observe the immemorial custom of opening the Fair in due form, and tasting his "Fair Ale." Accordingly, at the appointed hour, the Mayor, Corporation, and a good many besides, presented themselves in the Council-room to partake of the loving cup. A "sea coal" fire blazed in the chimney, a large silver bowl, containing the spiced ale, stood in the middle of the long table, two pair of silver guilt goblets, with highly chased covers, the work of the tool of the graver, stood at the higher end, accompanied by a silver flagon and large dishes bore the toast, well soaked in the good "home-brewed." After the Town Clerk had called over the names of the Council, the Mayor said he believed they had no particular business to attend to, and the adjournment of the Council being moved, he proceeded to congratulate the Council and their friends on the Pleasing circumstances under which they were met, and drank their health in a hearty draught of the "spiced–ale." The cup went round, and the toast went round, Whig and Tory, Cleric and laic, town and country, drank together, and, for the nonce, appeared to forget the past elections, briberies, and commissions. That part of the ceremony being over,

The Mayor, preceded by the mace-bearers, and accompanied by the corporation and officers of the Council, moved in procession to the High-cross — to the bottom of the High-street, and thence to the Quay: at each place the Proclamation announcing the opening of the Fair was read by the Town Clerk. It exhorted all men to deal justly, to wear no weapon, and keep the peace, and not to lodge "any rogue, vagabond, or suspected person." The procession then returned to the Hall. The company having again refreshed themselves after their tour, and the Mayor thanking them for their attendance on this, his fourth Mayoralty every man went about his business. The ceremony altogether, carries the mind back to the days of Athelstan who made Barnstaple a borough, and to the times of Henry I. who gave it a corporation. The wassail bowl, the ladle, and the "goblets high" wear an air of venerable antiquity, the youngest of the cups bearing the date of 1620, the 17th of James I."

The following proclamation used in <u>1606</u> during the reign of King James, is shown in its entirety (Much of it was used in the nineteenth century but a much shorter version is used today.)

Proclamation For The Faire
(King James, 1606)

Mr Mayor of the Towne doth give you knowledge that there is a free fair within this Towne and Liberty of Barnestaple for all manner of persons to buy and sell within the same which ffair began yesterday att noone an doth continue three days following, during which tyme Mr Mayor chargeth and commandeth in the Kings Majesty's behalf, all manner of persons reparing to this Towne and ffair to keepe the Kings peace, And all buyers and sellers to deale Justly and Truly And to use true weights and measures; And Truly to pay their Toll and Custome and Stallage with all other Duties as they ought to doe, upon the paine that shall fall thereof; And all wool and yarne to be weighed att the Kings Beame appointed for the same, and Duly to pay for weighing thereof as hath been accustomed upon the paine Lymitted in that behalf, And that all victuallers bring to the ffaire good and wholesome victualls and doe sell the same att reasonable prices And that noe person forstall or regrate any Kinds of victualls , nor other thing coming or brought to this ffaire to be sold upon pain that shall fall thereof; And that noe stranger be out of their hosts houses goeing or wandering abroad in the streets, after nine of the clock in the night, upon paine of imprisonment, and to make fine with Mr Mayor for their Disobedience, And noe inhabitant of this Towne or parish do Lodge nor take into his or her house any begger or vagabond rogue or suspected person or any other person having a Contagious dissease or coming out of an Infectious place upon paine that shall fall thereof; And that noe man beare any Armes: or weapon in disturbance of the Kings peace; nor make any assault or affray, riot, rout or unlawful assembly; upon payne of loosing their Armour and Weapon, And to suffer other punishment for the same; And if any offence injury or wrong shall be committed or done by any person within the Towne ffaire and Liberty the same being duly approved shall be redressed according to justice and the Laws of the Realme.

God Save the King.

> 19th September 1850 - *The Mayor (John M Fisher) extended the fair up to "Monday night next."*
>
> 1854 — *On the present occasion, the "Municipal Authorities" had to take a longer walk than usual and proceed to the New Cattle Market,to proclaim the fair, which they did a little after twelve o'clock.*
>
> 1873 — *"The Mayor's (Thomas May) health was then drunk with a most hearty three or four times three, the town-crier acting as a splendid fugleman. In addition to the usual toasts of the Queen, Mayor, and Barnstaple Fair, a new toast had to be honoured, "Success to the Agriculturists of North Devon." In walking through the fair it had been seen a larger influx of the beautiful produce of North Devon, in the form of their choice breed of red cattle, than had been here for many years past."*

Towards the end of the nineteenth century, speeches at the fair opening ceremony get longer and much more interesting in their content, and we see that in the 1890s the 'General Public' have now become privileged into the "goings-on" inside the Guildhall as well as the outside.

And what of the ladies? They are first mentioned in 1876 as "sitting in the gallery," and in 1896 there was such a large attendance of ladies that apart from the gallery and side benches, accommodation had to be found for them in the main body of the hall. Later on in 1907 the Journal mentions that although not many years previous the bench and side galleries sufficed for their accommodation, they now fill half the hall too! By this time the females had established a firm hold within the proclamation proceedings. At the turn of the nineteenth century a toast to "The Ladies" was introduced, but it would seem to have been dropped after 1935 - ah well, it was nice while it lasted!

However, perhaps this is an excellent time to mention Barnstaple's first Lady Mayor - Councillor Mrs. E.M. Fern - who took office in 1976. For those who might be interested, the "Barnstaple Fair" toast that year was Proposed by Clive Gunnell, Esq., of Westward Television, and the Response by

The Right Honourable Jeremy Thorpe, Esq., P.C., Member of Parliament for the North Devon Constituency.

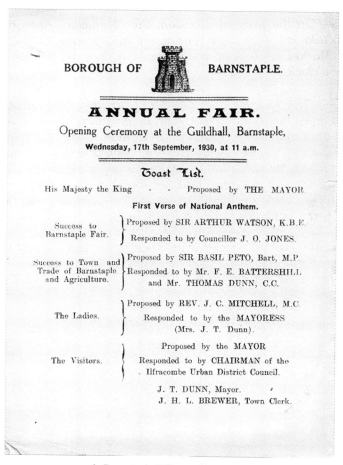

BOROUGH OF BARNSTAPLE.

ANNUAL FAIR.

Opening Ceremony at the Guildhall, Barnstaple,

Wednesday, 17th September, 1930, at 11 a.m.

Toast List.

His Majesty the King - - Proposed by THE MAYOR.

First Verse of National Anthem.

Success to Barnstaple Fair.
Proposed by SIR ARTHUR WATSON, K.B.E.
Responded to by Councillor J. O. JONES.

Success to Town and Trade of Barnstaple and Agriculture.
Proposed by SIR BASIL PETO, Bart, M.P.
Responded to by Mr. F. E. BATTERSHILL and Mr. THOMAS DUNN, C.C.

The Ladies.
Proposed by REV. J. C. MITCHELL, M.C.
Responded to by the MAYORESS (Mrs. J. T. Dunn).

The Visitors.
Proposed by the MAYOR
Responded to by CHAIRMAN of the . Ilfracombe Urban District Council.

J. T. DUNN, Mayor.
J. H. L. BREWER, Town Clerk.

1. Barnstaple Millenary Year (C.R.)

Noteworthy Snippets:

1930 — The year of Barnstaple's Millenary — J.T. Dunn, Mayor, and the Town Clerk, J.H.L. Brewer.

1932 — Bruce W. Oliver, architect and local historian, became Mayor. He was, together with Alderman Harry Ashton, instrumental in giving the public the story of Barnstaple's one thousand year record as a borough, for the millenary celebrations.

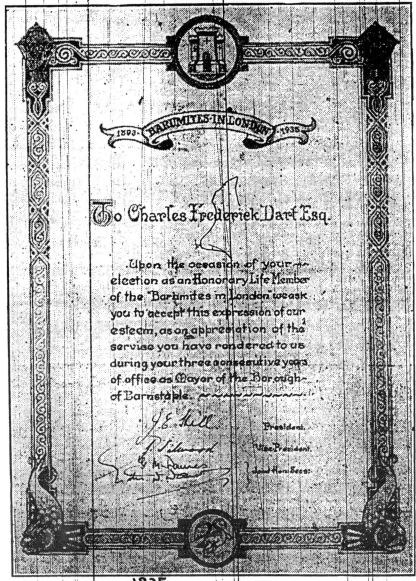

1893 · BARUMITES IN LONDON · 1935

To Charles Frederick Dart Esq.

Upon the occasion of your election as an Honorary Life Member of the "Barumites in London" we ask you to accept this expression of our esteem, as an appreciation of the service you have rendered to us during your three consecutive years of office as Mayor of the Borough of Barnstaple.

President.

Vice-President.

Joint Hon. Secs.

1935

Our photograph is of the handsome illuminated address presented at yesterday's Fair Opening ceremony at the Guildhall, Barnstaple, by the Barumites' in London, to the Mayor of Barnstaple. The text of the address explains the reason for this unprecedented gesture on the part of the "exiled" Barumites.— Photo: R. L. Knight.

<u>1935</u> — A representative of the "Barumites' in London" presented an illuminated address, to the Mayor of Barnstaple, Charles Dart, at the Fair Opening Ceremony.

The Fair Opening Ceremonies were kept up throughout the years of World War II. (The Pleasure Fair and Carnival were not.)

<u>1945</u> — During the Proclamation of the Fair ceremony, a presentation was made to His Worship the Mayor, Alderman C.F. Dart, J.P., C.C. and Alderman John Smale, J.P., C.A. with Freedom Scrolls and Silver Caskets, in admission of them being made Honorary Freemen of the Borough of Barnstaple.

<u>1946</u> - On Fair Wednesday, the freedom of the borough was conferred upon the Devonshire Regiment, and an impressive ceremony staged in the Market Hall. (A full report can be read in the 19th and 26th September 1946 issues of the North Devon Journal.)

<u>1949</u> — Patricia Hardman, was the first Carnival Queen to be invited to the Fair Luncheon.

<u>1951</u> — Mr. Chester Crocker, a Selectman of Barnstable, Massachusetts, was a guest at the ceremony. The Mayor presented him with a Carved Oak Casket containing greetings and a message of goodwill to the townspeople of Barnstable. (This was also the year of the 'Festival of Britain.')

<u>1956</u> - For the first time in the history of the Ancient Fair Ceremony, television cameras recorded the proceedings for a B.B.C. Newsreel.

<u>1961</u> - A Fair Salute in the form of a letter from President John F. Kennedy, was to be read out at the Fair Opening Ceremony. Unfortunately, the communication had been delayed but was eventually delivered to the Town Clerk. For the present time the letter appears to be mislaid. However, it has been recorded in the Town Council Minutes of September 1961 has having been received and read out at the committee meeting.

<u>1965</u> — Francis Chichester, Esq., C.B.E., F.I.N. (Later to become Sir Francis Chichester) gave a speech on "Devon our County" at the ceremony.

(During the opening of the fair in 1966 a milk churn was in place outside the market entrance to the Guildhall. For the duration of the fair itself, churns were placed at each entrance to the North Walk. It was a three-day effort to raise funds in aid of the Turkish earthquake relief.)

2. Town Crier (C.R.)

1985 — Napoleon Eugene Poyant, Town Crier of Provincetown, Barnstable, Massachusetts, was invited to the Fair Opening Ceremony where he gave a resounding performance at the Guildhall entrance, and during the procession. He was adopted as an Honorary Town Crier by our town of Barnstaple.

Many changes were made to the 'Toast List' throughout the twentieth century. Our all-important **"Agriculture"** was last mentioned in 1972, **"Success to Town and Trade of Barnstaple"** has now become **"The Prosperity of North**

Devon" and "**The Visitors**" changed to "**Our Guests.**" On special occasions as in time of war, inclusions were made such as — "**Our Allies**" - "**The Imperial Forces**" and "**His Majesty's Forces.**"

BOROUGH OF ⬛ BARNSTAPLE

SATURDAY, 27th SEPTEMBER, 1919.

Civic Entertainment for Ex-Service Men.

ALL OFFICERS, N.C.O.'s and MEN who have served during the Great War and are residents in the Borough, desirous of taking part in the above are requested to write stating their Rank, Names, Regiment, and present address to the Town Clerk, or to the Headquarters of the "Comrades," or to the local branch of the Discharged and Demobilised Sailors' and Soldiers' Association BEFORE MID-DAY TO-DAY THURSDAY, THE 25th INSTANT. The Entertainment comprises :—

2 p.m. Sports in the Sports Ground
5.30 p.m. Tea in the Market, and at
8 p.m. Smoking Concert (including Presentation of "Service" Certificates).

F. A. JEWELL, Mayor.
S. J. TAYLOR, Town Clerk.

23rd September, 1919.   [5366

Onward then to the last Fair Proclamation of the twentieth century, which reads in part, as follows:

Sir or Madam,

I hereby summon you to attend a SPECIAL MEETING of the TOWN COUNCIL of BARNSTAPLE, which will be held at the Guildhall, Barnstaple, on WEDNESDAY the 15 SEPTEMBER 1999 at 11 o'clock a.m. for the following purpose:

TO PROCLAIM THE FAIR

Yours faithfully
M.C. TAYLOR
Town Clerk

ORDER OF PROCEEDINGS

1. To Honour the following toasts:

"THE QUEEN"
Proposed by
The Worshipful the MAYOR OF BARNSTAPLE,
Councillor JOHN WILSHER

"BARNSTAPLE FAIR"
Proposed by
BERTIE AYERS Esq.,
President of the Showmen's Guild of Great Britain
Response by
DR TODD GRAY — Historian

"THE PROSPERITY OF NORTH DEVON"
Proposed by
LT. COL. C.W.P. HOBSON, RM -
Officer Commanding RMB Chivenor
Response by
NICK HARVEY M.P.
Member of Parliament for the North Devon Constituency

"OUR GUESTS"
Proposed by
The Worshipful the MAYOR OF BARNSTAPLE,
Councillor JOHN WILSHER
Response by
HERBERT MALEK Esq., Local Businessman

2. The Town Clerk to read the Proclamation

A procession will then be formed in the entrance to the
Guildhall in the following order:
POLICE
BEADLES
SERGEANTS AT MACE
MAYOR
HIGH SHERIFF OF DEVON
DEPUTY MAYOR
TOWN CLERK
MAYOR'S CHAPLAIN
CIVIC GUESTS
MEMBERS OF THE COUNCIL IN ORDER OF SENIORITY

And proceed to the following points where the proclamation
Will be again be read, viz :

(1) High Cross
(2) South end of High Street
(3) Queen Anne's

25

During the Guildhall ceremony, the ancient customs are still carried out. Spiced ale is still passed around for those who wish to sup. It is the responsibility of the head beadle to brew the concoction from a closely guarded, secret recipe — a legacy from those days so long ago.

The toast is soaked in the ale and passed around with the cheese, and the plates of toothsome fairings are handed out to those lucky enough to be near them! The loyal toasts and speeches are carried out, the proclamation is made at 12 noon to open the Fair and the glove is put out of the window, giving a sign to the crowds below in the street to raise a cheer. The procession starts its perambulation with those involved dressed in their full regalia. The proclamation is read at the relevant points along the way and the procession finally wends its way up through Cross Street and back to the Guildhall. From there the dignitaries, their guests and members of the Showmen's Guild, are whisked away to partake of the repast known as the 'Fair Luncheon.' The venues for this have varied in the past, and for many years it was held in the 'Queen's Hall' prior to the inception of the 'Queen's Theatre.' In recent years however, it has been held at the Barnstaple Hotel, Braunton Road. It has been the custom of many years now, that when lunch has been duly dealt with, the Mayor and all his guests are invited by the Showmen's Guild to attend the fair for the afternoon to round off the festivities. If you look closely, you just might see the Mayor and visiting Mayors cavorting about in the bumping cars and, hopefully, with their chains of office still intact!

BARNSTAPLE TOWN COUNCIL   **№   066**

Proclamation of Annual Fair

AT THE GUILDHALL

WEDNESDAY 16th SEPTEMBER 1981 at 11 a.m.

Admit Bearer to MAIN HALL for Opening Ceremony

No seat will be reserved after 10.40 a.m.   FAYE WEBBER, Mayor

3. Spiced Ale Jugs. Early 19th century. Formerly used at the Fair Opening Ceremony. On loan to the Museum of Barnstaple & North Devon by the Mayor and Corporation of Barnstaple. (Photograph Shane Woods © Museum of Barnstaple & North Devon).

4. Spiced Ale in silver 'loving cup', (presented by the Barumites in London association), prepared by Mr E.V.Stowell, Senior Beadle, c.1938 (C.R.)

5. Waiting to see the opening of the Fair ceremony, held inside the Guildhall in the earlier part of the 20th century. It was a 'first come, first served' basis — nowadays tickets are allocated. (© North Devon Athenaeum)

6. The Mayor, Mr G.T. Andrew, JP, is accompanied by the North Devon M.P. Mr E.J.Soares, seated to his right, and James Bosson, Town Clerk, to the Mayor's left. Alderman Alexander Lauder, Architect and accomplished artist, is sporting a full white beard and is seated at the table facing the photographer. Note that at this time the dignatories sit in front of the Bench with the ladies seated behind. (Photographer: W.S.Wood).

7. 1930 — Barnstaple Millenary year Fair Opening. (Mayor: J.T.Dunn; Town Clerk: J.H.L Brewer). Barumites in London association were well represented. (Photograph © R.L. Knight)

8. This was the first Fair Opening Ceremony after the Second World War had ended in 1945. (Mayor: Alderman Charles Frederick Dart) (C.R.)

9. (Mayor: Cllr. J.B.Cruse). It is interesting to note that the banner regarding the reigning monarch is missing at the ceremony in 1952. This was probably due to the fact that Queen Elizabeth II's Coronation did not take place until June 1953. (C.R.) (photograph: Barnstaple Town Council)

10. 'Will you let me speak'. Graham White's last opening cermony as Senior Beadle, 1999 (Photograph © Bob Scarboro).

11. 1985. (Mayor: Cllr. J.Nott). This was the year that the town crier, Napoleon Eugene Poyant, of Provincetown, Barnstable, Massachussetts, took part in the ceremony. The American 'stars & stripes' flag is displayed. Note the film cameraman to the left of the picture. (C.R.) (photograph: Barnstaple Town Council)

12. 1930. Mayor & Mayoress J.H.Dunn at the Guildhall entrance, after the 'Glove' ceremony in Millenary year. (Photograph © R.L. Knight)

13. Proclaiming the fair in 1886 at High Cross (top of Cross Street). Note the child with its Nanny viewing the proceedings from the balconied window. (C.R.).

14. Even more crowds — as far as the eye can see — c. 1907. The umbrellas indicate Barnstaple Fair weather! (C.R.)

15. People congregate as far as the eye can see in this 1920s photograph of the fair proclamation at 'High Cross'. In the far distance a man is viewing the scene from his horse and cart! Note the 'Post Office' sign pointing down Cross Street.
(© North Devon Athenaeum)

16. c.1906. The procession headed by the Police Beadles and Sergeants at Mace, makes its way down to the South Gate. Note the sign for Dominick ~ one of the 'fairing' suppliers. (Photographer: W.S.Wood). (© Tom Bartlett Postcard Collection EX34 9SE)

Opening of Barnstaple Fair—
Quaint Ceremonial.

A. E. Barnes Athenaeum Series

17. c.1907. The photographer 'snaps' a photographer picturing the scene at South Gate. Note the ornate post and sign to Lynton, on the right. (C.R.)

18. 1938. Proclamation at Queen Anne's Walk, accompanied by two buglers. Mayor: Capt. Slatter. (C.R.)

19. Proclaiming the fair open at Queen Anne's Walk, 1910.
(Photographers: Major, Darker & Loraine).

20. c. early 1930s. Crowds at Queen Anne's Walk for the proclamation of the fair.
The notice advises that the North Walk is closed to vehicular traffic, and indicates
the way to a char-a-banc parking ground. (C.R.)

21. 1933/4. Bill Forward (former Mayor of Barnstaple) is in the front row (the boy in the cap, first left)... doesn't he look happy! Mackintoshes and the wet ground suggest the crowds are suffering the effects of rainy fair weather. (C.R.)

22. c.1951, Queen Anne's Walk. Jack Nott (fair buff) is seen here on the right in the Trilby hat and glasses, carrying his daughter, Mary.
(Photograph courtesy of Mary Bellamy). (C.R.)

23. 1996. The procession following head beadle, Graham White (on left), wends its way from Queen Anne's Walk, via Cross Street, and back to the Guildhall. The crowds of yesteryear proportions are no longer evident. (Photograph © Dave Fry).

24. This Barnstaple Fair procession scene was captured by the photographer opposite his shop and studio in Bear Street. The horse-drawn Landau carries the Mayor, Frederick Willliam Hunt, and the Town Clerk, James Bosson, accompanied by their wives. Perhaps this was a special occasion for Bear Street?
(Photographer: W.S.Wood). (© Tom Bartlett Postcard Collection EX34 9SE)

25. 1907. The Mayor's Fair Dinner held in the Pannier Market. (C.R.)

The Proclamation of the Ancient Fair

LUNCHEON

Given by
THE MAYOR AND TOWN COUNCIL
OF BARNSTAPLE

THE BARNSTAPLE HOTEL, BRAUNTON ROAD

Wednesday, 15th September 1999

THE MAYOR AND MAYORESS OF BARNSTAPLE extend to all Persons residing within the Borough, of the age of 60 years and over, an INVITATION to a DINNER in the Vegetable Market, to be followed by a Concert and Entertainment in the Albert Hall, on Wednesday, 25th September inst., at 6-30 in the evening.

Any Person who desires to accept the Invitation of the Mayor and Mayoress can obtain a ticket for the Dinner and Entertainment on leaving, either personally or in writing, on or before Saturday, 14th inst., his or her name and address and age, at either of the undermentioned Offices :—

The Town Clerk's Office,
Municipal Buildings, High Street.
The Borough Surveyor's Office,
Strand.
The Chief Constable's Office,
Police Station, High Street.
Dated, Guildhall, Barnstaple, September 4th, 1907. [7542

The Tradition of the Glove

Those of us who have stood outside the Guildhall at Fair-time could not help but notice the "Glove" protruding from the window above the Guildhall entrance. It is a survivor of the days when fairs were established by virtue of the King's glove, and under whose authority a free mart or market was held. Traditionally, it is symbolic of the 'right hand of friendship' and welcomes those that wish to trade and buy for the duration of the fair. It has also been mooted, some time ago, that it was also probable that the Glove was intended to figure the "Hand" to be seen on Anglo-Saxon coins, notably of the mints of Norwich, Exeter and Barnstaple — all of which claim an Athelstan tradition and pre-conquest market. Whatever thoughts may be tossed around on this particular theory, we at least do not have to assume the existence of a "Glove" long ago — this is a fact. Mention of the glove occurs in 'The Accounts of the Collectors and Receivers of Barnstaple."

(Elizabeth 1st)
1569   *Paid for a Glove for the fair, 1d.*
(From this, it is evident that the custom of the Glove at fair time, is at least four centuries old.)

(James 1st.)
     Paid for a Glove put out at the Fair, 4d.

In earlier times, the Glove was put out at the 'Kay Hall' - N.W. Window. This is mentioned in the Barnstaple Town Records. (11, 26) A small square-mullioned window, looking towards 'Merchant's Walk.' (Queen Anne's Walk — site of our 'Heritage Centre')

26. The Old Quay (Kay) Hall, at West Gate, was the original site for the Ceremony of the Glove. It was suspended on its pole from the mullioned window, shown above the female figure in the drawing. (© North Devon Athenaeum)

(George IV)

1836   There is still mention of the Glove being suspended from the 'Quay Hall Window.' (The spelling has been altered by then from Kay to Quay.)

After this time, no reference to the glove appears to have been made until 1862 when it is revealed that the exhibition of the well-known symbol — the glove — was in place over the Guildhall entrance.

It was described as being of prodigious dimensions. The Fair report in the North Devon Journal of that time mentions that "For several years the practice of indicating the arrival of fair-time by displaying the glove had fallen into desuetude; but during the Mayoralty of Mr. Chanter, (1859) that gentleman caused search to be made for the relic of antiquity which was renovated and decorated and displayed to public view, as aforetime."

27. Old Guildhall before its demolition in 1826. (Site of this located near the Parish Church entrance from the High Street.)
(© North Devon Athenaeum)

The Guildhall (the third) at this time was built in <u>1826</u> and is for the most part, the familiar building we know today.

One can only surmise that the glove was still exhibited from the Quay Hall until that was demolished together with the West Gate in <u>1852</u>. Like many other of our town artefacts, the glove had probably been mislaid or lost over the years. Hurrah! say I for Mayor Chanter's perseverance.

In <u>1890</u> the senior beadle ascertained that the glove for the present year had been in use for at least 15 years past. It was described then as being "*some 18 feet long and a foot wide, and is roughly made of sheepskin leather, with a stuffing of sawdust. Decked with dahlias and other flowers and a bunch of ribbons, selected and purchased by the beadle, the glove is hoisted, at the top of a pole some twelve feet long, out of the window above the entrance to the Guildhall, on the Wednesday morning of the Fair, and is removed at its close."* Apparently, it then lay in the Guildhall attic for the rest of the year, and was at that time (1890) in a dilapidated condition. Proof then, that it had been in annual use since its revival by Mayor Chanter. No doubt it has been renovated or replaced at least once in the past 100 years or so!

Today, the customary white glove extends its welcome in much the same way as in those days of yore, and is still the responsibility of one of the beadles.

28. Ceremony of the Glove about to take place from the Guildhall window, Barnstaple Fair, 1927. (© North Devon Athenaeum)

Vagrancy & the Cholera

It was commonplace in olden times to send on their way, any vagrants that entered the villages and towns uninvited. This was particularly so in times of any outbreak of diseases such as the plague, smallpox, or cholera. It would be the responsibility of the local authorities to employ watchmen to make sure that no undesirables gained entry into the area, especially when festivals were taking place such as Barnstaple Great Fair. For the disease to be brought in and spread throughout such a large assemblage of people would be unthinkable.

A few examples of precautions taken and recorded in the "Accounts of the Collectors and Receivers of Barnstaple" are thus:

1568   *Paid to 15 Men for keeping out the Exeter men which came to the fair, 11s.*

1585   *Item paid to 6 Watchmen to kepe a watch at night at the fair, 12d.*

1591   *Paid to 13 watchmen appointed to keep out from the fair those that came from places infected with the plague, 13s.*

1614   *Paid to divers watchmen at fair time, 12s.*

1626   *For sending away hues and cries and for whipping and sending away vagrants this year, 15s. 4d.*

"Hues and Cries" were people employed to follow up the 'offenders' ensuring banishment was complete, and sometimes they were used for communicating news from parish to parish on the stirring events of the day. (Occasionally, we still hear the phrase — "There was a right hue and cry about it!")

In the nineteenth century, records show that Barnstaple and the neighbourhood had its fair share of the Cholera.

Guildhall, September 20th. 1830
"A vagrant was brought up from the Constables' Prison, and committed to gaol for one week, for having refused to obey the order of the "rout beggar to quit the borough."

In 1832 the following notices were issued by the Mayor and from the Guildhall:

BARNSTAPLE FAIR.

NOTICE IS HEREBY GIVEN, that, on account of that awful disease, (the Cholera,) which is at present existing in, and spreading through the County,

No Public Exhibitions or Amusements Will be allowed at the BARNSTAPLE FAIR, on Wednesday the 19th of September, and Two Following Days: that the Fair will be confined exclusively to the Sale of Cattle and other Commodities: and that all Vagrants will be apprehended, and treated with the utmost severity allowed by law, as well as all Persons harbouring such Vagrants.

WILLIAM LAW, *Mayor.*

Dated August 27th, 1832.

Guildhall, Barnstaple, September 17th, 1832
Thirteen special constables were sworn in, to exercise their office during the fair, for the purpose of guarding the avenues of the town, to prevent as far as possible the admission of improper persons, and to apprehend all suspicious ones.

The Barnstaple Board of Health requested that no public exhibitions or amusements be allowed as detailed in the copy of the original notice shown here.

(From the collection in the Museum of Barnstaple & North Devon)

BARNSTAPLE

FAIR.

☞ **AT** the request of the Barnstaple *Board of Health*, We hereby give Notice that **NO PUBLIC**

Exhibitions or Amusements

will be permitted or allowed in the Parishes of *Pilton, Bishops Tawton, Tawstock or Fremington*, during the approaching **BARNSTAPLE FAIR;** and that all Vagrants found in the said Parishes, will be apprehended and punished with the utmost severity of the Law.

BOURCHIER P. WREY,
JOHN DENE,   *Magistrates of the*
Z. H. DRAKE,   *County of Devon.*
JOHN MAY,

Dated September 15th, 1832.

The attendance of the pleasure seekers at the fair was greatly diminished, and it was said that it was never witnessed so few persons in the town on fair day.

Two vagrants — Thomas Baker and Charles Gilman — were charged with vagrancy, and committed to the borough prison for a fortnight, by the Chief Magistrate.

The *North Devon Journal* issued the CHOLERA MORBUS — DAILY REPORT from The Central Board of Health, Whitehall, September 18th 1832.

New Cases in the County - 394
Deaths - 127
Recovered - 295
Remaining -1303
(One month later shows new cases as 166, deaths 62, and recovered 123)

It is amusing to read some of the adverts advocating remedies for the disease –

"*Directions for taking the Universal Medicines in Cases of Cholera Morbus.*

As soon as the patient feels any symptom of the disease coming on, twelve, fifteen, or twenty pills of No.2, which will immediately allay the spasms (the most dangerous symptom) and procure easy evacuations, upwards and downwards, which at once carries off the disease. In severe cases the largest dose should be repeated in six hours; in more lenient ones, in twelve or twenty-four hours; but the most prudent way is, if perfect ease is not restored, to repeat the dose, and afterwards to continue with Nos. 1 and 2 alternately, and the powders throughout the day, till well. Warmth and rubbing over the stomach and heart are recommended. No other medicine is requisite, nor should be used. Weak diluting drinks, or warm water alone, are recommended.

N.B. The College will not be answerable for the consequences of any Medicines sold by any Chemist or Druggist, as none are allowed to sell the "Universal Medicines;" which can only be had genuine at the British College of Health, and of the regularly registered Agents in town and country.

The Vegetable Universal Medicine is sold in boxes at 1s. 1d., 2s. 9d., and 4s. 6d., And, in Family Packages of three boxes, by which there is a great saving."

(Agents are then listed for the North Devon area; they include grocers, stationers, booksellers, and printers!)

September 23rd, 1841
Henry Williams, a vagrant from the Emerald Isle, was brought up in charge of Policeman Chanter, and ordered to be conducted without the borough boundaries.

Barnstaple Police, Sept. 19th 1844
(Before John Law Esq.)
John Richards, a young man in the attire of a mariner, and describing himself as a native of Lynton,was charged with vagrancy, and committed for seven days.

<u>1849</u>, sees another epidemic of Cholera starting a few weeks before the fair. General alarm attributed to the outbreak, caused a fall in numbers attending the fair and was an unsatisfactory business time for the farmers and trades-people.

On the 13th September of that year, the health of the town was reported in some detail by the *Journal* and is recorded here in its entirety:

"We are thankful to be enabled to give a more favourable report of the health of the town and district than that which fidelity constrained us to publish last week. Two only fatal cases have occurred in the town since our last, and one at Pilton. The latter was the second child of the ill-fated Oatway's family, whose hopeless illness were mentioned in connexion with the record of the death of her father, mother, aunt, and brother. The two deaths in this town occurred on Friday morning last, in a house in Maiden-street. They were the children of Abraham Land, hairdresser; they were seized in the course of Thursday night, and died next morning. What added to the painfulness of the calamity was the fact that the parents (who are very respectable people) were away at the time at Tiverton to attend the funeral of Mrs. Land's father.

There was another case or two in the same house, which yielded to medical treatment. The house was one which the inspecting committee had particularly remarked upon as among the most unhealthy they had visited in their district.

The room in which the family lived was over a close pigstye, and the stench proceeding from it was such as to induce the committee, on their visitation three weeks ago, to recommend some of the inmates to remove. They have since, we believe, acted upon the advice, admonished by this sad fatality. With these exceptions there have been no deaths, nor any aggravated cases of the epidemic. The applications for diarrhoea medicines have also very much diminished; and, on the whole, there can be no doubt that the health of the town is considerably improved. When we bear in mind that the first case of cholera appeared here above five weeks ago, we cannot be sufficiently thankful for the leniency which has characterised the visitation; not more than about 12 fatal cases having occurred out of a population of almost as many thousands."

Present day readers might be interested in the suggestions given for "Anti-Cholera" for that period of time.

"Be careful of taking cold. Don't fatigue yourself excessively.

Avoid raw acid fruits, nuts, and much pastry, or whatever you find it difficult to digest. Eat fresh meat in preference to salt, and brown bread in preference to white, and don't cut the loaf the day it is baked.

Let your vegetables be well boiled.

Drink no spirits, and very sparingly of fermented liquors.

Keep your mind easy, and divest yourself as much as possible of fear.

Eat light suppers, if any.

Be temperate and moderate in all things.

Keep your person clean by frequent ablutions and changes of linen; and let your house be kept clean, whitewashed, and well ventilated.

Keep your sewers clean, and remove all accumulations of offensive matter about your premises.

Attend to the state of your bowels. Do not neglect the premonitory symptoms, pains in the stomach and bowels, with diarrhoea. In such cases, lose not a moment in applying for medical relief.

Pray for God's grace and protection for yourself and others. And lastly,
"Prepare to meet thy God," for "Though knowest not what a day may bring forth.""

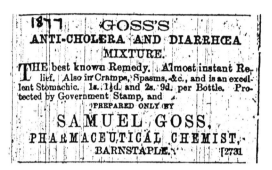

1877. GOSS'S ANTI-CHOLERA AND DIARRHŒA MIXTURE. THE best known Remedy. Almost instant Relief. Also in Cramps, Spasms, &c., and is an excellent Stomachic. 1s. 1½d. and 2s. 9d. per Bottle. Protected by Government Stamp, and 'PREPARED ONLY BY **SAMUEL GOSS, PHARMACEUTICAL CHEMIST,** BARNSTAPLE. [2731

Maybe this information made a difference. At least with the introduction of the Public Health Act, diseases such as these gradually became contained, and epidemics of Cholera appear to have abated by the mid. 19th century.

The whipping and hounding of vagrants is certainly a thing of the past, and so too are the fair watchmen. The police constable has taken over.

ffair Tolls

or centuries the collecting of Market and Fair Tolls, was made by the Bailiffs of the town on behalf of the Lord of the Borough or the Mayor, Aldermen and Commonalty. A Clerk of the Market was also responsible, and sometimes even the Town Clerk was paid for toll duty, as can be seen in one of the account entries.

From Articles of Covenant etc:

1566 *"Indented made the 5th day May, in the 8th year of the reign of our Sovereign Lady Queen Elizabeth and between Sir John Chichester, Knt. Of the one part, and the Mayor, Aldermen and Commonalty of Barum of the other part.*

Item 12. That the mayor and aldermen to have the profits and commodities of the markets and fairs."

From the Accounts of Collectors & Receivers of Barnstaple:

1577 *"Item to the Bailiffs of the Town, for the Fee-Farm Rents of the Markets and Fairs, X11. V1d."*

1614 *"Paid to Mr. Thomas Davie, steward and Town Clerk, for keeping the Tolsewill at the fair, 1s. 4d."*

1614 *"To the bailiffs of this town for the fee farm of the fair and market there this year, 2s. 6 1/2d."*

1657 (Charles II) *"Toll of Fair Markets (for cattle) except of quick cattle, which the Town Clerk for the time being hath used to take to his own use in Fair Time, £7 15s."*

Much later, the land on which the fair took place was "farmed out" to the highest bidder for the privilege of becoming the lessee, and collecting the tolls for themselves.

At a Town Council meeting in <u>1848</u> some discussion took place regarding the exorbitant charges made by the renter of the Square, during the fair. According to the report, two respectable exhibitions decided to take their leave of Barnstaple when the payment of £12 each, was demanded by the lessee. As the Council's fee for rent to him was only £5 and the site brought in a revenue of at least £30 for the lessee, it was felt that future investigation be made as to the principle of keeping the Square in the hands of the Council, instead of letting it during the fair.

By the next decade the Council are apparently managing things themselves again, but in <u>1857</u> the Square is being leased once more, for the period of the fair.

A confectioner, named Spark, who had attended the fair for several years, asked to be relieved of some of the charges for setting up his standings in the Square. Pleading his case, he informed the Mayor that he had never been charged so much as at the present fair; he had stalls occupying a space of ten feet by three feet each, for which he was required to pay 10s.each. The charge used to be 6d. the running foot, he stated. The Mayor said that he couldn't assist him, as the Council had leased the site of the fair without any conditions as to the scale of charges, therefore, the lessee could charge what he liked!

Other complaints were clearly made, as the following year it was decided that the letting of the Square would be retained in the hands of the Council. It was stated that the lessee of the tolls rented the Square at £15, and made £45 by charging the stalls and exhibitions an exorbitant 500% above the customary rate of charge.

Further on into the 19th century, the letting of the tolls of Barnstaple Fair & Markets, were being put up for auction.

One such auction took place in the Guildhall in <u>1873</u> for the lettings which were for one year, from the 30th day of June. Mr. James Martin, of Cross Street, was the auctioneer, and the attendance of bidders was said to be small.

Lot 2 was the tolls arising from the Sheep & Cattle Fair and Markets, and the Horse Fair. Mr. Squires the then present lessee started the bidding off with £75. Possession of the lot seemed to rest between Mr. Squires, Mr. John Manning, and

Mr. Parkin, of the Golden Fleece. It was finally knocked down to Mr. John Manning, for £100.

In June 1878, a large company assembled for the bidding of various lets. The tolls and dues of the Sheep & Cattle Fair and Markets, and the Horse Fair were in the present ownership of the lessee, Mr. Yeo, who made a bid at £101, but the lot was knocked down to Mr. Green at £117. The tolls of the Pleasure Fair, (now re-sited at Castle Street and part of North Walk) was knocked down to Mr. Williams at £20. At the end of the proceedings, the auctioneer adjourned with the bidders for refreshments at the Royal Exchange Inn.

At the end of the next decade auctioning the tolls etc., has become obsolete. The report for 1889 gives the Town Council as collecting the tolls themselves, instead of the usual practice of letting them. It was said that this would result in a substantial addition to the borough funds, as when let by auction the tolls fetched around £20; the Council now would clear £100 over the Pleasure Fair.

North Devon Journal — 25th September 1890

> *"For many years the Barnstaple Fair tolls were sold by auction, the highest sum obtained being £20. The Town Council now "farm" the tolls themselves — with a result highly advantageous to the burgesses. Last year the tolls produced*
>
> *£89 18s.7d., and the nett sum received last week just exceeded £100. These figures amply justify the Council in the course they have adopted, and afford a very decisive argument against those who urge the decadence of the annual event. It is gratifying to know that there was a substantial increase in the cattle and horse department, the augmentation being particularly noticeable in the case of the horses. Barnstaple Fair holds its own — and there is every probability that it will continue to do so."*

The 1892 receipts from the tolls exceeded those of any previous year, netting £100 from the spaces let in the North Walk alone.

In 1894 the sum of £115 exceeded 1893 by £28 although the 1896 tolls only yielded £81 - £20 less than the previous year.

<u>1889</u> Mr. J. Jordan (the borough accountant) and Mr. T. Lee (foreman of works "laid out" the ground for the shows, booths, and stalls, which was said to be a great improvement upon that of former occasions.

Brief research into the 20th century gives a few snippets of information.

In the year <u>1913</u> (pre-first World War days) the amount received in tolls and lettings in connection with the fair, was £220 16s.6d. <u>1918</u> receipts were only £96 18s. but the <u>1919</u> tolls yielded £282 1s. 6d. of which £270 17s.9d. were in respect of the Pleasure Fair.

The year of Barnstaple's Millenary celebrations in 1930, showed the fair tolls amounting to the record amount of £720.

<u>1945</u> The general agreement on the planning of the Fair was that it was the best there had ever been. More space had been allowed for the public and there was not so much congestion.

Further details on the <u>1945</u> fair give the Councillors remarking on it being the most orderly they had ever seen — there were no drunks or quarrels.

It was wished the committee had some means of regulating the sudden rise in charges owing to the popularity of the festival, and the Showmen's Guild should be approached in an endeavour to stop the exorbitant prices, particularly on a Friday night. Another Councillor retorted "This racket has gone on for years," and he saw no reason for it.

In turn, the Showmen's Guild thought the council's charges were too high! Money for the rentals was more than ever before which were to go towards the relief of the rates.

Moving on to <u>1953</u> it was said that customers at the fair for the Wednesday and Thursday nights were very scarce, and although attendance was better the following day, the traditional Friday night increase in prices were seldom put into use.

Tolls collected were not affected however, as the charges from the pleasure section of the fair created yet another record of £1,449. The increase was due to more stalls and shows being crowded into the Fairground and North Walk.

1961 Mayor Stan Woolaway, and Guests toured the North Walk Fairground in customary fashion. There was a complaint made to him by the Showmen regarding the wall having been built along the length of North Walk. They said it was causing them to cram sideshows too close together, and Mr. Tom Whitelegg (77) confirmed that he was dissatisfied with the distribution of the sites for the sideshows.

A few years later in **1967** the Pleasure Fair was moved to its present site on Seven Brethren Bank. This year was the first time, the allocation of positions on the fairground, were undertaken by the Showmen's Guild. Most of the major exhibitors had by now, become members of the Guild.

At the end of the 20th century, the fair tolls are still in the hands of the Town Council.

The charges for rental in **1999** were £13 per run-out (old running foot).

Our 19th century confectioner, Mr.Spark, would most likely turn in his grave at the thought of it!

Us be Goin' to Barnstaple Fair

Extract from "The Maid of Sker" by R.D. Blackmore – (1872)
set in the year 1782

"The town is a pleasant and pretty one, and has always been famous for thinking itself more noble than any other; also the fair was a fine thing to see, full of people, and full of noise, and most outrageous dialect; everybody in fine broad humour, and no fighting even worth looking at."

Up to well into the nineteenth century, such was the importance of "Barnstaple Great Fair" to the populace of North Devon and beyond that it was an event in their lives to anticipate with pleasure. People converged into Barnstaple in their masses from all directions; from isolated moorland farms, rustic hamlets, villages near and far, and bustling towns. A combination of all walks of life could be seen jostling their way, side by side about the fair - The drover of sheep and cattle, and the dealer in horses hoping to strike a bargain. The Farmer would bring his stock to dispose of or replenish his own, and at this time of year it was customary for him to settle his accounts with local businesses and look forward to the hospitality afforded to him and his family. With savings of a twelve month, the Farmers wife and her offspring most certainly came to sample the delights and wonders of the fair. If the weather had been kind and their labours of bringing in the harvest ended, stalwart farmhands were free to attend, and rosy-cheeked buxom lasses dressed in their "Best" and new bonnets made especially for the occasion. Released from their servitude for a short time, you can almost hear the peals of laughter and shouts of banter rising above the rumble of the cartwheels, as they all rode in together for come-what-may! To the very remote parishes and its inhabitants of hard-working and honest country folks, Barnstaple Fair was as much a subject of wonderment as many people would find in going to a foreign country today. (An amusing tale is told in 1838 of when someone enquired of the road from a dame in the neighbourhood of Parracombe, she asked whether they had come from *Bastable*, or the strange countries!) Naïve rustics were continually being warned of tricksters after their hard earned money at the fair. Many did not take heed and were left with empty pockets before they had made full use of all the fun of the fair. As with any large gathering, pick pockets abounded and confidence tricksters tried their shameless tactics on the gullible.

Extract from "Lorna Doone" by R.D. Blackmore (1869)
(To quote John Ridd on his return to
Plover's Barrow Farm from his sojourn in London)
"Before breakfast was out of our mouths, there came all the men of the farm, and their wives, and even the two crow-boys, dressed as if going to Barnstaple fair, to enquire how Master John was."

The higher classes went to see and be seen. They paraded in a fashionable array of waistcoats and stocks, dresses and highly ornamented bonnets. The ladies would look upon the cattle fair with disparagement and fear and would stay away, but would tolerate the parade horses at the horse fair. Most importantly to them, they had come to partake in all the fun and festivities, not least the Fair Ball and Fair Stag Hunt.

Romance was looked for by many a lass, lad, young lady or gentleman. All hoped for a beau or belle to come their way at Barnstaple Fair.

Children were expected to don the best of their clothes to visit the fair. Great excitement rippled through the younger generation as they set off clutching varying amounts of money. Confectionery and gingerbread — known as fairing, and toys would be high on their list of purchases. But, like any child past or present, to be "amused" was the most exciting priority of the event.

The local inhabitants and tradesmen went to great lengths and expense to smarten up their houses and premises. All was cleaned and painted' to get rid of the smut and dust of the past long months. Hospitalities, freely offered to customers and friends alike, and the tradition of providing huge rounds and ribs of beef, apple pie, stewed pears, all of which was accompanied by Barnstaple ale, was of great importance. Hostelries and taverns vied with each other for custom and enticed the fair-goers with an abundance of food, and the ale readily quaffed in great quantities.

Shops looked inviting with their displays of eye-catching baubles, unusual gifts and novelties especially bought in for the annual event. Silk ribbons, bonnet trimmings, toys from London, Milk of Roses for the complexion, leather leggings, boots & shoes, winter clothing, and all manner of toothsome delicacies. The list goes on and on in the endeavour to tempt - "They that be comin' to Barum Fair."

Grand Gala and Fancy Dress Ball,

AT THE

1827 **VAUXHALL ROOMS,**

In the Horse Fair, every Evening during the Fair.

THE Public are respectfully informed that the above Rooms are elegantly fitted up for their reception, and may be inspected every Morning.

THE BALL

Will commence at Seven o'clock in the Evening.—Admission only One Shilling, and no further charge made.

The nature of this Establishment is so well known as to render any description superfluous; but those who have been in the habit of attending, will acknowledge that it is the cheapest and most agreeable Entertainment in the Fair. The Proprietor respectfully invites an early attendance of his Visitors.

N. B.—Refreshments of every description on the most reasonable terms.

Barnstaple, September 20th, 1827.

"Heigh Ho! let's go to the Fair." And so they did, on foot, horseback, cart and carriage, even the River Taw played its part in conveying whomever to the celebrations. In 1828 the North Devon Journal reported the steady approach of the boats from Bideford etc., bringing up their freights of holiday folks to join in the festivities of the Fair.

BARNSTAPLE FAIR 1858

MARINE PLEASURE EXCURSION.—The 'PRINCE OF WALES,' WM. POOKETT Commander, will leave Swansea on an Excursion to *Ilfracombe* on THURSDAY, September 23rd, 1858, leaving Padley's Quay at Five o'clock, and the Lock Bridge punctually at Half-past Five o'clock in the Morning, and will return from *Ilfracombe* on Friday Evening at Four o'clock, thus giving Excursionists TWO DAYS AT BARNSTAPLE FAIR.

A Special Brass Band will be in attendance.

Tickets To and Fro:—Best Cabin, 4s. 6d.; Fore Cabin, 3s.—Tickets may be had of Mr. J. W. POOKETT, and Mr. H. POOKETT, Steam Packet Office, Swansea; of Mr. DAVEY, Agent, *Ilfracombe*, and of the Captain on board. Special Rates will be given for Cattle, Sheep, and Pigs, in large quantities. Excursion Fare only available when Tickets are taken before leaving Swansea.

With the opening of the Crediton (Exeter) to Barnstaple Railway in 1854 (now Barnstaple Junction) several hundreds more visitors took advantage of the transport to attend the fair. Over twenty years later, the September 23rd 1875 issue of the *Journal* reported — "It is computed that no fewer than 12,000 strangers made their home in Barnstaple for the day: whether that be an extravagant estimate or not, certain it is that much more than half that number were passengers from the different lines. At the Victoria Road site, the first train of the Devon and Somerset (opened in 1873) came in with 15 carriages bringing between 800 and 1,000 visitors; and it left hundreds behind to come by a later train. So also the new Ilfracombe line (Quay Station — opened 1874) introduced numbers of its summer folk to see the gaiety of Barnstaple fair; while the older line, the

London and South Western, with its larger accommodations, brought traffic from both directions — Exeter and its intermediate stations, and Bideford (opened 1855) Torrington, (1872) and their neighbourhoods."

"The stations were all crowded as the hour for the last train at each drew on. All were conveyed back without the slightest accident that we heard of. Not all however; for many, having missed the train, were constrained to stay overnight, to whom the terrible gale which came an hour or two after midnight was an unwelcome variation of experience."

1893 — During the Fair 3,100 persons alighted at Barnstaple Junction, and 1,500 at the Quay Station. A large number also arrived by way of the Great Western Railway.

1894 — 5,000 were conveyed on Friday alone by the London & South Western Railway.

In 1898 the Barnstaple to Lynton Railway was opened providing even more opportunities to go to "Barum Fair." How times have changed since then for our North Devon Railway facilities, with only one line in existence at the end of the twentieth century!

1858   NORTH DEVON RAILWAY.

B A R N S T A P L E   F A I R.

ON THE THREE DAYS OF THIS FAIR, the 22nd, 23rd, and 24th of September, ADDITIONAL TRAINS will run to Barnstaple from *Exeter* to *Bideford*, and intermediate Stations. A TRAIN will leave *Exeter* on FRIDAY, the 24th, at 9:50 a.m., taking from the South Devon third-class Train. ☞ The 7:40 a.m. down Train from *Exeter* will be A THIRD-CLASS TRAIN TO BARNSTAPLE, for the three days. R. OGILVIE, Manager.

Dated Barnstaple, September 16th, 1858.

LYNTON & BARNSTAPLE RAILWAY

BARNSTAPLE FAIR.

CHEAP TICKETS will be issued to Barnstaple on September 16th, 17th, and 18th. On Wednesday and Thursday a SPECIAL TRAIN will leave Barnstaple Town for Lynton at 6.20 p.m. On Friday the 7 33 p m. train from Barnstaple will be Suspended, and SPECIAL TRAINS will leave at 5 15 and 9 30 p.m. The 1 55 train Barnstaple to Lynton will not run on Wednesday, September 16th. See bills.

AUCTION SALES.—Special Train to Barnstaple from Blackmoor at 4 25 p.m. on Tuesday, September 15th. 1914

C. E. DREWETT, General Manager.

GREAT WESTERN RAILWAY.

BARNSTAPLE FAIR,

SEPTEMBER, 19TH, 20TH, AND 21ST.

ON the above dates MARKET TICKETS will be issued to BARNSTAPLE.

On FRIDAY, September 21st, the 9.0 p.m. Train from Barnstaple will run to DULVERTON, and a SPECIAL TRAIN for SOUTHMOLTON will leave Barnstaple at 11 p.m., both Trains stopping at Intermediate Stations. Holders of Market Tickets can return by these Trains.

J. GRIERSON, General Manager.

Paddington Terminus. 1877 [2410

SPECIAL ANNOUNCEMENT

BARNSTAPLE GREAT FAIR

TODAY (THURSDAY) AND TOMORROW (FRIDAY),
SEPTEMBER 15th and 16th **1955**

To BARNSTAPLE

Leave Eggesford 12.21, 2.20 p.m. (2/9), King's Nympton 12.29, 2 27 p.m. (2/3), Portsmouth Arms 12.35, 2.33 p.m. (2/-), Umberleigh 12.42. 2.40 p.m. (1/6), Chapelton 12.47, 2.45 p.m. (1/3).

Return by any train same day.

On FRIDAY, SEPTEMBER 16th a SPECIAL RETURN TRAIN will leave BARNSTAPLE TOWN at 9.30 p.m. and BARNSTAPLE JUNCTION at 9.40 p.m. for all Stations to Eggesford.

Leave Ilfracombe	12.20, 2.20, 3.00, 4.48, 5.45, 7.42 p.m.	2/3
Mortehoe	12.32, 2.32, 3.12, 5.00, 5.57, 7.54 p.m.	2/3
Braunton	12.44, 2.43, 3.25, 5.12, 6.11, 8. 5 p m.	1/3
Wrafton	12.47, 2.46, 3.28, 5.15, 6.14, 8. 8 p.m.	1/2

Return by any train same day.

On FRIDAY, SEPTEMBER 16th a SPECIAL RETURN TRAIN will leave BARNSTAPLE TOWN at 10 p m. for all Stations to ILFRACOMBE.

Leave Bideford	12.27, 2.24, 2.56; 4.47, 5.55, 7.47 p.m.	1/9
Instow	12.35, 2.32, 3. 6, 4.56, 6. 3, 7.56 p.m.	1/6
Fremington	12.43, 2.40, 3.14; 5. 4, 6.13, 8. 4 p.m.	11d.

Return by any train same day.

On FRIDAY, SEPTEMBER 16th, a SPECIAL RETURN TRAIN will leave BARNSTAPLE TOWN at 11.15 p.m. and BARNSTAPLE JUNCTION at 11.30 p.m. for all Stations to Torrington.

FRIDAY, SEPTEMBER 16th.

To BARNSTAPLE (Great Fair)

Leave Hatherleigh 11.7 a.m.(3/3), Meeth Halt 11.20 a.m. (3/3), Petrockstowe 11.30 a.m. (3/-), Dunsbear Halt 11.40 a.m. (2/9), Yarde Halt 11.45 a.m. (2/9), Watergate Halt 11.59 a.m. (2/6).

The 8.30 p.m. train from BARNSTAPLE JUNCTION to TORRINGTON WILL BE EXTENDED to HATHERLEIGH on FRIDAY, SEPTEMBER 16th.

Further information obtainable from Stations, Offices, and Agencies.

BRITISH RAILWAYS

61

Barnstaple Fair in Poem & Song

JOHN GAY & BARNSTAPLE FAIR.

(Extract from Shepherd's Week, 1712)

Now he goes on, and sings of fairs and shows,
For still now fairs before his eyes arose:
How pedlars' stalls with glitt'ring toys are laid,
The various fairings of the country maid:
Long silken laces hang upon the twine,
And rows of pins and amber bracelets shine:
How the tight lass knives, combs and scissors spies,
And looks on thimbles with desiring eyes:
Of lott'ries next with tuneful note he told.
Where silver spoons are won, and rings of gold:
The lads and lasses trudge the street along,
And all the fair is crowded in his song:
The mountebank now treads the stage, and sells
His pills, his balsams, and his ague spells:
Now o'er and o'er the nimble tumbler springs,
And on the rope the vent'rous maiden swings:
Jack Pudding in his party-coloured jacket
Tosses the glove, and jokes at ev'ry packet:
Of rareeshows he sung, Punch's feats,
Of pockets pick'd in crowds, and various cheats.

BARNSTAPLE FAIR IN THE OLDEN TIME

(Published in "The Cave" periodical, 1824)

Oh! Devonshire's a noble county, full of lovely view, miss!
And full of gallant gentlemen for you to pick and choose, miss!
But search the towns all around about there's nothing to compare, miss!
In measurement of merriment, with *Barnstaple Fair,* miss!

Then sing of Barum, merry town, and Barum's merry Mayor, too,
I know no place in all the world old Barum to compare to!

There's nothing happens in the year but happens at our Fair, sir
'Tis then that every thing abounds that's either new or rare, sir!
The misses make their start in life its gaieties to share, sir!
And ladies look to beaux and ball to Barnstaple Fair, sir!

Then sing of Barum, merry town, and Barum's worthy Mayor, too,
I know no place in all the world old Barum to compare to!

The little boys and girls at school their nicest clothes prepare, ma'am!
To walk the streets and buy sweetmeats and gingerbread so rare, ma'am!
Their prime delight's to see the sights that ornament our Square, ma'am!
When Powell brings his spangled troop to *Barnstaple Fair,* ma'am!

Then sing of Barum, merry town, and our indulgent Mayor, too,
I know no place in all the world old Barum to compare to!

If milk be scarce tho' grass be plenty, don't' complain to soon, dame!
For that will very often happen in the month of June, dame!
Tho' cows run dry while grass runs high, you'll never need despair, dame!
The cows will calve, and milk you'll have, to *Barnstaple Fair,* dame!

Then sing of Barum, wealthy town, and our productive Fair, too,
And drink "The corporation, and the head of it, the Mayor, too.

If pigeon's wings are plucked, and peacock's tails refuse to grow, friend!
In spring; you may depend upon't in autumn they will show, friend!
If feathers hang about your fowls in drooping style and spare, friend!
Both cocks and hens will get their pens to *Barnstaple Fair,* friend!

Then, friend, leave off your wig, and Barum's privileges share, too,
Where every thing grows once a year, wing, feathers, tails and hair, too.

If winter wear and summer dust call out for paint and putty, sir!
And Newport coals in open grates make paper hangings smutty, sir!
And fusty shops and houses' fronts most sadly want repair, sir!
Both shops and houses will be smart to *Barnstaple Fair,* sir!

And Barum is a handsome town, and every day improving, sir!
Then drink to all who study its improvement to keep moving, sir!

King George the Third rode out to Staines, the hounds to lay the stag on!
But that was no great thing of sport for mighty kings to brag on;
The French, alas! go *à la chasse in ron po shay* and pair;
But what's all that to Button Hill, to *Barnstaple Fair.*

For we will all a-hunting go, on horse, or mule, or mare, sir!
For every thing is in the field to Barnstaple Fair, sir!

To Button Hill, whose name to all the sporting world sure known is,
Go bits of blood, and hunters, hacks, and little Exmoor ponies,
When lords and ladies, doctors, parsons, farmers, squires, prepare,
To hunt the stag, with hound and horn, to *Barnstaple Fair*.

Then up and ride for Chillam Bridge, or on to Bratton Town, sir!
To view the rouse, or watch the Yeo, to see the stage come down, sir!

There's nothing else in jollity, and hospitable fare, sir!
That ever can with Barnstaple in Fair time compare, sir!
And guests are very welcome, hospitality to share, sir!
For beer is brew'd, and beef is bought, to *Barnstaple Fair*, sir!

Then sing of merry England, and roast beef, old English fare, sir
A bumper to "the town and trade of Barum and its Mayor," sir!

Boiled beef, roast beef, squab pie, pear pie, and figgy pudding plenty,
When eight or nine sit down to dine, they'll find enough for twenty,
And after dinner, for desert, the choicest fruits you'll share, sir!
E'en walnuts come from Somerset to *Barnstaple Fair*, sir!

Then sing of Barum, jolly town, and Barum's jolly Mayor, too,
No town in England can be found old Barum to compare to!

I will not sing of Bullock Fair, and brutes whose horrid trade is,
To make us shut our window blinds, and block up all the ladies:
Nor of the North Walk rush and crush where fools at horses stare, sir!
When Mr Murray brings his nags to *Barnstaple Fair*, sir!

But sing of Barum, jolly town, and Barum's jolly Mayor, too!
No town in England can be found old Barum to compare to!

The Ball one night, the Play the next, with private parties numerous;
Prove Barnstaple people's endless efforts, sir, to humour us;
And endless, too, would be my song, if I should now declare
All the gaieties and rarities of *Barnstaple Fair*.

Then loudly sing, God save the King, and long may Barum thrive, O!
May we all live to see the Fair, and then be all alive, O!

Roger Clodpole pon Bastabel Vair
(1829)

Vrasl wurk vor Roger! aw the vools!
Aw that I'de gawt but better rules!
    I'd cut and zlash away;
Than wid I zeng wa vess subblime,
And zaterize ech dedly crime! ~
    But doant the provarb zay,
"Was wishes hosses, beggers then
"Wid ride abowt leek gentlemen!"
Wull than I'l be conteynt vor creap
    Wa hobblin staps alung;
Veel glad eef I doant zeng asleap
    The peeple wa me zung.

Leek awther vokes I went vor stare
A leetel round abowt the vair,
    Awl the vine zites vor zee;
An thare the jans and jones was drengin,
Zom awem hollerin, dancin, zengin,
    Happy es they kude be;
Blind vokes zo drunk they kudden stand,
Sawt down an houlded out thar han
    An axd vur charitee,

An kickshaws ov awl zoarts was thare~
    Zum awem crewel vunny;
Wan theng pertikkerler I zeed,
They awl zimd verry wull agreed,
    Vor rub the peyple's munny.

Et only maed ma laf vor zee
The vokes zo trikk'd wi voolery~
    Et didden gee ma no zurprize~
    Cubwebs, I knawd, wid ketch the vlies;
But when the vokes kemmd hum, at nite,
Zo drunk es pegs, in zich a plite,
I kudden bare for zee the zite,
    I rinn'd and zhet me iys.

Aw Drunkinness! thou feind ov hell,
Wus than the plaeg! thou zimmst to me,
Man's crewelest, wust henemy.
Aw wy will vokes so voolish be
Vor breng tharzelves zich missery!
Et awfen makth me heyve a zi,
Et awfen makth poor Roger cry,
Vor zee the stewpid craturs vly
    To drenk a vrendly zup.
Aw wy want voolish men taek kear,
Aw wy want voolish men beware,~
    Thare's poyson in the cup.
Twill maek yore poor ould noddys shaek~
Twill maek yore poor ould boddys craek~
    Twill maek yore pukkets zore.
Aw that ech nasty drunkin codger,
Wid taek advise from thare vrend Roger,
And nivver drenk no mear.

Zatterday nite, Sept. 26.

OYEZ, OYEZ, OYEZ!
(BARNSTAPLE FAIR)

(Sung by the Loveband family over a period of 165 years...
Rev. Chorley Loveband was one-time Rector of West Down.)

Now, all you good people, come hearken to me,
King Athelstan bids me declare
This day of all others shall notable be.
Through Devonshire, Cornwall, and over the sea,
As the foundling of Barnstaple Fair.
The King he devised the affair,
The students of history swear.
So let us all sing
Long life to the King
Who founded our Barnstaple Fair.

There are Honiton laces and ribbons that gleam,
And woollens for wintery wear,
And sheep, and fat cattle, and fish from the stream,
And junket, and cider, and Devonshire cream,
To be bought at our Barnstaple Fair.
So banish all trouble and care,
And flock in your myriads there;
Loud praises recite
To the monarch of might,
Who founded our Barnstaple Fair.

The lads and the lasses they open their eyes
At the noise and the fun and the glare,
The merry-go-rounds and the coconut shies;
Ah! It's right to be merry and wrong to be wise
When flocking to Barnstaple Fair.
Oh! I doubt if the King is aware
Of the joy that it gives to be there,
But I'll venture to bet
He will never regret
The founding of Barnstaple Fair.

A VERSE BY MR. PAUL PRY, 1827

Dear Sir ~ at Barum's well-known fair

Last week, I had a famous stare;
Highly delighted all day long,
Most gaily bustled thro' the throng,
Popp'd into ev'ry booth and show,
Enquir'd of all, both high and low,
What they were doing, how they far'd,
And whether things went smooth or hard;
Heard many strange and curious jokes,
About the good old Barum folks;
Which with great pleasure I'll relate,
When we are snugly títe-a-títe,
But from the fair I mustn't ramble,
So, now, Sir without more preamble-
There was a crowd of girls and boys,
All sorts of gaudy, glittering toys;
First-rate beaux with quizzing glasses,
Ogling all the pretty lasses;
Groups of simply country fellows,
Jugglers, Jews, and fortune-tellers;
Great droves of cattle, learned pigs,
Youngsters playing curious rigs;
Ginger bread stall, ups and downs;
Giants, dwarfs, tom-fools, and clowns;
Big rogues in plenty, bang-up swings,
And several strange outlandish things.
Whichever way my steps I bent,
All seemed happy and content.
'Twas in truth rare fun to see,
So many people in high glee;
Great bargains ev'ry day were made,
Lots of cash received and paid.
To amuse the folks in various ways,
At night were concerts, balls and plays;
To Vauxhall Rooms I went parading,
And view'd the gentry masquerading;
To merry music, light and gay,
In motley garbs they danced away.
May Barum rise in wealth and pow'r,
And gain importance ev'ry hour;
And as each annual fair comes round,
Improv'd in every way be found.
'Tis now high time, my worthy friend,
To bring my letter to an end.
Were I to mention all I saw,
On the delightful banks of Taw,
I really think that you would whistle,
At the length of my epistle;
So that I mayn't your patience try,
Believe me, truly yours, PAUL PRY. (1827)

A POEM, 1864

"What! Betsy Jane, you, up and down,
And dressed so, I declare!
But I forgot, you're going to town,
To be sure, 'tis Barnstaple Fair."

The matrons all like this exclaim,
Till it seems to ring in the air,
For all are off with might and main,
Hurrah! "Us be going to Fair".

Lads and lasses come trooping along,
And none to gainsay them dare,
Just list to the bells, how they go, ding dong,
"Come along, come along to the Fair!"

And now the dust rises all in a cloud,
'Tis Brown with his high-stepping mare,
He dashes past and exclaims aloud,
"Hillos! Aren't you going to the Fair?"

And so like this along the road,
Till you get to the town, and there
If ever a doubt your mind bestrode
'Twill vanish — 'tis Barnstaple Fair.

Just like an ocean of wild commotion,
Chatting and laughing and lemonade quaffing,
No merriment lacking, and nuts ever cracking;
No faces sad and no hearts sair, this my friend, is Barnstaple Fair.

Here's blooming Betsy, and John to meet her,
So stupid and bashful and loving a pair;
Of course she knows he's going to treat her –
She's to give him his answer this Barnstaple Fair.

Here's Brown and his six fine sisters,
All style and dash and glare;
And after following six young misters,
Dancing attendance at Barnstaple Fair.

And now between the elms we're strolling,
Meeting beauties rich and rare,
Love and horse flesh round us rolling,
Oh! The pleasures of Barnstaple Fair.

But the best of the Fair is down in the Square,
When the bells are ringing, and the boats are swinging,
The shouting of many, "walnuts ten-a-penny,"
Organs and monkeys, not a few human donkeys,
A clashing of bands, a few trembling hands,
A noise and a rout, a continued shout;
If this my friend, you think you can bear,
Pray hasten away to Barnstaple Fair.

A YOUNG LADY'S LAMENT FOR THE WET FAIR, 1864

Oh dearie me, oh dearie me, my heart is very sair,
Did ever anybody know such a drenching, stupid Fair?
My bonnet new, and dress so smart, I had fondly hoped to don,
But the rain came down in torrents and I could not put them on.
Gazing idly through the window I saw no one I knew,
Then glancing upward to the sky "no, not a bit of blue."
I'm not at all a moping, down-hearted little lass,
But to hear my uncle saying "Twas splendid for the grass"
Was almost I can tell you, too much for me to bear,
With dress and bonnet all put by expressly for the fair.
In knowing specs and stately silk, there sits my dear grand-dame,
She ever looks as tranquil, no matter clear or rain,
She chat away to uncle of gents, and ladies beaux,
"Things are changed so much," she says, "since by times used to be;"
Then peeps below her spectacles and glances round at me.
But I'm staring through the window at all things far and near,
My senses all engaged of course, I'm not supposed to hear.
But I listen to her lecture (wisdom's good in time of need)
And methinks gents must be changed — changed very much indeed,
But a grim old maid, of course, I know that I shall be,
Just then upstairs there came a gent, and said he'd come for tea.
He talked of plays and concerts and the country round about,
And then walked off quite nonchalent and never took me out.
Of course, I did not hint to him by gesture, word, or look,
How very much I should have liked to see Miss Charlotte Cooke.
At last the rain took breathing time, it turned a little fair,
And I and uncle sallied forth to "do" the Barum Square.
The Barum pavement I should say would beat most any town,
Sometimes 'tis up a little bit and then a little down,
And one thing we made sure of as onward we did go,
If water came not overhead 'twas plentiful below,
But never mind the water, we splash and dash along,
And in a very little time we reach the noisy throng.
The country lasses said the noise "their heads could not abide",
But how 'twas made and what I saw I'm sure I can't describe.
Here were travelling theatres and here a waxworks show,
And somewhere else I do not care and I'm sure I do not know.
So round we turn'd, and home we came, my heart was very sair,
And grand-ma meets us smiling, and "hopes I liked the Fair!"
But when the rain in torrents came, and I could not get a beau,
I could not help thinking to myself it was a little slow;
And never for the Barum Fair will e'er I start again,
If there should be the slightest chance of some of Devon's rain.

BARNSTAPLE FAIR
(By W. E. Heard, 1894)

Our town is full; we welcome in
The good old-fashioned Fair,
One relict of the olden days,
That glads us year by year.
Though many of us have out-grown
The noisy mirth and fun,
Yet many more are springing up
Just where our lives begun.

Our children now, with flushing cheeks
And joyous sparkling eyes,
Look on the scene of merriment
With just the same surprise.
"The Living Wonders of the Age"
Are still the same to-day
As they were in our youth, that's now
Hidden by time away.

Although so old 'tis ever new,
This good old-fashioned Fair~
A happy meeting, too, of friends,
Who come from far and near.
The farmer leaves all care behind,
Among the golden grain;
His wife and bonny daughters all
Are "fairing" once again.

Long may the Western Hills resound
With honest mirth and glee,
And troubles for the hour become
Only a memory.
And those who would condemn the law
That gives our town this right,
Need only see the happiness
On every face to-night.

GOING TO BARUM FAIR
(By W. E. Heard, 1900)

The scythe is silent on the hills;
The children seek no berries gay;
A new, sweet rapture each heart thrills ~
It is the old-time Fair to-day.

The maid is singing as she goes
About her duties merrily;
The farm boy dons his Sunday clothes ~
A dandy Johnny now is he.

The smiling lassie meets her swain;
The farmer gets the old mare out;
His bonny wife, quite young again,
The children greet with noisy shout.

Joy rings along the stubble grass,
And tunes the song-birds in the air;
It is a joyous throng that pass
The highway to old Barum Fair.

And over all the sweet bells ring;
Their merry voices seem to say:
"We unto old-time customs cling,
And ring in Barum Fair to-day."

FAR AWAY FROM BARUM FAIR
(By W. E. Heard, 1914)

Across the scented sweetness of this fair September
    day
We hear the glad bells ringing in their old-time
    merry way.
Unchanging 'mid Time's changes is the dear familiar
    strain~
That we, amid our sadness, can look up and smile
    again.
In spite of all the partings that have come to us this
    year,
We love their merry music as they ring in Barum
    Fair.
Though many have responded unto England's call
    to War,
And many vacant places about us all there
    are;
They gather not the harvest who so hopeful sowed
    the corn,
Nor fruit that now has ripened round the home
    where they were born~
Yet still, as bells are ringing, we see peopled
    everywhere
"Our darlings" who are fighting far away from
    Barum Fair.

AT BARUM FAIR, (AN INCIDENT).

(By Albert Ash Allen, 1937)

Of course I went to Barum Fair,
The third week in September,
And many Farmers I found there
Whose names I can't remember~
But one I know, was farmer Yeo,
His wife and daughter, and her beau!

Oh my, what caravans we saw,
All glittering ~ painted fine;
They fairly kept my mind in awe,
For how the things did shine!
And maidens fair, with golden hair,
And shoulders brown, but rather bare.

And there were clowns with painted face,
Bespangled, like the stars,
And columbines, in coloured lace,
And there were fat mamma's~
Who oft did say, "now walk this way"~
Sixpence is all you have to pay!"

And when the drums began to beat
A giant came in view~
"This man," she said, "knows no defeat,
A Cornish wrestler true~
In Barum Fair, if any dare,
Come now, and toss him, I declare!"

At this, a yeoman, bold and stout,
Said "I will have a try;
But if I knock the boaster out
What will his money buy?"
At which she said, "A sovereign red~
If you can toss him on his head."

And then a maiden's woeful cry
Was heard amongst the throng~
"Jan come away, and do not try
To wrestle with the strong~
For much I fear ~ oh Jan, my dear ~
Why do you leave me lonely here?"

But Jan had gone within the tent,
And never heard the sound;
His thought was on the giant spent,
And well he held his ground~
With muscles fed, he deftly led,
And threw the giant on his head.

And as he slowly left the scene
And sought the outer air,
The daughter of old Yeo, I ween,
Had lost her look of care~
And quickly ran, and said, "Oh Jan,
You are the dearest, bravest man!"

At this, we'll draw the veil, but show
Though women's hearts are true,
They have a weakness that we know

Will often see them through~
But valour more, will surely score,
As Jan's did, at the showman's door.

And as they left old Barum's Fair,
When all the fun was over;
Old Farmer Yeo did then declare
That Jan should live in clover:~
The wife said "Nay!" the daughter "Aye!"~
And Jan, the valiant: "Name the day!"

THE CRAFY PLOUGHBOY SONG

There was an old farmer in Devon did dwell,
He had a young son and to him he did tell,
"Go take yonder cow up to Barnstaple Fair:
Tho' she's a good cow, I can her well spare."

Derry down, down, down, derry down.

Young Dan started off with the cow in a band,
To Barnstaple Fair as you all understand,
But alack at an ale-house he met with three men,
And sold them the cow for nine pounds and ten.

Derry down, down, down, derry down.

There sat an old highwayman drinking his wine;
Said he to himself I will make that gold mine.
Quoth he "my young sir, if you're going my way,
Pray mount up behind, 'twill lighten the day."

Derry down, down, down, derry down.

They rode 'till they came to a very dark lane,
When the highwayman said "I do ward you quite plain
To deliver your money with out any strife,
Or else I will certainly take your sweet life".

Derry down, down, down, derry down.

Dan opened his coat and the money pulled out,
And on the green grass he did strew it about,
And while the old robber was filling his purse,
Young Dan saw his chance, rode off on his horse.

Derry down, down, down, derry down.

The highwayman shouted and swore he would fire,
But Dan crouched low and rode off thro' the mire,
And back to his father safe home he did bring
Horse, saddle and bridle a very good thing.

Derry down, down, down, derry down.

They opened the saddle bags there to behold
Five hundred good pounds in bright silver and gold,
With a brace of good pistols I'll swear and I'll vow~
"Why dang it!" said the farmer "you've well sold the cow."

Derry down, down, down, derry down.

BARNSTAPLE FAIR

(A song by Amy Cavan, 1931.)

I'm a rosy-cheek'd Devonshire maiden,
And I love all the fun of the fair;
I've got a most beautiful jumper,
And ribbons to match, for my hair.

But, father, he says I'm too flighty,
And mother says many a pray'r;
For Harry and Tommy, and Billy and Johnnie,
Are waiting for me at the Fair!

The organs are playing so sweetly,
The horses are swinging along,
I can hear all the noise and the laughter,
I'm longing to join in the throng.

Then I see mother's dear eyes look anxious,
And father pretends he don't care;
But, Harry and Tommy and Billy and Johnnie,
Are waiting in vain at the Fair!

Fair Hospitalities

From earlier times until the 1870s it was a recognised thing for the merchants and tradesmen to keep a free table for country customers and friends during the Fair. It was a time for settling outstanding debts to the firms who supplied seeds and other agriculture commodities. Accounts for clothing and footwear would also be paid at Barnstaple Fair. In return for their custom it was traditional to provide those that had travelled long distances to complimentary food and drink. The tradesmen dined friends from the locality too, the hospitality being enjoyed by all who were invited. A few references to this fact can be found in the newspaper reports of the day.

1828 *"The good old hospitable customs of our ancestors are still being kept up. The Dinner Tables of most of the inhabitants during the fair bending beneath the Weight of the rounds and ribs of their matchless oxen, to which all their Customers and friends were expected to do homage."*

<u>1836</u> *"The proverbial hospitality of our tradesmen has suffered no abatement; and the roast beef and pear pie, with other good things which smoaked on every board, and generous Barnstaple beer received ample honor from the numerous visitants."*

<u>1844</u> *"Many tradesmen dined several hundreds — some well on to a thousand each on the principal days of the fair."*

In <u>1856</u> it was said that one draper alone dined 500 people. From these two reported facts on numbers entertained, it gives us some idea of the extent to which the annual open house hospitality was carried out.

Moving on to the next decade, the year of <u>1863</u> was said to be never more generously dispensed with roast beef, apple pie and stewed pears having their accustomed attractions; "and potent liquors have their wonted exhilarating effects."

Ten years on the hospitalities are not maintaining their former greatness. Tradesmen are talking of either discontinuing or restricting it. According to W.F. Gardiner, the hospitality was very much abused with customers only owing small amounts making the house they patronised the headquarters for themselves and families. It is no wonder the custom gradually fell from favour! At the end of the 19th century just a few traders observed the old custom although in a much modified form. Early in the 20th century after the 1914-1918 War, the free lunches disappeared.

Out of interest:

Between 1850 and 1873 one trader's meat purchases to supply his fair table for that period of time was approximately, 40 cwt. It consisted of, all round rump of beef, chandler's cut, and pin round. Prices varied from 5d halfpenny per lb. in 1850, 7d for rump and 9d chandler's cut in 1860, to 10d all round in 1871.

The Cattle & Sheep Fair

Extracts taken from the 3rd vol. Of the "Borough Court Records of Barnestaple"
"Tolls for ev'y bullock 2d. viz., 1d a peece of the buyer and seller; for ev'y pigg 1d. a peece; for ev'y sheepe 1d a peece; for ev'y calfe 1d a peece."

17th century:
Richard Thomas, of Swansey, sold to Thomas Merchant, of Tawstock, 2 Welsh oxen, collared blacke.
George Coates, of West Down, sold to John Lee, of Combe Rawley, 8 heifers, black like; price £30 10s.
George Harris, of Marwood, sold to Henry Voysey, of Temple, 2 Black oxen, top cutt on the farther eare, price £13; the buyer takes the seller's word.
John Eller, of Rober, sold Jno. Hobbes, of South Molton, 2 heifers and one steward; the steward black, and the heifers, one red and the other rugged, price £6 13s. 4d.; buyer takes the seller's word.

Many hours before the proclamation of the opening of the Fair had been performed, farmers, and drovers had been busy bringing in their stock for sale from all districts leading into Barnstaple. By the time the Mayoral Procession had wended its way around the traditional focal points, the business of the Cattle and Sheep Fair was well under way with many a bargain struck at an early hour. For many years and well into the nineteenth century the cattle fair was held throughout Boutport Street. The noise, smell, and havoc wreaked by all the animals, must have been horrific for those living in the vicinity.

In <u>1828</u> the scene was described thus: *"The first day of the fair is filled with horned cattle in such numbers, that the houses in one of the principal streets, in which this portion of the fair is held, look as though they were besieged, being barricaded throughout with shutters, poles, and other fences to keep the cattle from breaking the windows or entering the houses."*

Things seemed to have calmed down marginally for the next few years as in <u>1837</u> it was agreed that, *"a great number of beasts was never remembered for the past twenty years."*

"Boutport Street was literally thronged, and the line of beasts extended beyond the Golden Lion, at one end, and around by

Pilton Bridge, up the North Gate, nearly to the Red Cross, at the other, branching also into Bear Street, Joy Street, and Vicarage Lane." For all that, it was remarked that the beasts were all of an ordinary description, and the fair did not exhibit any specimens of extraordinary prime North Devon Oxen, which were usually furnished by the principal neighbouring breeders on those yearly occasions. However, prices were good and sales many, to the extent only a small proportion were driven home unsold. Apparently, the best steers in the market were in a lot of ten belonging to a Mr. Fisher of Yarnscombe, which sold at £15 a piece.

Regarding the North Devon Oxen mentioned here, perhaps some readers would be interested in a Cattle Fair report from the *North Devon Journal* and re-produced here with the *Journal's* kind permission.

24th September 1824

"Our Fair on Monday last , presented as fine a shew of Cattle as was perhaps ever seen together; from the abundance of Grass which the late summer produced, the cattle were in very high condition, and the justly celebrated North Devon breed never appeared in greater perfection. Amongst the number of beautiful Oxen, we heard the ploughs of several Farmers mentioned as possessing peculiar merit; but the "Pride of the Fair" was that of Sir A. Chichester, Bart. Which consisted of 10 Bullocks, for fineness of hair and colour, symmetry of shape, and highness of proof, unrivalled, not only in the Fair, but probably in the West of England; this beautiful plough was sold at £24 per head. We have seen more Bullocks in the fair, but never was more business done; no Cattle were brought in but were, or might have been, sold, and at prices which the Farmers themselves call good. Cows and Calves were in great request; fat beasts in proportion to their quality from 8s.6d. to 10s. per score. Some idea may be formed of the immense number, and the proportionate Sale from this circumstance, that of 1440 Bullocks which came into the fair by the northern entrance of the town over Pilton Bridge, not 300 were driven out by that road. And of those perhaps more than half were sold. And by a calculation we have just seen, more than £20,000 was expended in the purchase of Cattle."

With the Cattle Fair monopolising all the attention, Barnstaple Fair was not at this time, regarded as a market for Sheep, and perhaps the scant mention (if any at all) is the reason for the lack of its report in the *Journal*? In any event, the Sheep and Cattle Fair took place on the same day and at the same venue in the nineteenth and twentieth centuries.

<u>1828</u> - Fat Wethers sold on an average of 5d per 1b.

<u>1838</u> - The Sheep fair was not abundantly supplied, and in ten years the fat sheep did not fetch more than 5d.1/2d. per 1b.

<u>1839</u> - A slight change of fortune for the Sheep Fair as it was plentifully supplied, the sales brisk with fat sheep and lambs fetching up to 6d per 1b.and horn breeding ewes, 15s.to18s each.

In <u>1841</u> the Cattle Fair was reported has having a brisker sale and better prices than the farmers had seen for many a long year, and thought that the dear days of Buonaparte had returned upon them again! At a very early hour, a great number of bullock dealers from Cornwall and the far eastern counties, had been anxious to make purchases. It is evident from this report, the importance of Barnstaple Fair to the dealers, who really did travel vast distances to attend and make their purchases. It is noted that the sales ranged from £7 fetched for yearlings to £21 for three year old steers. Mr Fisher is mentioned again with among others — Mr. Ridd of Bratton Fleming, Mr. Merson of North Molton, and Mr. Umbers of Warwickshire.

<u>1848</u> - The Town Council had recently enlarged the accommodation for the Sheep Market and the show of sheep was larger than ever before known.

<u>1850</u> - At the Cattle Fair scarcely any oxen were on show; a solitary pair of working oxen belonging to Mr. John Snow of Boode, fetched £30 and a coming pair of four year olds fetched £25 for Mr. William Crang of Knightacott. (Very little mention is made of oxen after this date.) A purchase of 27 heifers by Mr. John Turner by order of Earl Fortescue, was intended for his Lordships model farm at Castle Hill.

It was also in the September of 1850 that much debate was made at a Town Council Meeting over the Cattle Market site, and the welfare of the animals. A former proposal for the market's removal to the Rackfield, was deemed most unlikely that consent would be given by Sir Peregrine Acland, Bart. This was due in part to advice given him by his steward, Mr. Riccard. The Mayor's (John M Fisher) opinion was that the Rackfield would not be suitable, even if it could be had; for the approaches to it were altogether insufficient. Alderman Cotton although not despairing of the Rackfield, he had hoped before the last fair, the inhabitants of Boutport Street would have been relieved of the dangerous nuisance to which they had for too long been subjected, in having the cattle fairs held there. "It was a relic of a barbarous age which ought not to be tolerated any longer," he added. He went on to say that a large dealer in cattle — a Mr. Southcombe — had told him of the great injuries sustained by the beasts to their feet, by standing for so many hours on the hard pavement, which consequently disabled them from travelling. He did not believe there was a respectable town in the Kingdom in which so great a nuisance was suffered, and he trusted that a very short time would elapse before they should be rid of it. Alderman Latham called attention to the extreme cruelty carried out every fair towards the bullocks when they were being driven from the market by the toll-collectors and the drovers, who apparently beat the poor creatures shamefully about the head with their bludgeons. He trusted means would be taken next year to punish such brutality. This statement was concurred by Mr. Young, who, living in that part of the town for many years had witnessed this misconduct.

Following on from that, Alderman Cotton recollected that a child had lost its life due to the cattle in Boutport Street, and reminded everyone of the danger of the bullocks going into the houses there; an animal had intruded into the dining-room of the occupants of one house, and upset their dinner!

(It was to be another four years of turmoil in Boutport Street before any changes were made.)

1853 -The Sheep Fair was deemed worthy enough this year to get a good mention!

It was said that never, within the memory of the "oldest man living" nor since Barnstaple was Barnstaple, had there ever been seen so large a number of sheep in the fair. People wondered where they had all come from, as it had been said there really were no sheep in the country — none to be had for love or money! Evidently, there were so many brought together at the fair that there were more than the Sheep Market could accommodate, all the pen-room had been occupied and sheep still came pouring in. The Council had to muster some hurdles to improvise as pens; these were soon used up and the over-spill had to take up quarters in Tuly Street. The congregated flocks were stuffed into every corner and were running over. With such a supply, demand was easily met causing sellers to submit to a reduction in prices. They came with high expectations but many felt keen disappointment; one seller was reported to be so mortified that he declared he would sooner throw his sheep over Barnstaple Bridge, than accept the reduced offers made to him!

At least the sheer numbers of sheep at the fair, put paid to the grumblings of a few people regarding the more commodious sheep-market that was soon to be provided. "The room would never be wanted for markets and fairs" they said, "and all would be going to Davy Jones!"

1854 - At last the issue of the Cattle and Sheep Fair has been resolved by its removal to the area we now know as Victoria Road, but was then adjoining Cooney-bridge. In the *North Devon Journal* on the 19th September, 1854 it was described thus:

> "*Another change took place yesterday, the removal of the Cattle Fair from its ancient site, the streets of the town, to one prepared for it by the Council, between the town itself and the village of Newport.*
>
> *The New Cattle Market is a very wide macadamised road, bounded on each side by a well-built wall into which rings are inserted at intervals, for tying the cattle to, a wide foot-walk being laid down for them to stand on. The Sheep Fair is provided for on a piece of similarly prepared road, going off at a right angle with the other.*"

As is often the case for Barnstaple Fair, rain made its presence known for much of the day. It delayed active business to such an extent that there was no selling before 8 o'clock in the morning much to the impatience of the sellers. But by noon the best lots had changed hands, and animals of inferior quality hung on hand. The non-appearance of some dealers was attributed to "bullock fever," a disease then not curable by (doctors.) The sellers who stuck out for late prices had to drive their beasts' home again.

(As a point of interest, when passing through Victoria Road, just take a few moments to stand and stare. You will find a few remaining tethering rings embedded in the left hand wall leading up from Rock Park - just before the roundabout. Iron remnants of the past nearing 150 years old!)

29. Cattle tethering rings. Site of former cattle fair, Victoria Road, Barnstaple. (Photograph © Shane Woods).

On the whole, the new site went down well, especially the Sheep Market. It was felt however that a shed roof would be desirable for the sheep in the wide pens, to shelter them from the rain. It was everybody's opinion that far more sheep could be exhibited than could be penned in the old market.

The value of sales on Fat Sheep was adjudged to be 3s. a head lower than Bratton Fair.

1854 - Numbers of sheep penned were around 3,000 and relatively greater than the gathering of cattle.

1858 - A nice lot of mountain sheep were exhibited by Mr. Smith of Emmett's Grange. 300 sheep of all kinds were shown by Mr. Jewell, of Langtree.

The Cattle seem to be back to their usual standards in the report of the day in 1858 The Cattle Market adjoining Cooney-bridge was filled with men and animals from end to end. There were stated to be from 1,700 to 1,800 beasts exhibited, mostly in prime condition. A vast number of beautiful animals were on view and Devon cattle reflected the highest praise for the breeders.

1859 - Heavy showers of rain had fallen throughout the morning, and, as the sewers and drains had been neglected, the ground resembled a quagmire that "reflected great discredit upon the Town Council." The show of cattle exceeded anything that had been witnessed for ten years past, and the leading breeders and agriculturists of the district were present and those noticed were:

William Hole, Esq., of Hannaford, Mr. George Lovering, of Chappletown; Mr. W.B. Fisher, of Pottington Barton; Mr. Edwin Maunder, of Heasleigh; Mr. Richard Turner, sen., of Grange; Mr. Richard Turner, jun.,of Dowland Barton; Mr. John Turner, of Abbotsham; Mr. Wm. Turner, of Bideford; Mr. George Burden, of Kerscott; Mr. George Langdon, of Strand House, Ashford; Mr. Southcombe, of Arlington Barton; Mr. Thomas Stone, of Tree; Mr. J. Buckingham, of Clatworthy; Mr. T.D. Ridd, of Chelfam; Mr. Philip Rock, of Gratton; Mr. N. Chammings, of Highbray; Mr. Norman, of Exmoor; Mr. Thomas Yeo, of Dinuaton; Mr. Norman, of Frithelstock; Mr. Norman, of Heanton Court; Mr. George H. Day, of Liscott;Mr. James Day, of Westdown; Mr. James Harris,of Bittadon; Mr. George Downing, of Pickwell Barton;Mr. Joshua Downing, of Horwood Barton; Mr. John Shapland, of Heale; Mr. John Dennis, of Sticklepath; Mr. Wm. Buckingham, of Landkey; Mr. John Andrew, of Umberleigh Barton; Mr. W. Balsdon, of Westcott; Mr. Jas. Moore, of Week; Mr. Shapland, of Damage; Mr. Cawsey, of Alverdiscott.

Besides these, Earl Fortescue sent a splendid lot of steers, and Dr. Yeo, of Fremington House, made drafts from his flock of choice and healthy sheep.

<u>1861</u>-During the previous night and on the morning of the fair, heavy rain had fallen rendering the ground into a complete swamp. *"A most comfortless place for men and beasts."*

The Sheep Fair was fully supplied but few fine flocks exhibited due to some of them being afflicted with "Caw." Nott Ewes fetched 28s.to 35s.Horn Ewes 20s.to 25s. Breeding Ewes 35s.Wether Mutton, 6d per 1b.and Ewe Mutton 5d half-penny.

Again, among the exhibitors were:

Mr. Geo. Lock, of Instow; Mr. Richard Pethebridge, of Pill; Mr. John Dennis, of Sticklepath; Mr. Richard Packer, of Herton; Mr. John Ware, of Hollamore; Mr. John Ching, of Dean; Mr. Stone, of Tree; Mr. Crocker, of Fremington; Mr. Stanbury, of Viveham; Mr. T.D. Ridd, of Chelfam Barton; Mr. R. Pethebridge, of Alverdiscott; and Mr. Dyer, of Tadscombe.

<u>1864</u> - It seems that weather and conditions have not improved — the *North Devon Journal* reporter is quite appalled over the state of affairs, (quite rightly so) and berates the Town Council in his account.

"The Cattle Fair was held in the new Cattle Market, Victoria Road, which was in a comfortless state that beggars description. The roadway was a quagmire, and both men and beasts were exposed to the cold and the rain which heavily descended in incessant showers. To charge toll for the use of such a place is a gross imposition; and we cease to wonder that graziers could not be induced to incur the risk of sending their beasts, to such a market. The civic wisdom of the borough has not provided any means of shelter."

However, at the opening of the Fair Ceremony, the Mayor (Thomas Guppy) stated he hoped he should live to see the time when a more convenient site for holding the cattle fair should be provided.

<u>1874</u> - A statement was made that in order to keep the road open from the Devon & Somerset Railway into town via Barbican, the Sheep Fair would be held in the field opposite the station. This was now to be the accustomed venue until 1892.

<u>1875</u> - Due to an outbreak of Foot and Mouth Disease in the district, some doubt existed as to the Annual Cattle & Sheep

Fair taking place. Although it did go ahead, the knowledge of the outbreak (mild as it was) seriously prejudiced the fair, both in quantity of stock for sale and numbers of buyers.

<u>1886</u> - There was cause for some special interest when the "Queen of the Bay" came up the river Taw, bringing for the first time, a consignment of stock from Lundy Island for Barnstaple Fair. The importer, who personally supervised the operation, was a Thomas H. Wright, Esq. The stock included 200 sheep, 20 beasts, and a horse. The embarking of the animals afforded the inhabitants of the Island great excitement, each animal having to swim alongside the vessel and then be slung-up aboard! Loading commenced at 5 o'clock in the morning, the Queen of the Bay steaming away from the Island at 3p.m. It arrived before dark at the Quay at Barnstaple. An incident along the way of two bullocks "attempting suicide" by jumping overboard, was a lively diversion for the owner and the steamer's company!

At the fair, the auctioneers Messrs. Sanders & Son, disposed of the stock at good prices for Mr. Wright, and it was the opinion of many that the Island mutton was the best fed in Devon. It was said that several persons looked forward to the privilege of dining on it during the coming week.

<u>1891</u> - Victoria Road as a venue for the Cattle & Sheep Fair is in its last year.

<u>1892</u> - After 36 years that saw many changes in the development of the area now known as Victoria Road, the Annual Cattle & Sheep Fair had, at long last, been removed from this site much to the relief and delight of the local inhabitants. The Town Council were congratulated on this turn of events. They had previously purchased some property next to the town Cattle Market (opened in 1848) to enlarge the facilities and accommodate the Fair market. (Up to 1837 the only enclosure for livestock for market purposes was a Pig Market — a narrow strip running from Castle Street towards Tuly Street, and on Fair days livestock lined Boutport Street. The Council extended the Pig Market in 1846 and 1852 to make accommodation for other stock.) All who had business to do at the Fair were delighted with the change of venue. The attendance of the agriculturists was above average, and many

up-country dealers attended and made extensive purchases. The highest quotations for any animal in the Fair appeared to be between £17 and £18.

With the change of venue the Sheep Fair was accommodated in the new section of the Cattle Market. There was an exceptionally large supply of sheep and they were penned on the North Wall, for many years known as the showground. The new entrance to the Cattle Market at the site of the old Oxford Hall (formerly Bell's School) afforded ready communication between the two sections of the fair. At the sale held by Messrs. Sanders & Son, of Barnstaple, a large number of Ewes made from 16s. 6d.to 30s. 6d.and Rams from £4 to £7.

1896 - 1,000 Bullocks were driven into the Cattle Market.

1899 - The last Cattle Fair of the 19th century saw the amount of bullocks brought in as not exceeding 300. It was thought that the long drought and the consequent scarcity of keep had a lot to do with the low numbers. The only "head" for which any enquiries had been made, was for fat beef, there being little or no trade for store stock. One farmer offered his steers for the comparatively low price of £15 per head, but even at this price he could not clear them.

G.H. Gould was another auctioneer mentioned conducting business in the Fair Ground that day. Business for both Cattle & Sheep was concluded at 1 o'clock.

The last Barnstaple Sheep Fair of the 19th century turned the tables on the Cattle Fair in its size — scant mention is a thing of the past! So far as numbers were concerned, thousands were penned and probably proved a record with special pens having to be erected in the middle of the market and reserved spaces in the North Walk apart from all the usual pens being filled. However, business was slow until vendors decided to reduce prices!

Exmoor Ewes making 24s to 30s., and Horn Ewes 23s to 35s.

Sanders & Son had previously advertised their auction for "Barnstaple Great Fair on Wednesday 13th September for the important sale of — Devon Longwool and Hampshire Down Rams from noted flocks." The sale was consequently reported as "Seventeen very fine Devon Longwool ram lambs belonging to Mr. W. Copp, of Woodbury, sold at from £3 5s.to £3 10s.each;

and fifteen splendid Hampshire Down ram lambs owned by Mr. W. Coles, of Warminster, at from £2 2s 6d.to £4 4s. each."

30. Barum Sheep Fair, 1908. The young girl is the photographer's
daughter, Elsie Wood.   (Photographer: W.S.Wood)
(© Tom Bartlett Postcard Collection EX34 9SE)

Settling nicely now into the twentieth century, we will venture forward to the year 1914

The Great War (1914-1918) seems to have had little effect on the Cattle & Sheep Fair. The attendance was large, bringing dealers from Wiltshire, Dorset, and other counties. Mr. F. Chanter of Barnstaple disposed of a batch of fat heifers at £19 a piece, 36 steers from £16 - £19 a piece, and a number of fat cows at £20 each. From even further a-field, Messrs. Murphy, of Cork, Ireland, had on offer 100 shorthorns and polss heifer yearlings, which were disposed of from 5 to 10 guineas.

The sheep section was good in quality and numbers regardless of a large auction, that had been held two weeks previously. Mr. P.B. May, Barnstaple had 900 sheep on offer. A batch of 200 Exmoor ewes were sold to Mr. Jeffrey, of Wiltshire, for 45s.each. A pen of 70 sheep were disposed of by Messrs. R Isaac & Son, of Barnstaple which included black faced store rams at 39s. 6d. each.

The well-known Barnstaple auctioneers Messrs. Sanders & Son, were now accompanied by — Messrs. Blackford & Son, Southmolton and Messrs. Slee & Sons of Torrington.

However, things were not so good by 1918. Interference of the weather for the corn harvesting affected both supply and attendance. One farmer voiced his opinion by saying "people have not the heart to buy cattle when corn is growing out and rotting."

Mr. J.M. Metherall, J.P., CC, responding to the Mayor's (F.A. Jewell) toast to the "Success to Barnstaple Fair and Agriculture," at the Fair Opening Ceremony, appealed for volunteers to help garner what remained of the corn crops, (during the War, over 50% of men had been taken from the land) for although wheat had been mostly saved the other half of the crops remained out, and were being badly damaged. Fewer up-country buyers were in attendance due to difficulties of transit in wartime.

The consensus of opinion regarding the Sheep Market was "A fairly good trade."

1939 - With the outbreak of the second World War not only are animals understandably down in numbers for the fair - again, attendance was sparse and trading very small.

Messrs. Sanders & Son were still auctioneering, and one other mentioned as Messrs. Cockram, Dobbs & Stagg, of South Molton.

By 1946 the traditional Cattle Fair appears to have given way to the weekly cattle market auctions we know today, and has disappeared in its own right. Places such as Blackmoor Gate and South Molton became known as the venues for annual animal fair and auctions.

The Sheep Fair was still part of the scene, but it is apparent that it was in a gradual decline, in popularity. The last mention for the Sheep Fair as such, appears to be in 1955. But a mention of the sale of Dorset Down Rams making 38 guineas at Barnstaple Fair Ram Sale appeared in 1966.

The Annual Cattle & Sheep Fair as a traditional part of "Barnstaple Great Fair" has ended. But the weekly auction for the Cattle & Sheep market is still a customary event at Barnstaple on a Friday. Who knows however, what may happen to this in the future!

BARNSTAPLE GREAT FAIR, 1863.

ALTERATION OF TIME.

NOTICE IS HEREBY GIVEN, that in pursuance of the New Bye Laws, approved by One of Her Majesty's Principal Secretaries of State, on the 8th July, 1863, the GREAT

ANNUAL CATTLE FAIR

Will be held this Year and henceforth on the Wednesday, preceding the 20th September.
The Fair for the present Year will be
ON WEDNESDAY, SEPTEMBER 16TH, AND TWO FOLLOWING DAYS.

MICHAEL COOKE, MAYOR.

Guildhall, Barnstaple, August 12th, 1863. [723

Sales by Auction.

NOTICE.
BARNSTAPLE FAIR.

MR. WM. COLE will Sell by Public Auction, in the Sheep Market, on Wednesday, the 14th day of September, 1881, 7 Hogg and 2 two-year-old LONG WOOL RAMS, of very superior quality, the property of Mr. Courtney, Eastacott, Chittlehampton.

Sale at 12 o'clock.

Dated the Unicorn Hotel, Southmolton, 7th Sept.

W. O. SMITH & CO. 1886

ARE NOW OFFERING

PURE ENGLISH LINSEED, FINEST COTTON AND WATERLOO ROUND CAKES,

AT EXTRAORDINARY LOW PRICES

STORES:—POTTINGTON, BARNSTAPLE,

1898

QUIBELL'S
SHEEP DIPS

For Curing SCAB,

For Killing TICKS,

For Improving WOOL.

To Prevent the Fly Striking,

— USE —

QUIBELL'S POWDER DIP.

——o——

Agent for Barnstaple and District:—JAMES PARTRIDGE, Apothecaries' Hall, Barnstaple.

1907

BOROUGH of BARNSTAPLE

THE ANNUAL CATTLE, HORSE & PLEASURE

— FAIR —

WILL BE HELD ON

☞ WEDNESDAY, THURSDAY, AND FRIDAY,

18TH, 19TH & 20TH SEPTEMBER, 1907.

———o———

The CATTLE AND SHEEP FAIR will be held on WEDNESDAY, the 18th, and the HORSE FAIR on THURSDAY of the Fair week only.

There will be no Horse Fair on the Wednesday.

N.B.—ALL TOLLS at the Cattle and Sheep Fair MUST BE PAID at the time the Animals enter the Market. This rule must be strictly observed. Animals will not be received without the Tolls being paid.

———o———

NOTICE IS HEREBY GIVEN that the Sale and Use of CONFETTI, TEASERS, or the like, at or during the Fair, are STRICTLY PROHIBITED.

By order of the Town Council of Barnstaple.

. JAMES BOSSON, Town Clerk.

Dated, Municipal Buildings, Barnstaple, August 27th, 1907. [7337]

The Horse Fair

Extract from "The Maid of Sker" by R.D. Blackmore — (1872)
— Set in the year 1782

"And so we pushed on, and the people pushed us. After a little more of this, and Ikey bragging all the time, though I saw nothing very wonderful, we turned the corner of a narrow street, that opened into a broader one. Here there seemed to be no bullocks such as had made us keep springs on our cables, but a very amazing lot of horses, trotting about, and parading, and rushing, most of them with their tails uphoisted, as if by discharging tackle. Among them stood men, making much of their virtues, and sinking their faults (if they had any), and cracking a whip every now and then, with a style of applause toward them.

I had just hailed a man with a colt to show off, and commodores pendants all over his tail, and was keeping clear of his counter to catch the rise of the wave for boarding him, when a hush came over all the hands as if the street had been raked with chain-shot. And on both sides of the street all people fell back and backed their horses, so that all the roadway stood as clear as if the fair had turned into Sunday morning."

Traditionally held on the second day of Barnstaple Great Fair, and spilling over into the next day, the horses were paraded in fine style to tempt prospective buyers into parting with their money. Things were often kept in perpetual motion by the constant galloping to and fro of the horses by their riders, and it was sometimes wondered if those on horseback were more interested in showing themselves off as well as their horses, rather than get down to the serious business of striking a bargain! The clatter of hooves on ground, accompanied by the whinny of horse and colt and the pitched voices of the horse jobbers jabbering their peculiar jockey slang, added to the excitement of the scene. A rich tapestry of noise, colour and smell. The customary venue for the Horse Fair has been quoted as *"from time immemorial held in the North Walk,"* and in <u>1828</u> was described as *"near the North Walk, which is one of the most beautiful promenades in the West of England."* In <u>1829</u> confirmation of the site was given as *"held as usual, in the waste and road adjoining the North Walk, formerly part of the 'Castle Manor'."* The site was to change later on in the nineteenth century, but for now we will slip a little further back in time for some 'horsy' information!

References made to the buying and selling of horses can be seen in the extracts taken from the 3rd volume of the 'Borough Court Records of Barnestaple' noted by Thomas Wainright.

*"**Barnestaple, the register of horses and mares bought, sold, and exchanged in the ffayre there holden on the feast day of the Nativitie of our Blessed Virgin Mary, the 8th day of September, in the fowerth yeare of our Sov'eigne Lord Charles of England, &c. Tolls for ev'y horse, mare, or colt, 8d. Viz., for record 4d., and for custome 2d a peece of the buyer and seller."***

This fair attracted buyers and sellers not only from the North Devon Parishes, but also from the remoter districts. In the 1600's, among the distant places from which the buyers came are — Kirckly (Lancaster), Lyfton, Bristol, Sampford Courtenay, Milverton, Thornbury, Exeter, London, Stratton, Hawkridge (Somerset), Launson (Launceston), Seaton, Lanruddean (Wales), Morebath, Mumbles (Wales), St. Gerrans (Cornwall), Whiteson (Cornwall), Winsfard (Somerset), Tavistock, Temple (Cornwall), Dunster, Combe Raleigh, Cheddar (Somerset), Camelford, and Padstow.

The seller of an animal had to give "surety" for his trustworthiness, unless "the parties knew each other." It can be seen in the register of horse fairs, that the marks on each animal are always given. The most common were those cut in one of the ears, as a halfpenny, a square, a slit, a "top," a stubb, a hitch, a snip, or in some cases, there were brands on the buttocks as letters or a horseshoe.

Edward Frye of Dulverton in the county of Somerset bought of Mary Richards, wife of Henry Richards of Kentisbery, in the county of Devon, one little chestnut nagge slit in the farther eare, and a spade cutt in the neare eare, price 40sh. The parties knowe eache other.

John Bishopp of South Molton hathe exchanged with Walter Symon of Rackingford a taddie woo mare for a little bay nagge with a white face, and Bishopp hadd 10sh. boote.

Arthure Serjante of Kirchbe in Lancaster sold unto Richard Chapple of Ilfarcombe in the county of Devon one greye geldinge, snipt in the bottome of both eares, Price £3 2s. 6d. The Parties knowe each other.

An example of the "Fair" transactions and prices fetched for horses bought before 1629 are as follows:

Thomas Garland, of Mort, sold unto John Pell, of Woostree, one bucke colt, colour brown baye, with a slit in the near eare, price 43s. John Combe, Ilfracombe, knoweth the seller.

Abraham Hearson, of Tawton, sold unto Wm. Earle, of Biddiford, one black mare, with a hitch in the near eare, price 33sh. John Dillon knoweth the seller.

Henry Puggesley, of Bratton, sold unto Walter Thomas, of South Molton, one little bay nagge with a square halfpenny under the farther eare, price 27sh. The parties know each other.

The total number of horses disposed of at this fair was 44; six were exchanged; the price of two are not given; the remaining 36 average £2 0s. 0½d.each, the highest price paid being £4 5s.for "one bay nagge" sold by Wm. Mare, of Fremington and the lowest 10s. 6d.for "one little nagge" sold by Richard Mule, of Tawton. (Mare and Mule — how appropriate!)

At this period of time, animals were sold at low prices and the horses were very cheap. This was probably due to the difficulty of moving them as roads were little better than rutty

lanes in those days, and the invention of the railways for
transportation was far into the future.

	Horses Disposed of.	Average Price.	Highest.	Lowest.
		£ s. d.	£ s. d.	£ s. d.
1629	39	2 9 8	7 0 0	9 0
1630	97	2 9 9	5 2 0	9 0
1631	60	2 19 8½	6 9 0	14 0
1632	26	2 16 2	6 0 0	13 4
1633	33	3 5 0	8 16 8	17 0
1634	29	2 18 0	5 0 0	18 0
1635	21	2 1 10	4 10 0	4 8
1636	17	2 15 7	3 18 4	1 6 0
1637	22	2 19 1	5 10 0	19 6
1638	31	2 18 0	7 10 0	19 0
1639	56	2 14 0	4 10 0	18 0
*1640				
1641	9	2 14 5	5 6 0	13 0
+1642	3			
1643	2	1 15 6	2 0 0	1 11 0
‡1644				
‡1645				
‡1646				
1647	46	4 3 4	5 6 0	15 0
1648	5	2 14 0	5 0 0	1 1 0
1649	37	3 15 10	7 10 0	1 7 0
1650	17	4 5 8	7 3 0	1 0 0
1651	12	3 16 0	5 5 0	1 0 0

* Not entered.
† No prices given.
‡ No entries during these years of Civil War.

The accounts of the years 1650 — 1651 show the rise in prices
most likely caused by the demand for horses occasioned by the
English Civil War. Examples are given as:

*John Curry of Yarnescombe sold unto David Fosse of
Chumeley a black nagge, a halfpenny under the farther
eare, price £4. Mathew Lovebone of Yarnescombe
pledge.*

*Abraham Cudmore of Alverdiscott sold unto William
Kelland of Chittlehampton a sorrel nagg with a white
starr in the forehead, price £3 17s. The buier takes the
sellers word.*

*William Lewes of Tawton Epi sold unto Richard Udy of
Greate Torrington a gray nagg, stubbed under the neer
eare, price £6 13s. 4d.Anthony Heddon of Swimbridge
pledge.*

*Humfrey Langdon of Barnestaple sold unto Richard
Dunscombe of Ringsaishe a ireon gray nagg, top cut in
the farther eare, price £3 13s. 4d. Christopher Hill
pledge.*

97

Thomas Bragg of Berrynerber sold a browne bay nagg (noe marke) unto Nicholas Dennys of Braunton, price £4 15s. The buier takes the seller's word.

Mr. Robert Dennis of Bideford sold a browne bay mare, a starr in the forehead, unto Frauncis Heale of Chumeley, price £3 13s. 4d The buier takes the seller's word.

John Earnestt of Ilfordecombe sold a surle (sorrel) nagg a stubb upon both yeares with a black list, unto Joane Nickels of Wesley, price five pound.The byer takes the seller's word.

Moving swiftly now into the nineteenth century, we can see how things have changed and not necessarily for the better! Reports from the *North Devon Journal* are varied regarding the horse dealer's fortunes.

<u>1827</u> - "The Horse Fair was very full; very high prices were asked, but it is difficult to ascertain what they were really sold for."

<u>1829</u> - Horse dealers who had for a number of years frequented the fair, said they never knew of so little business done in the horse department.

<u>1830s</u> - Business appears to be very poor in this decade and not worthy of note.

<u>1840</u> - This year saw the Horse Fair transacting business on Saturday, Monday and Tuesday. Although exhibiting a number of cart colts, there were very few good hunting or carriage horses, although six or seven belonging to, John Knight, Esq., of Simonsbath, fetched from £20 to £45 each. A good deal of business was done by way of bartering and it was said "some who had not their wits about them bitterly lament their bargains!" Prices appeared to be downwards due to grass being short and winter keep high.

<u>1845</u> - There was a demand for horses fit for hunters or roadsters, but they were not to be had, except in the hands of one or two dealers. The price asked for promising colts was from £20 to £23.

Any case of "sharp practice" was an unwanted feature at the fair, but there was always someone destined to become a ready victim! An instance in this year was of a young farmer from Lynton who bought and paid £7 for a horse. He had not taken the precaution of removing his purchase immediately and upon his return after an hours absence found his horse had been exchanged for a "miserable beast, not worth a sovereign." It culminated in a take it or leave it situation — the farmer chose to leave it and left the fair minus £7!

1846 - The breeding of horses in the area had been neglected for a few years. It was feared that the idea of a railway extension to the district would extinguish the demand for them. This was found to be groundless as good horses were in great demand, and prices obtained by the breeders at the fair made a handsome profit. Mr. Matthews of Exmoor had a string of young galloways and ponies, and some good hunters for which high figures were demanded. A few cart colts fetched from £23 to £28 and a very handsome pony 12 hands high, fetched £18.

1853 - Horses displayed were brought in chiefly by dealers, and as usual, it was Reported, no great number from the neighbourhood. There had been some horse "jockeying" (sharp practice) business methods used, and the *Journal* reporter seems to have taken great delight in informing readers - "*A farmer of a neighbouring parish — we don't mean to give his name, as the man who thinks himself "up to snuff" does not like to have it known that he has been duped — was " regularly done" in the purchase of a horse. He was negotiating a bargain with a horse dealer for an animal he had taken a fancy to, but finding the owner "full tough" to deal with, a third party, having the appearance of a country clergyman came at his request, to the assistance of the buyer, and the bargain was by and bye concluded. The money was paid, the dealers disappeared, and the farmer found himself possessed for his forty guineas of a rosinante, half blind,aged, and infirm, which he afterwards sold for 35s.*"
(No wonder the farmer wanted his name kept quiet!)

<u>1854</u> - This year the horse fair was held on the site of the new sheep market. *"There were some flashy-looking animals, flashily got up, but there were some very sober contrasts to them."* The time during the afternoon appeared to be occupied in inspection and galloping about. The fair was continued into the next day where a considerable amount of horse flesh was gathered there, *"from the superior beast sold for £40 down to the most pitiable collection of animated bones, about which, whoever brought it there must have made a mistake, and taken it to the fair instead of the knacker's yard."* The general show of horses was described as inferior, with no great business done, buyers fighting shy of strange dealers! Several gipsies were reported among the sellers, and some other jockeys of a more respectable class. No evidence of *"flagitious acts of jockeyism so frequently occurring at fairs"* was found.

<u>1855</u> - Held on its old site at the North Walk, several gipsies attempted to practice their jockeyism at the horse fair, on the *"duller wits of heavy customers from the country."* (It can only be assumed that this quote refers to strapping country lads of the time — strong in the arm and weak in the head!) There were also several instances of conflicts between the collector of tolls and people riding in and out from the fair. When asked for tickets to be shown, some riders refused and had their horses seized as a consequence, which led in some cases to blows being dealt!

<u>1862</u> - Of the 200 horses offered for sale only 22 were shown by *"jockeys."*

<u>1863</u> - *"There were some wretched old 'screws' offered that would be dear in any money."*

<u>1871</u> - Demand for horses was great, and reported to be stimulated by the void left by the consumption of large numbers as human food during the siege of Paris. Never before had horses been remembered to be so scarce; they had been eagerly sought out and bought up in all parts of the district. Few fine animals were shown, and they were sold at very high prices. Neat riding horses 15 hands above, fetched £50, which a few years previous would have been considered

well sold at £30. Such was the enquiry, that anyone who had a good thing to sell had no difficulty in getting its full value.

1873 - Formerly, strings of horses — of young cart horses especially — used to be brought to the fair from up the country. Now the dealers were coming from a distance to buy and not to sell.

The highest price made was 80 guineas for a fine young hunter sold by Mr. Shapland, of Fylden, North Molton. Mr. Smyth, of Westland Pound, sold a hunter for £75. Mr. Allen, of London purchased a string of 25 hacks at prices from £20 - £35. Mr. Brookes, of Heanton Satchville, sold a pair of fine young cart horses, bought for Mr. Gould, of Poltimore, for £100. A sale by auction took place of some of the surplus horses of the railway contractor, Mr. Taylor: 17 were advertised for sale, but only a few found buyers.

1874 - Many eager buyers were present from Birmingham, Bristol, Bath, Exeter, Plymouth, and elsewhere. A great deal of money changed hands. Many farmers made £50, £60, £80 and even £100 being paid for a first-class hunter. Weight carriers and posting horses were worth up to £70. Ponies and galloways made from £15 to £25. It was noted that an invariable feature of the fair in former years — the strings of cart colts – were entirely absent.

1879 - Since 1877 the venue for the Horse Fair had been changed to the Strand, due to the removal of the pleasure fair from the square to North Walk. The Strand was reported to be crowded with buyers, sellers, and lookers-on. Among the horses for sale was a few offered from the stud of the Right Hon. Earl Fortescue, but only two were sold for breeding purposes, and those at low figures. Overall sales were down between 20 & 40% on the previous years figures.

1882 - It would appear that although the Horse Fair was customarily held on the Thursday each year, it had now become usual for its commencement on the Wednesday afternoon immediately after the Cattle Fair had ceased to be the centre of attraction. The space between the bottom of Cross Street and the end of the Bridge was utilised for the purposes of exhibiting the animals. The Bridge itself and the Taw Vale Parade made very suitable trying grounds for intending purchasers. It was stated - "*as might be expected, such a large Fair as the Barnstaple September one could scarcely be without some excellent animals. Mr Tom Horn, of the Horse Repository, Bear Inn, tied up a very creditable lot, among them being several sound and clever hacks, carriage-horses and hunters. He sold several of them during the two days of the Fair at prices ranging from £40 to £60.*" ·

For the next few years the Horse Fair "jogged along at a steady pace" with not much of a change to speak of. In <u>1887</u> there is mention of animals suitable for tram-work being much in demand and <u>1888</u> saw the scarcity of drays. Mr Edward Mugford, of Barnstaple sold one of his colts — out of his well-known mare and sired by the Earl of Portsmouth's Sailor — for £26 in <u>1889</u>. Moving to <u>1894</u> it is clear that the observance of Thursday for the Horse Fair is speedily becoming a thing of the past. Farmers and dealers find that making their business transactions for all of the animals on the first day of the fair, more convenient. Practically the whole of the horses were paraded on the day before and a large amount of interest centred in the Strand and a portion of the Taw Vale Parade. Around 400 horses were shown.

By <u>1898</u> the Thursday Horse Fair is in a serious state of deterioration and seen as in danger of becoming a farce. It is feared that unless something is done. "Barnstaple Horse Fair — as it has been known for generations — is doomed."

At the end of the 19th century, the Horse Fair sees very little change in the dispute over the traditional day. Thursday is still hanging on by the skin of its teeth, but as a rule now, most of the business is being done on the Wednesday. Several hundred horses were being paraded along the Strand and a few were exceptional – A fine weight-carrying hunter belonging to Mr. J. Alford and the well-known winner "John Barleycorn" belonging to Mr. W. Edger, was selling for £130 each. Mr J. Smallridge was asking £65 for a smart lightweight hunter. Mr. Warren Jnr., of Heale Farm, Kingsnympton, was mounted on a pony in the fair, when he received a terrific kick in the leg by a horse. Having treated the injury, Dr. Harper advised Warren to proceed to the North Devon Infirmary. Fortunately no bones were broken. (Over the years many accidents occurred at the animal fairs.

This was to be expected considering the huge numbers of beasts attending.)

1899 - Barnstaple Fair Wednesday September 13th Several lots on view morning of sale At the Golden Lion Stables Sale 2 o'clock — Frank Trapnell of Bideford (Includes Bay Cob 14.3 perfection. Single & Double Harness. Wheel Gig.)

1899 - G.H. Gould will conduct his usual Auction for Horses outside the Old Quay Station on Wednesday 13th Sept. at 4 o'clock and on Thursday 14th at 2 o'clock. There are numerous enquiries for Posters And Carriage Horses.

At the beginning of the 20th century people are still bemoaning the fate of the traditional Horse Fair. A lot of the business is being done in the hotel yards long before the commencement of the fair, and the parade of horses along the Strand is fewer by consequence.

1914 - With the outbreak of the Great War and the demand on the district for horses in connection with the hostilities, the number paraded along the Strand did not exceed 150 animals. "Thursday" seems to be back in favour but there were no big price horses in the fair. A few useful harness horses sold readily up to 40 guineas apiece and a batch of young Irish Hunters made from £20 to £35 apiece. The remainder of the horses were mostly in the hands of visiting dealers and trade for the most part was dragging. Superior horses were undoubtedly very scarce and the advice given to agriculturists by Councillor T.W. Pearce at the Fair opening ceremony was, "to breed only the best, with the old-fashioned type of Exmoor pony as the foundation."

1918 - Most of the best "blood" horses were acquired early by a Remount Officer, for the Army. Mr. Withecombe, of Littleham, sent a number of useful vanners, which realised up to £120 apiece. Mr. Payne of Newton Abbot, introduced a lot of heavier horses with one magnificent specimen fetching £180.

1919 - Although only 120 animals were assembled on the Strand it proved to be more than the previous year. Many North Devon farmers had by this time, introduced steam tractors on their holdings. This was probably the reason so many cart and heavy draught horses were seen at the fair this year. However, ready sales were made for these fine animals and one of the best cart horses seen in the fair, was that belonging to Mr. C. Southcombe, of Berrynarbour. The asking price was £90.

In <u>1926</u> the question being asked was "Is Barnstaple Horse Fair a decadent Institution?" The number of horses paraded had fallen to just 83! When Mr. Russell a well-known Barnstaple dealer, was asked for his views he remarked that he had never seen such a bad trade. He declared that the motors were running the horses off the roads. Another dealer put forward the opinion that people wanting, for example, hunters, no longer went to the fairs for them, but to the breeders. It would now only be a few years before all types of steam and motorised transport, deeply affected the "horse" business. By the <u>1930s</u> the Horse Fair was gradually In decline. After the building of the Bus Station on the Strand in 1922 the horses were moved to the cattle market site for the Thursday transactions. The outbreak of World War II in <u>1939</u> saw many changes and the Horse Fair appears to have outlived its purpose. Tractors came into more general use and horses were being used less and less on farms. Only two horses were brought into the market for sale on that Fair Thursday in 1939 — the Barnstaple Annual Horse Fair was sadly at an end.

SALES BY AUCTION by GOULD & SANDERS.
1876
SALE IN BARNSTAPLE FAIR.
GOULD and SANDERS will Sell by Auction, at the Quay-end of the Horse Fair, on Thursday, 14th September, at Two o'clock, several good POSTERS, HUNTERS, CART HORSES and PONIES; also a PHAETON, with Shifting Seat; a good DOG CART; and 4 handsome DARTMOOR PONIES, four years old, three have Foals at foot, property of John Dovell, Esq. [8341

31. Horsefair, The Strand, 1908. (C.R.)

32. c.1910. Barnstaple Horsefair, outside Queen Anneís Walk. The man is Mr Laythorn. (© Beaford Archive)

33. Horsefair, The Strand, 1910. Note the Angel Hotel by the lamp-post with the smaller Bell Hotel alongside. (© North Devon Athenaeum)

34. Horsefair, The Strand, 1910. (© North Devon Athenaeum)

Fair Week Events

The Fair Stag Hunt:

W.F. Gardiner states in his 1897 book on Barnstaple – "The Stag Hunt which was for generations associated with the opening of the Fair was abandoned many years ago." This has given me the encouragement to delve a little deeper into the past for some information on the subject.

The poem "Barnstaple Fair in the Olden Time" (which can be read in its entirety in the 'poems' section) seemed to be a good place to start. It includes the verse –

> "To Button Hill, whose name to all the sporting world sure known is,
> Go bits of blood, and hunters, hacks, and little Exmoor ponies,
> When Lords and Ladies, doctors, parsons, farmers, squires, prepare,
> To hunt the stag, with hound and horn to Barnstaple Fair.
> Then upland ride for Chillam Bridge, or on to Bratton Town, sir!
> To view the rouse, or watch the Yeo, to see the stag come down sir!"

This was published in the 'Cave' periodical of 1824 and from this it can safely be assumed that this custom dated back to at least the 18th century. The Barnstaple Records also confirm this with a report in 1795 "*Sept. 22. Staghunting day – nearly 400 horses out, but did not kill.*"

From the Accounts of the Collectors and Receivers of Barnstaple

1582 - *Paid to Mr. Richard Avery, Mayor. The cost of a dinner at the eating of the venison, the whole Town Council being present, £1 14s 4d.*

Looking back through the 19th century reports, many references can be found to this fair week tradition. In the first year edition of the North Devon Journal in September <u>1824</u> it was noted that — *"On Tuesday last, the Stag Hounds met at Bratton, and turned out a "Galloper" from North Wooley, which was lost under Yeotown, by three Hinds starting up before the dogs; this together with the heavy rain rendered further pursuit impracticable, and disappointed the expectations of a large field of Sportsmen, we are informed to the number of 300."*

It was customary for a Stag Hunt Dinner to be held after the hunt itself had finished, and in this same year *"it was respectably attended by admirers of the chace."* In the chair was J. Knight Esq., supported by the treasurer J. Law Esq.

<u>1828</u> - Sees Sir Arthur Chichester's Hounds meeting at Bratton Town. By eleven o'clock, upwards of 200 horses were in the field, and a great number of pedestrians. A fine five year-old Deer was turned out from Smithapath Wood which made off through Bratton Town, to Haxton Down, and Leworthy Bridge; then on to Boscombe, Shoulesberry Castle, Mole's Chamber, and over the Forest to Exford Town. Although so large a concourse of Huntsmen were present at the rousing of the Deer, only half-a-dozen were in at the death, which was two miles below Exford, in the parish of Winsford.

Barnstaple Stag Hunt
VENISON
Part of the stag, which was hunted and killed
on Saturday last,
Will be dressed at the GOLDEN LION, on Thursday
September, 25th. –
To be on the Table precisely at Four o'clock.

<u>1838</u> - The deer was brought out at twelve o'clock, and let off on Bratton Down, and the hounds were laid on half an hour later. Their course was taken across Kep-combe, and Challacombe Common, to Exmoor following the deer to Simonsbath. The quarry then went from Simonsbath House to the woods, in view of the field and proceeded down the bottom

towards Winsford. About 150 horsemen were in at the taking in the river, and the chase was considered to be one of the smartest as well as the finest that the "Devon and Somerset Stag Hounds" had hunted.

1841 - *North Devon Journal* — **23rd September 1841**
"The Stag Hunt, which used to be one of the most attractive sports of the fair, came off on Tuesday. The meet was on Yard Down; a field of about 300 horsemen assembled. Intelligence was brought that a heavy deer had harboured in Buttery Wood, and on the tufters being thrown into the wood at half-past 11, they immediately gave tongue and a fine stag broke from the cover. The pack was very soon laid on and took directly over the forest pointing for Simonsbath; but unfortunately, they came upon a herd of deer in the forest, and divided into three or four parts. Some of the horsemen followed a few couple of hounds, and after rather a sharp run killed a deer in a garden belonging to Lord Poltimore, at Court Hall."

1843 - This year the meet took place at Kempland-cross (8 miles towards Exmoor); a very large field assembled to witness the start. However Disappointment was keenly felt as after a delay of an hour and a half it was announced that some difficulty had arisen to prevent the uncarting of the stag. Inconveniently, the field was invited to Yard-gate several miles away. Some people who had come out in gigs and chaises merely to see the start, returned home less than pleased. Eventually the hunt came off and nearly 200 horses were in at the death. It was reported — *"Foremost among them were two ladies whose bold riding excited the imagination of the field."*

1844 - It will give many of today's readers the satisfaction of knowing that The Fair Stag Hunt of this year was a failure in terms of the hunt not getting their kill. The event of the chase was making for Cornham from Keynesford-water, when a fox sprang up in full view of the hounds! The temptation was too great for the pack and in full cry they hunted their new quarry until it was driven to ground at Ashcombe earths near Simonsbath. The hounds were brought back to their first object of pursuit who after nearing Scob Hill took refuge in Badgers Wood where he joined two companions. — *"It was now nearing*

four o'clock, and Mr. Fellowes and Mr. Knight deemed it advisable to let the noble animal remain for another years sport."
Stag and Fox — ONE. Hounds and Horses — NIL!

<u>1845</u> - The curse of the fair — bad weather had set in. Rain poured down in torrents preventing any large assemblage; the meet comprised of around 130. The deer made away for the Radworthy covers then ascended the hill again, going over the forest wall near Five Barrowdown, then made away for Hawkridge. She was finally taken alive at Westwater, in the parish of Hawkridge and conveyed to the preserves of Sir Peregrine Acland, at Little Bray.

<u>1846</u> - It was reported that the field this year included many ladies who, it would appear, were among the most intrepid in the chase. There was very little detail given about the hunt itself.

From here on in, the Fair Stag Hunt appears to be in its death throes. In <u>1847</u> it was omitted for the first time in nearly half a century, and no information was given as to the cause. The following year scant mention revealed the hunt to be a failure with no stag being roused, and 1850 seems to be the last year for reporting the event in any detail. The following particulars speak for themselves:

"The Stag Hunt is but a shadow of its former self; for, instead of the red deer aroused in his native covers by the noble staghounds, whose deep-toned voice, was wont 'to make the welkin ring,' a four year old stag, who had spent the last 18months in captivity at Winkleigh, was brought to Bratton-down enclosure, and hunted by a right merrie pack of harriers." The fixture was made for half past ten, but the heavy rains of the preceding night, prevented the Master of Hounds (Mr. Luxton, of Winkleigh) crossing the River Taw, delaying the event for two hours.

TO SUM UP: Traditonally ushered in on the second day of the Fair. The event started from the borders of Exmoor, the stag being driven Barumwards in order that the weary huntsmen could sit down and dine there in the evening. It mattered not if things didn't always go to plan, just as long as discussions could be made on the incidents of the day, when it was time to partake of the walnuts and wine!

From ancient times, when this sport formed one of the chief attractions of Barnstaple Great Fair, the Stag Hunt has disappeared as a customary event by around the middle of the nineteenth century. It has made its farewell 'Tally Ho!'

The Fair Ball:

THE Nobility and Gentry of *Barnstaple* and the *North of Devon* are respectfully informed, that **THE ANNUAL FAIR BALL** 1841 Will take place at the *Public Rooms*, in *Barnstaple*, on WEDNESDAY the 22nd day of SEPTEMBER instant (the Evening of the Horticultural Exhibition).

LADY PATRONESS.

LADY ELIZABETH BUCK.

STEWARDS.

SIR BOURCHIER WREY, BART.

JAMES WHYTE, ESQ.

STEPHEN BENCRAFT, ESQ.

THOMAS WREY HARDING, ESQ.

JOHN BUDD, ESQ.

THOMAS HOOPER LAW, ESQ.

** *Dancing to commence precisely at nine o'clock.*

LADIES' TICKETS, 3s. 6d.; GENTLEMEN'S TICKETS, 4s. 6d.; *Tea included.*

TICKETS TO BE HAD AT THE ROOMS.

BARNSTAPLE FAIR BALL.

1827

THE Nobility and Gentry are respectfully informed that

THE FAIR BALL,

Will be held at the Rooms, (as usual) on Thursday, the 20th of September instant.

Dr. BIGNELL, Master of the Ceremonies.

Ladies .... 3s. 6d.

Gentlemen .... 4s. 6d.

Tea Included.

Dancing to commence at Eight o'clock.—Tea at Ten.

Tickets may be had at the Rooms.

Dated, September 6th, 1827.

This was indeed a most propitious occasion for the young ladies of Barnstaple and the neighbouring areas. It was an opportunity for them to be "seen". Making their appearance at the Fair Ball was to all intents and purposes, a sign to the various eligible gentlemen in attendance, of their availability. To hope for a beau at this venue was an exciting contemplation.

In the nineteenth century the Fair Balls were held at the Assembly Rooms in Boutport Street. (Now the Conservative Club) The building was built in 1800 and was first known as 'The Rooms' then the 'Public Rooms' eventually becoming known as the 'Assembly Rooms' around the middle of the century.

114

35. Former Assembly Rooms (venue for the old Fair Balls). Boutport Street. Barnstaple. Now the Barnstaple Conservative Club. (Photograph © Shane Woods).

36. Interior of Ballroom in former Assembly Rooms. Boutport Street. Scene of the traditional Fair Ball. (Photograph © Shane Woods)

Several references to the rooms and the ball itself have been described in the *'North Devon Journal'* of that period.

1824 - This was the year of the *Journal's* inception. A small report of the ball reads- *"Our Annual Fair Ball on Wednesday, was attended by nearly 200 of the most respectable Families in the Town and Neighbourhood. The Ball was opened by Miss Bury and Car Clay Esq. and the dancing was kept up until a late hour."*

It is interesting to note that at this time, the Lord Chamberlain had issued orders through the medium of the newspapers that the Court was to be in Mourning for His Majesty Louis XV11 of France who had died on the 16th of September. In consequence, the fair fashionables had exchanged their gay attire for the 'sombre trappings of woe.' There was no doubt that the example of the Court would be generally followed among the higher classes. But I wonder how many of the younger ladies attending Barnstaple Fair, succumbed to the tempting array of 'London Female Fashions' which were then described in the following manner:

"**PROMENADE DRESS** — Pelisse of lilac *Gros de Naples*, **made high and full, with a circular collar, which turns over, having a double cordage at the edge. The sleeve is plain, and very large at the top, and confined twice between the shoulder and the elbow by corded satin bands, which are decorated about two or three inches apart on each side of the front of the sleeve by campanulus or Canterbury bells made of lilac satin. The skirt touches the ground and is trimmed with five satin tucks of the same colour elevated on the right side, and fastened by Canterbury bells of lilac satin; shaded lilac waist ribbon, and gold buckle in front. Very full worked muslin ruff a little open at the throat, and fastened with a gold buckle. White chip bonnet, with a band of lilac satin introduced midway of the brim, which is circular and deep in front, but shallow behind. The crown is low, and surrounded with a puffing of lilac satin ribbon and ears of corn; the strings are of *crepe lisse* bound with lilac satin. Ear-rings of amethyst set in gold. Primrose colour kid gloves and shoes.**

EVENING PARTY DRESS — Dress of white *crepe lisse*, **with the broad flounces of blond; each flounce headed by a full plaiting of *tulle*, of which plaiting there is a treble row next the hem, laid so close to each other, as to form a *ruche*. The *corsage* of white satin, made, according to the present mode, extremely plain, having no other ornament than a small *bouquet* of roses, with one sprig of myrtle, placed almost under the arm. A very full plaiting of blond finishes the tucker part of the *corsage*, which is confined round the waist by a belt of white satin, with a pearl buckle. The short sleeves are of *crepe lisse*, made plain and full; at the shoulder they are ornamented by a piece of broad blond, which falls over, and is set on rather scanty; next the arm they are finished by two rows of blond, headed by a**

white satin *rouleau*. The hair is arranged in curls and bows, and ornamented in a very elegant manner, with short white feathers, beautifully disposed in various directions; among these feathers, and also among the tresses, are scattered full blown roses, without foliage. The ear-rings are of large pearls detached from each other, and set in a form of a cross; the necklace consists of two rows of large pearls, the under one fastened in front with a garnet brooch, set round with small pearls, and a cross depending, close to the under row, to correspond with the ear-rings. Pearl bracelets are worn over the gloves, fastened with a garnet clasp."

(Sounds good enough to eat, doesn't it!)

1828 - The proprietors had at great expense, painted and furnished the rooms with new drapery and according to the *Journal* — *"The Ball Room is surpassed but by a few in the County, and on Monday evening presented a most tasteful and splendid appearance. The Dresses of the Ladies exceeded in elegance any thing we ever before witnessed in this Town. Dancing commenced about Nine o'clock, and continued with undiminished vivacity until an early hour on Tuesday morning."* (Could it be the 'London Female Fashions' are making the news again!)

1829 - The ball was genteely attended and was opened by Miss Buck, of Daddon, and J. Moyser Esq. It was reported that, *"the witchery of the 'light fantastic toe' was indulged, till the streaks of morn reminded the delighted party of the time of separation."*

Very little is mentioned regarding the Fair Ball during the 1830's so perhaps the event needed a little boost at that time.

1841 - It was said that so large a party and so agreeable a meeting, brought back to the old frequenters of the ballroom the recollection of palmy days gone by. Lady Elizabeth Buck was the patroness.

1849 - This year the ballroom had undergone redecoration, and was for the first time brilliantly lighted by gas for the Fair Ball.

1856 - It was well attended by members of the principal families of the neighbourhood, comprising rank, beauty, and fashion. "The stewards were assiduous in their attentions and the catering of Mrs. Britton was admirable."

<u>1864</u> - *"It was patronized by an un-usually large assemblage of the rank and beauty of the neighbourhood."* Dancing was to the orchestra of 'MR BRIDGEMAN'S QUADRILLE BAND.' (I have no doubt that the writer of "A Young Lady's Lament for the wet Fair, was in attendance. I wonder if she found her beau!)

<u>1871</u> - It would seem that the gas lighting mentioned in 1849 had diminished over the years as the report on the Ball for 1871 reads in part — "The large room was nicely decorated, and the improved lighting by gas, instead of candles as before, which has been done by the lessee, Mr. Thomas May, gave great satisfaction. MR. WALDRON'S QUADRILLE BAND WAS IN ATTENDANCE.

Over the next few years the Fair Ball reports (if mentioned at all) consisted mainly of lists of the people attending, although the year of <u>1875</u> gives the information that "It did not preserve its ancient glory, when hundreds protracted the pleasures of the night far into the 'small hours'." Among the company in <u>1879</u> was Alderman Sir Robert Carden, Knt., who was on a visit to the town for the purpose of addressing the Conservative elctors with a view to being accepted as their candidate. The Rhine Band, from Ilfracombe, had been retained for the occasion and dancing was kept up "with abundant zest" for several hours. An elegant supper was served by, Mr. Brooks, confectioner, of Barnstaple High Street. In <u>1877</u> the Rhine Band was engaged again and the dances included - Lancers, Madame Angot; valse, Blue Danube; Mazurka Lillien; valse, Sweethearts; quadrille, Sultan of Mocha; and polka, Cuckoo. The supper and refreshments were supplied by, Mr. Verney, confectioner, of Barnstaple and Ilfracombe.

<u>1884</u> - A more prolific report appears in the *North Devon Journal* –

"The old Fair Ball was revived at Barnstaple on Wednesday evening at the Assembly Rooms, Boutport Street. The whole of the rooms were occupied for the occasion, and great pains were taken into furnishing and decorating as to give them the appearance of a private dwelling. The ante-room on the right was furnished as a drawing room by Messrs. Symons and Son, and the room

on the left was used for light refreshments before supper. This room was very prettily adorned with evergreens and firs, and was lit with small variegated lamps. From the entrance door up the stairs to the different rooms the walls on either side were covered with evergreens, &c. In the ball-room, extending over the balcony, was the huge white-gloved right hand used by the Corporation at the Fair opening, and indicating the hand of welcome. Messrs. J.J. and R. Harding personally undertook the decorations, assisted by one or two gardeners. Mr. Brooks, of High Street, supplied the supper and other refreshments. The dancing was conducted to the strains of a string band from Taunton."

The report then went on to list all those present. Some of the names are even familiar to us today. For your interest here are just a few that were mentioned:

Mr. And Mrs. Chichester (Hall)
Miss Davie (The Elms)
Dr. Berry
Mr. C.E.R. Chanter
Mrs. And Miss Chanter
Mr. Pitts Tucker (2)
Mr. W.H. Toller
Mr. P. Northcote
Miss Vicary
Mr. Incledon Webber and Mr. W. Incledon.

1896 - Music was supplied by, the BAND of the ROYAL NORTH DEVON HUSSARS. (This was also the time of the completion of the then band-stand in Rock Park, and the Hussars gave a pre-formal opening concert in it, to test the adaptability of the structure. It would appear that all was "eminently satisfactory.")

The days of the "*light fantastic toe*" as one of the events for fair week are apparently at an end. By the end of the 19th century the Fair Ball seems to be of lesser importance, and has faded into obscurity.

Gone for all time are the days, when the very early advertisements for "Barnstaple Fair Ball" included the description as being of - "The size of the Balls held at Exeter," to show its importance.

The Theatre & The Music Hall:

Entertainment for fair week was amply provided for in the 19th century and the Theatre and Music Hall were well attended. In the 1760s the Theatre was situated towards the rear of Honeypot Lane (to become the site of the Regal Cinema in the 20th century) and seated around 350 persons. The Barnstaple Records contain an entry for <u>September 18th 1768</u> (first day of the fair) quoting "*The Exeter Players played first this evening.*" From early theatrical reports and advertising, it is evident that performers came from far and wide. The theatre-going public had their favourites, especially in fair week. The theatre in Honeypot Lane ceased in <u>1833</u> — nothing remains except the passageway from the Strand to the High Street officially known as Theatre Lane. However, a new theatre was erected in <u>1834</u> on the site in Boutport Street previously occupied by a row of cottages known as 'The Seven Drunkards' and next door to the George & Shakespeare Inn! (The cottages had been in a state of complete dilapidation before their demolition, and not as one might think as a result of their proximity to the inn!) The new building was opened in fair week and was first known as 'The Grecian Hall'; later it was re-named 'The Theatre Royal'. Its first lessee was a man named Davis who paid £20 for the privilege.

The following fair week dates give some idea of the performances the audiences came to enjoy:

<u>1824</u> - The selection of plays for Fair Week was varied and the theatre opened on the Monday with, the 'Vampire' and 'A Roland for Oliver'. The house was well attended and the Tuesday evening performance of 'Cherry' and 'Fair Star' by Simpson & Co. played to an overflowing house. Wednesday's drama of 'Clari' or the Maid of Milan went down only tolerably well with Mr. Chaplin not at his best. It seems the critic preferred that gentleman "in the genteel comedies and lively

37. The Theatre Royal, Boutport Street,
formerly known as the Grecian Hall – venue
for many 'Fair Week' productions. Built
around 1835, demolished in 1930.
(© North Devon Athenaeum)

38. Poster for theatre events in
Barnstaple Fair week, c.1831.
(Photograph © R.L. Knight)

farce performed in his former visits to Barnstaple." Miss Norton's performance of Clari was considered good, but would have been even better had she acted less!

Thursday evening's entertainment went off with much Èclat and to a full house. Mr. Chaplin was back in favour as Frank Poppleton in the farce 'Too late for Dinner' and it was reported that "Our old acquaintance Woods, as usual, kept the Piece alive, and his learning of French, from a Vocabulary, and humorous application of the words, excited many a hearty laugh from the Gallery, and many a half smile from the elegant occupiers of the Boxes."

<u>1831</u> - The Manager of the Theatre — Mr. Herbert Lee — advertises the fact that he has at considerable expense, had the "THEATRE THOROUGHLY REPAIRED, NEWLY PAINTED, and altogether improved and rendered more comfortable." Two years later, the Honeypot Lane Theatre closed its doors. A photograph copy of an original playbill is featured in fig. 38.

<u>1835</u> - Mr. Lee has resigned the new Theatre into the hands of Mr. Davis. Attendance has been very thin regardless of the attraction of the new house and new company.

The <u>1840s</u> Theatregoers for Fair Week seem to have lost interest with scant attendance. Even the *Journal* appears to perceive it as *"of lesser importance than in days of old."*

<u>1856</u> - Pleasure seekers had the choice of "Whittington and his Cat" at the Theatre or two "grand concerts" at the Music Hall.

<u>1873</u> - Mr. William Montague and Company enlivened the town during fair week. The play selected for the fashionable night of Friday, was "The King's Favourite." It was noted that Mr. Morgan Smith, a coloured tragedian, had been performing in Shakespearian plays during the week.

<u>1879</u> - One of the last accounts given by the North Devon Journal for the Theatre Royal, refers to Mr. Wybert Rousby as one of the most talented and popular provincial actors, and that he had given a splendid performance.

By 1882 the Theatre building had become disused for dramatic purposes, and until 1893 was under lease by the Salvation Army. From then on the building was put back to its original use and eventually demolished in 1930/31 to make way for the Gaumont Cinema.

Theatre, Barnstaple.
1824
By Permission of the Worshipful the Mayor.

MR. LEE has the honor of announcing to the Ladies and Gentlemen of Barnstaple and its Vicinity, that the THEATRE will OPEN on MONDAY Evening, September 20th, 1824; on which occasion his Majesty's Servants will act a favourite COMEDY and FARCE; Particulars of which will be expressed in the bills of the day.

Stage Manager Mr. CHAPLIN.

A variety of New Pieces are in active preparation, and will speedily be produced.

The Theatre will be open every Evening during the Fair.

Barnstaple, September 16th, 1824

THEATRE, BARNSTAPLE.
1829

MESSRS. SHATFORD and LEE, beg leave most respectfully to inform the Families and Public of Barnstaple and its Vicinity, that this Theatre will open under their management, for the usual season, at the FAIR. Messrs. S. and L. being most anxious to give every satisfaction in their power, pledge themselves to produce a Variety of Novelties in succession; and trust, that by unwearied diligence and attention to each department of the Theatre, they may merit and receive the patronage which has been so long and liberally bestowed on the former Management.

The Company at present engaged consists of

Mr. Herbert Lee	Mr. Heathcote	Mr. Davis
Mr. Horsman	Mr. C. Heathcote	Mr. Lewis.
Mr. Hughes	Mr. Kent	Mr. Crickmore and
Mr. Woods	Mr. Fuller	Mr. Hill, Musicians.
	Mr. Gilling Stage-keeper.	
Mrs. Horsman	Mrs. Woods	Mrs. Kent
Miss Lee	Mrs. Davis	Miss Lewis
Miss E. Lee	Mrs. Lee	

On SATURDAY, September 19th, 1829, will be presented the MUSICAL OPERA, called

Guy Mannering or the Gipsy's Prophecy.

A CELEBRATED AIR, by .... Miss. E. LEE.
A COMIC SONG, by .... Mr. HUGHES.

To conclude with the Admired Entertainment, called
The Children in the Wood, or the Cruel Uncle.

☞ *The Wardrobe Department (which has been greatly added to and improved,) will be under the Superintendance of Mr. and Miss LEWIS, from the Theatre Royal, Bristol.*

September 16th, 1829.

THEATRE ROYAL, BARNSTAPLE,

UNDER THE MANAGEMENT OF

MR. J. DAVIS,

WILL OPEN ON MONDAY NEXT, SEPT. 17TH,
WITH A TALENTED

DRAMATIC COMPANY,

FOR THE PRODUCTION OF STERLING
DRAMAS, COMEDIES, AND THE LATEST
NOVELTIES.

1817 ☞ For particulars see day bills. [2489

New Theatre, Barnstaple.

(Under the Management of Mr. Walter Summers.)

——o——

MONDAY, TUESDAY, AND WEDNESDAY,

SEPTEMBER 13TH, 14TH, AND 15TH. 1897

Great Attraction for the Fair Week.

*ASTOR and DU CANE'S COMPANY IN THE
CELEBRATED DRAMA—*

" THE STOWAWAY "

(From the Surrey Theatre, London).

TIME AND PRICES AS USUAL.

——o——

SATURDAY, MONDAY, AND TUESDAY, SEPT.
25TH, 27TH, 28TH, Welcome Return Visit of

" THE SIGN OF THE CROSS."

[9657

Theatre Royal

'PHONE 194.

MONDAY & SATURDAY at 6.15 & 8.45.
TUES., WED., THUR. & FRI. at 7.30.
Matinees Wed., FRI. and Sat. at 2.30.

☞ EXTRAORDINARY ATTRACTIONS FAIR WEEK. ☜

TO-NIGHT (THUR.), FRIDAY, & SATURDAY, SEPT. 16, 17, & 18.

CORINNE GRIFFITH and KENNETH HARLAN in a Thrilling and Sensational
Photo Play in an Astounding Exposé of Social Savagery, entitled—

'Modern Madness.'

MONDAY, TUESDAY, & WEDNESDAY, SEPTEMBER 20, 21 & 22.

YET ANOTHER GREAT DOUBLE FEATURE PROGRAMME.

BOB CUSTER in a Thrilling Dramatic Story of the great open-hearted West—

"GALLOPING VENGEANCE."

DOUGLAS MACLEAN in a Screaming Comedy Drama of Two Strangers in Love, entitled—

Introduce Me.

THUR., FRI. & SAT., SEPT. 30, OCT. 1 & 2. Matinee on Sat., Oct. 2, at 2.30.

Bannister Howard's Coy. in "TONS OF MONEY."

Box Office now open to all above Attractions at White's, High St., Phone 35. [8515

The Music Hall:

39. The Music Hall on the right was built in 1855 by R.D.Gould, the Borough architect. It was later renamed the Albert Hall, and then the Queen's Hall. It is now known as the Queen's Theatre. (© North Devon Athenaeum)

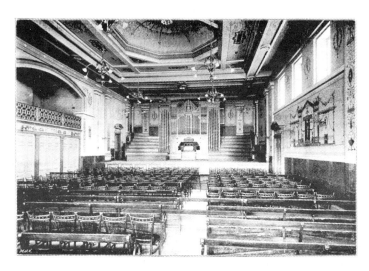

40. c.1904. Interior of the Music Hall. Seats were removable for dancing. (Photographers: Vickery Bros © North Devon Athenaeum)

The gradual decline of the Theatre in the 19th century was most likely due to the introduction of the Music Hall. It was designed by the Borough Architect, R.D. Gould, and built in 1855 at the top end of Butcher's Row facing Boutport Street. Later on the name was changed to The Albert Hall, and so it remained until one night in November 1941 during the Second World War when the building caught fire after a dance had been held there. By the next morning only a shell remained of its former glory. The ground floor was then roofed over to become a British Restaurant where wartime workers were provided with meals. Later, a stage was added and it became known as the Civic Hall. In 1952 it was rebuilt with the façade almost exactly as originally designed by Gould, and the name changed to the Queen's Hall. Towards the end of the 20th century in the year 1993 it became the Queen's Theatre. Appropriately, Theatre and Music Hall have now become one!

MUSIC HALL, BARNSTAPLE.

1869

MONSTER ARRIVAL OF TALENT.

OPEN EVERY NIGHT DURING THIS WEEK.

SPECIAL ENGAGEMENT from the Alhambra Palace of

MR. G. RAINSFORD,
The Great Baritone Vocalist; and
MONS. DUVALLI,

The greatest Wonder of the Day on the Half-inch Wire, performing all the feats of BLONDIN on an incline of 35; ascends blind-folded, with his head in a sack; wheels a barrow up the wire and descends backwards; ascends the wire in convict's chains and takes his supper on it, &c. The Sensation of '69 is

MR. J. DAVIS,

The Cure Upside Down; the greatest Novelty of the age. The whole forming one of the best Companies that ever visited Barnstaple.

Doors open at 7.30. Commencing at 8.

By particular desire there will be a MID-DAY PER-FORMANCE ON FRIDAY, at Three o'clock.

ADMISSION: 2s., 1s., and 6d.   [2178

ENTHUSIASTIC & DELIGHTED AUDIENCES.

MUSIC HALL, BARNSTAPLE.

POOLE AND YOUNG'S

PANORAMA OF PARIS,

NOW EXHIBITING until SATURDAY NEXT,
28th inst,

DAY EXHIBITION, Saturday at Three o'clock.
Evenings at Eight   [133

ROYAL GRECIAN HALL.

(Late Theatre,) Barnstaple.

ENTHUSIASTIC RECEPTION OF THE
NEW ARTISTES –

Mr. MALVERN, From Drury Lane.
Mr. STREETON, Sadlers Wells.
Miss FRANKLIN, Theatre Royal, Birmingham.

Now forming the most powerful and numerous Company
ever seen in Barnstaple.

WEDNESDAY & THURSDAY, September
24th and 25th, 1872, will be produced for the first
time here, the powerful and Romantic Drama, played in
London over 200 Nights, entitled

NOBODY'S CHILD!

WITH NEW SCENERY AND EFFECTS BY
Mr. TALBOT.

GRAND COMIC and SENTIMENTAL CONTEST!
ON THURSDAY NEXT.

Notice to Amateur Comic and Sentimental Singers
In order to encourage Native Talent Mr. Francis will
give a SILVER WATCH to the best Amateur Comic
Singer, and a splendid SILVER MOUNTED CIGAR
CASE for the best Sentimental Singer.—Open to All
Comers.

Parties wishing to contend must send their Names in
to Mr. Francis, at the Theatre, before Seven o'clock on
Thursday.

Song, Comique, Mr. HOLLIDAY.

To conclude each evening with A LAUGHABLE
FARCE.

NOTICE!!

GRAND FASHIONABLE NIGHT, Friday next!
under distinguished Patronage.

In active Preparation the two great Sensations
Dramas, entitled—
THE STEAM FORGE HAMMER, AND THIS
HOUSE TO LET!
WITH NEW SCENERY.

Doors open at 7.30, to commence at Eight precisely.
The Box Plan may be seen and Tickets obtained at
S. Nearis and Co.'s, Booksellers, &c., 15, High Street.
No places secured, unless Tickets are taken.   [4293

MUSIC HALL, BARNSTAPLE.

For Two Nights Only,
FRIDAY AND SATURDAY, Sept. 18th and 19th,
1874.

PRICES :—3s., 2s., 1s., and 6d.

TICKETS and Plan of Reserved Seats of Mr.
H. T. COOK, Librarian, 95, High-street.

Doors open at 7.45 for 8.15—Carriages at 10.15.
Children in arms not admitted.

VANCE'S VARIETIES

(From the Crystal Palace, St. James's Hall, Hanover
Square Rooms, etc.).

PATRONS — Their Royal Highnesses the Prince and
Princess of Wales.

N.B.—It is a noted fact that the Aristocracy, Clergy,
and Gentry of the Three Kingdoms recognise Mr.
Vance's Entertainment as the most refined "Melange
d'Enjoyment" extant, and, to quote the London 'Daily
Telegraph' of Jan. 7th, 1873, is "one that affords real
enjoyment to the audience."

VANCE'S CONCERT PARTY!

ARTISTES.—Miss KATE HARLEY, Soubrette and Con-
tralto ; Miss AMY BELMORE, Soprano ; Mr. ALFRED ST.
JOHN, Solo Pianist and Accompanyist, R.A.M. ; Mr.
ALFRED G. VANCE, Author, Composer, and Vocal
Comedian.

N.B.—All Mr. Vance's songs and Impersonations have
been written and composed by himself expressly for his
world-famed Entertainment of VARIETIES; "and
can be sung in any Drawing-room, the Music being original and invariably pretty, and the words funny, without
being calculated to cause a blush to the most fastidious."
'Court Circular.'

New and Original Impersonations by Vance.
Nouvelle Operetta Comique, THE THREE GRACES,
or Fashion's Daughters. A Damsel of the Past, Miss
Amy Belmore ; A Girl of the Present, Mr. Alfred G.
Vance ; a Belle of the Future, Miss Kate Harley.
Roars of Laughter at this New Extravaganza.
Town Address—Fulwood House, Gray's Inn, W.C.
Proprietor and Manager, Mr. Alfred G. Vance.
Business Agent, Mr. E. Houston Pelham.

ROUTE NEXT WEEK—Monday, Sept. 14th; Dorchester;
Tuesday, Bridport; Wednesday, Lyme Regis; Thursday,
Taunton; Friday and Saturday, Barnstaple.

LAST GRAND PROVINCIAL TOUR OF
1875   MESSRS.

STRANGE AND WILSON'S

MARVELLOUS ÆTHERSCOPE, AND
PROFESSOR PEPPER'S

GREAT OPTICAL WONDER,

PROTEUS, OR, WE ARE HERE BUT NOT HERE.
Will Open in the

MUSIC HALL,

BARNSTAPLE,

MONDAY, Sept. 13th, and Five Following Nights.

GRAND
ILLUMINATED DAY ENTERTAINMENT
ON WEDNESDAY, SEPT. 15TH.

Doors open at 2.30 p.m., to Commence at 3.

MESSRS. STRANGE AND WILSON have the
honour to announce to the Nobility, Clergy,
Gentry, and General Public of this town and its vicinity,
the above Exhibition of the new Scientific, Literary, and
Ætherscopic Entertainment, which combines all the
astounding effects of Spectroscope and Phantoscope,
and, in fact, all Optical Contrivances which have of late
separately astonished and delighted the civilised world.
By means of this astounding combination Angels are seen
floating in space and gliding imperceptibly through walls
—Human Beings vanish or appear at will—Demons roll
in mid air—Fairies dance on walls and ceilings—Spectres
creep up walls and gyrate in space—Ladies dance amidst
flames of real fire—one being dissolves into another ; in
fact, it would be utterly impossible to convey in language
any adequate idea of this extraordinary and seemingly
miraculous invention, which transcends anything hitherto
attempted.

It has been exhibited in all the principal cities in Great
Britain with a degree of success unequalled by any similar Entertainment.

The present Programme is entirely new. Every acces-
sory to give effect will be employed, it being the earnest
desire of the managers, who have spared neither expense
nor trouble, to make this, they confidently believe, the
Best Entertainment of its Class in Great Britain.

Children under 10 years of age and Schools of not less
than 10 in number Half-price, Back Seats excepted.

Reserved Seats and Tickets may be secured at the Hall
from 11 till 2 o'clock daily.

Open each evening at Half-past Seven, the Entertainment to commence at Eight o'clock.

Half price at Nine o'clock, Back Seats excepted.

Carriages ordered for Ten, and for Day Entertainments
at 4.45.

ADMISSION—6d., 1s., 2s., and 3s.   (3624

1867 - 19th September. *"At the Music Hall, the Avonmouth Company are astonishing the "natives" by extraordinary gymnastic feats and charming large audiences by vocal and other interesting entertainments."*

1873 - 18th September. *"Tonight and to-morrow night the "Great Vance" and Company give their annual concerts in this town. The Music Hall is sure to be crowded both this evening and to-morrow."*

MUSIC HALL, BARNSTAPLE.
POSITIVELY FOR FIVE NIGHTS ONLY.
DURING THE FAIR WEEK.
COMMENCING TUESDAY, SEPTEMBER 16TH
GRAND FASHIONABLE NIGHT
FRIDAY, SEPT. 19TH.
Engagement of the Celebrated Young
ACTRESS, ELOCUTIONIST, & VOCALIST—

MISS LYDIA HOWARD,

AND
HER TALENTED COMPANY,
Who have created such a sensation in London, Edinburgh, Liverpool, &c.
The following are some of Miss Howard's most celebrated Impersonations :.
Prince Arthur !......................From "King John."
Jack Bluff ! (With Sea Songs }
and Sailor's Hornpipe) } A True British Sailor.
Fergus O'Botherwell ! (With }
Irish Songs and Dances) } A Lad from Old Ireland.
Effie Heatherbloom ! (With } A Blossom from the
Scotch Songs and Dances) } Highlands.
Little Nell and the Mar- } From the "Old Curi-
chioness } osity Shop."
Jenny Wren ! (One of Mr. Charles } The Person of the
Dickens's strange Child Creations) } House
Mademoiselle Dumplino ....From "Le Grand
Opera à Paris."
Reserved and Numbered Seats, 2s. ; Second Seats, 1s.
Third Seats, 6d.
Doors open at 7.30. Commence at 8. Carriages at 10.
Plan and Tickets at MR. SEARLE'S, High-street.
COPY OF
TESTIMONIAL FROM THE QUEEN :—
Windsor Castle, May 15th, 1877.
To Miss LYDIA HOWARD.
THE QUEEN has desired me to convey to you
her thanks for the great pleasure you afforded her by your
interesting Entertainment. The Queen was especially
delighted with your very touching portrayal of the
character of " Prince Arthur," and your very charming
elocution.
Your obedient Servant,
[1419] T. M. BIDDULPH.

1879 — 18th September. **"MISS LYDIA HOWARD. —** This very gifted young lady — eminent as an actress, elocutionist, and vocalist — is now, with her talented company, giving her entertaining performances in the Music Hall, commencing on Tuesday evening, when there was a fairly good audience, and continuing to the end of the week. Miss Howard was preceded by a high reputation, for she had been much complimented by the daily and weekly press, and honoured with a testimonial from Her Majesty the Queen, who was particularly delighted with her "charming elocution" and her "very touching portrayal, of the character of Prince Arthur."

ALBERT HALL

BARNSTAPLE, 1931

THE HOME OF TALKIES.

Continuous Nightly 6 p.m. to 10.30 p.m. Saturdays, separate houses, 6 and 8.30.
MATINEES: Wed., Friday and Saturday at 2.30.
Seats at 1s. 6d. and 1s. 10d. for Saturdays may be booked at Nicklin's Music Stores, The Square, (Telephone 6).
Resident Manager: E. C. BETTY.   Tel. 469

Special Attractions for Fair Week.   **Monday, Tuesday and Wednesday.**

A Riot of Colour and Laughter— **Present Arms,** *with* **Irene Dunne, Louise Fazenda, Lilyan Tashman, Ned Sparkes,** *and the 60 Tiller Sunshine Girls.*

Also **Molly O'Day** *and* **Edmund Burns** *in* **SEA DEVILS.** *A romance on a windjammer.*

TWICE WEEKLY. THE BRITISH MOVIETONE NEWS.

Thursday, Friday and Saturday.

A delightful English Romance by Thomas Hardy— **UNDER THE GREENWOOD TREE.**

An old-time romance of Dorset, with village music and dancing, starring **John Batten, Marguerite Allen** *and* **Nigel Barrie.**

Also the Rambling Reporter in **WILD MAN'S LAND**—*Secrets of Nature (The Frog).*

Special Buses leave this Theatre on Saturdays only at 8.50 p.m. for Swimbridge, and at close of last performance for Bickington and Fremington.
EVERY WEEK-DAY: A 10 p.m. 'bus from Strand to Fremington, Instow, Bideford, and Westward Ho. and a 10 p.m. 'bus to Braunton and Ilfracombe. Hourly service between Ilfracombe and Barnstaple. See Southern National Time Tables.

PRICES (including Tax), 1s. 10d., 1s. 6d., 1s., and 8d.

Music Hall, Barnstaple.

Two Nights Only!

THURSDAY & FRIDAY, SEPT. 20 & 21.

1900

MR. ALBERT

CHEVALIER'S

RECITALS.

SUPPORTED BY

MISS FLOSSIE BEHRENS (Soprano & Siffleuse).
MR. WEIST HILL (Solo Violoncello),
MR. NELSON HARDY (Ventriloquist & Mimic),
AND
MR. ALFRED H. WEST, Solo Pianist & Accompanist

Mr. CHEVALIER'S Latest Impersonations:—
"Anky Panky," "Waxwork Show," "A Fallen Star,"
"It gets me talked abaht," "Mons. Armand Thibaults,"
"An old Bachelor," "Mary had a little Lamb," and
"Mafekin' Night" (New Coster Song), &c.

Tickets obtained on application to :

☞ Nicklin's Music Saloons,
which will Admit Holders by Early Doors
at 7.15 *without extra charge.*

PRICES OF ADMISSION:—Reserved, 4s. ; Unreserved, 2s. ; Admission, 1s. Ordinary Doors open at 7.30, commence at 8. Carriages at 10.   [4511
MANAGER .... MR. CHAS. INGLE.

ALBERT HALL, BARNSTAPLE.

FAIR BALL

(Under Distinguished Patronage)

will be held on

FRIDAY, SEPTEMBER 19th, 1919

Dancing 9 — 3

Tickets (including refreshments) Gentlemen 7/6 Ladies 6/-
may be obtained from

The Mayoress, Messrs. O. Nicklin & Son, J.T. White and A.E. Barnes.

Proceeds for the Parish Church Bazaar Fund.

Wrestling Matches:

> Extract from "The Maid of Sker" by R.D. Blackmore —
> (1872) set in the year 1782
>
> "Up the centre, and heeding the people no more than they would two rows of trees came two grave gentlemen, daintily walking arm in arm, and dressed in black. They had broad-flapped hats, long coats of broadcloth, black silk tunics, and buckled breeches, and black polished boots reaching up to the buckles. I asked Ikey who they were. 'Why them be two passons,' he cried with indignation. (The taller of the two was Parson Jack) This was 'Parson Jack' his surname being 'Rambone'. His business in Boutport Street that day was to see if any man would challenge him. He had held the belt for seven years, they said, for wrestling, as well as for bruising."

It was expected that wrestling matches would take place during fair week at Barnstaple and it was considered to be an excellent venue. Competitors came from far and wide to hold on to their championships, or hopefully gain one. Spectators were many, but not all were enamoured with what was seen as a brutal sport.

It would appear that for many years the fair week event had lain dormant, and attempts were being made in the 19th century to revive the custom.

In 1842 the report from the *North Devon Journal reads* –

"The Wrestling Match in this town during the fair was a failure, so much so, we trust, as to discourage any future attempt to renew this brutal sport. In consequence of the heavy rains, the ground was in a very bad state, and the company thin. Pile won the first prize. An unfortunate fellow named Lavercombe dislocated his shoulder-bone in the contest, and was taken off the ground to the Infirmary."

1844 brings further condemnation of the sport, with a recommendation to imitate the excellent example shown by the town of Tiverton of protesting against 'this degrading exhibition.'

"We are ashamed to record that among the "amusements" of the fair the brutal sport of Wrestling was revived. It is a reproach to the times we live in that so barbarous and cruel a practice should find countenance even among the humblest classes; but that it should be promoted by men who boast the refinements of education is not more to be condemned than wondered at. Yet we have heard that some "gentlemen" so called, both aided by their purse and patronised by their presence this demoralising and infamous pastime in which the physical endowments of nature are abused, the worst passions excited, and the "human form divine" engaged in a contest perfectly brutish, and subject to be mangled and disabled, if not destroyed. We learn that an illustration of the dangerous character of the sport was furnished on this occasion; a poor fellow who was tempted to engage in the ring having his shoulder dislocated. The play is said to have gratified the low taste of those who witnessed it, and the Devonshire champion (Chappell) was awarded the first prize."

(What would they make of the televised versions today!)

The following year we are told that the play was good and the sport got up to pander to the admirers of the brutal pastime. For the next few years very little mention is made of the event, but in 1868 an advertisement shows a lot of money to be won.

BARNSTAPLE ANNUAL WRESTLING.

A WRESTLING MATCH will take place in a Field on the Braunton Road, Barnstaple, on Wednesday, the 16th of September, 1868, and Three following Days, when the following Prizes will be awarded :—

	£	s.	d.
To the First Best Man	7	0	0
„ Second ditto	3	10	0
„ Third ditto	1	10	0
„ Fourth ditto	0	10	0

Refreshments of all kinds will be supplied on the Ground by Mr. J. PARMINTER, of the 'Braunton Inn;' and Mr. J. HASKINS, of the 'North Country Inn.''

By this time the earlier condemnation of the sport has seemingly abated.

The wrestling matches in 1870 had passed off successfully with prizes awarded to competitors as follows: MARSHALL, KINGSBRIDGE, first prize; TAPPER, NORTHTAWTON, second; WESTACOTT, BARNSTAPLE, third; GUBB, SWIMBRIDGE, fifth; PAVEY, BARNSTAPLE, sixth.

In 1871 the *North Devon Journal* gives a comprehensive report on the wrestling matches for fair week –

"The wrestling matches which have been held during the past week in a field adjoining the Barnstaple Workhouse, were brought to a termination on Tuesday morning. No less a number than 148 men have been in the ring and some excellent play has taken place. There were 25 standards made. On Tuesday morning the final play between Hooper, Lynton, and Ash alias Jack in the Box, Plymouth, took place, and resulted, after a very severe struggle, in favour of the former. Hooper thus won the first prize of £4 and a silver cup; Ash the second of £4; Burnett, Exeter, and Gerry, Swymbridge, divided the third and fourth prizes of £2 10s. and £1; whilst the fifth prize of 10s. was won by Webber, of Barnstaple. Those men who made single standards received 1s. each, double standards 2s 6d., and the treble standards 5s. each. The Silver Challenge Cup, value £23, presented by Sir Bruce Chichester, Bart., was not played for. The triers were Mr. Cooper, Drewsteignton, ex champion of England; Mr. Sanders, Bishopstawton; and Mr. Smallridge, Barnstaple. The wrestling was got up by Mr. Garland, of the Rising Sun, Boutport Street."

The year 1880 appears to be the last time any report worth mentioning was made on the accustomed wrestling. The matches took place at the Rising Sun, Newport, on the Friday afternoon of fair week. Among the competitors was Thomas Gubb, of Swimbridge, who once wrestled Samuel Rundle for one hour and apparently stood his ground to the finish. On this occasion he contested with J. Clatworthy for eight rounds but as play was not concluded until the Saturday no report was given as to the outcome. Other competitors named were: Edward Simmons, George Stone, Wm. Spurrier, Henry Holland, and John Baggot.

This then, as a separate event for fair week, is probably at an end as the tail end of the 19th century begins.

Horticultural Exhibitions:

From newspaper reports it is evident that the 19th century fair week events included horticultural exhibitions. In the 1830s the North Devon Horticultural Society held their event in the Assembly Rooms in Boutport Street. The 1837 (21st September) report was given as: "This interesting society held its autumnal exhibition this day, at the Public Rooms. The company was very numerous. The Rooms were decorated with more than usual taste and elegance, and the exhibition, both in quantity and quality, was equal, if not superior, to any that the society has ever witnessed. The fruit was particularly fine, and the vegetables were all remarkably good; indeed every branch of the exhibition was worthy of the highest commendation."

The following year it was said that the Horticultural Meetings presented and displayed an animated loveliness and improvement to the many other attractions at Barnstaple Fair.

The society held its twenty-first exhibition in 1840 (being two a year since its establishment.) The report reads:

"Although the extremely unfavourable weather in the morning must have operated most prejudicially, and family affliction preventing the attendance of some of the society's patrons, yet the company exhibited an increase upon the meeting in the spring, and was tolerably numerous, and highly genteel, the attractions of the fair and the ball in the evening having drawn many of the most fashionable country residents to the town. We may remark, however, that the room was filled principally with ladies, a vast number of gentlemen being engaged in the pursuit of more masculine amusement after the hounds."

In 1845 a large house in the High Street was bought and used as a Literary and Scientific Institute. A generous amount of money was provided by one of Barnstaple's benefactors — Mr. William Frederick Rock — towards the purchase of the building, and subsequently endowed it with £100 a year which provided free admission for a hundred members and students. Mr. J.R. Chanter was the first Hon. Secretary of the Institution, and continued in office until 1860.

By the year 1849 the Horticultural Society appears to have changed its name to the Barnstaple & North Devon Cottage Garden Society, and a change of venue for their exhibitions has been made to the Literary and Scientific Institution. The second show of the year took place on the Thursday, the second day of the fair, and the opinion being, that good as the first exhibition of the year was considered, the fair week one was far better.

"The specimens were both more numerous and finer. The garden and lecture-room were crowded with baskets, chiefly of useful vegetables, in the highest perfection. Potatoes were particularly fine and abundant, not the slightest symptom of disease. The beauty and attractiveness of the show were greatly augmented by the display of a profusion of charming flowers, plants, and shrubs, from the gardens of the resident and neighbouring gentry. A choice and elegant floral device, from the Arlington gardens, surmounted the front of the premises, and was an object of unusual admiration."

The fair week exhibition for 1851 was favoured by the most brilliant weather and it was said that never had the society displayed its wealth to greater advantage. A semi-circular entablature erected at the entrance to the Literary Institution, presented the "Cottage Garden Society" defined in dahlias of various hues. The approaches and avenues were adorned with a profusion of laurels and evergreens, and perfumed with the fragrance of floral garlands. Performances by a local band added the charms of music to the scene. From the time opening the promenade was crowded with people, comprising of the members of most of the principal families of the town and neighbourhood, and fashionable strangers who had come to visit the fair.

In the absence of the President, Sir Bruce Chichester, Bart., one of the most honourable members of the borough, Richard Bremridge Esq., made the appropriate address to the assembled visitors. He congratulated them on what was the sixth exhibition of the society and the finest in its history with the greatest number of competitors. He remarked that each department teemed with results of the taste, skill, and industry of the cottagers, and said that the success of the society must be particularly satisfactory to those who had originated it.

Indeed, reading through the full report the details given make the show come alive for the reader. A few examples have been extracted for anyone interested in the information given.

"The fruits, under which the spacious tables in the great room groaned, were of striking excellence, particularly the pears and apples; nor were there wanting highly creditable specimens of the rarer kinds. The room acquired much of its attractiveness from the several very gorgeous devices of flowers, which graced the walls, and gave evidence of the taste and emulation of the humble producers."

One contribution from the gardens of Sir Bruce Chichester, was in the shape of the fountain in the Crystal Palace, and set out with countless dahlias, fuchsias, and specimens of moss, and was an object of universal admiration. Among the gardeners and nurserymen were: Mr. Mallet, Mr. Ireland, and Mr. Pontey exhibiting far sale in the great room, large varieties of beautiful cut flowers. The vegetables were in great abundance; the potatoes never looked in better health, and, for the first time in years several baskets of the old favourite - reds, were among them.

The names of the prize-winners were read out by the Honorary Secretary –Mr. John R. Chanter Esq.

Prizes varied from 5s.to 1s. the first, second, and third, positions being awarded for the several classes. A few winners in each class are listed below.

FLOWERS:

Brompton stock, double — Norman
Carnations — Guard, Harding
Dahlias — Smallridge, Bennett

Hollyhock — Guard, Crang
German Asters — Smallridge
Flowers in device — Manning, Smallridge, Crang.

FRUIT:
Currants, red or white — Gough
Culinary apples — Rook, Scott, Collins
Dessert pears — Cook, Moorman, Rook
Grapes, white — Bennett, Down, Sanders
Plums, Damson — Collins, Groover
Plums, culinary — Smallridge, Rook
Ribstone Pippins — Crang, Guard
Filberts — Mock
Walnuts — Rook, Latham
Nectarines — Rook,
Mulberries — Rook,
Melon — Norman.

VEGETABLES:
Borecole, Siberian — Bennett, Dark, Dunn
Beans, scarlet runners — Allen, Bennett, Harding, Lancey
Beet root, true red — Lancey, Bevans, Groves
Cauliflowers, true — Lancey, Dark, Thorne
Carrots, long orange — Lancey, Hellier
Cabbages, any sorts — Bennett, Lancey, Nicholls
Celery, red — Dunn, Collins
Leeks — Dark, Diamond, Bennett, Featherstone
Onions — Featherstone, Lancey, Norman, Bennett
Potatoes, York Red — Ridge, Harding
Potatoes, Queen's Nobles — Bennett, Nicholls
Potatoes, Cups — Harding, Ridge
Peas, Great Britain — Bennett, Collins
Pot Herbs — Thorne, Scott
Parsnips — Harding, Thorne, Britton
Savoys, green curled — Dark, Fisher
Tomatoes — Norman, Rook
Vegetable Marrow — Scott, Crang
Cucumbers — Lancey
40 days' Maize — Thorne, Britton, Pidler

A prize of 10s. donated by, Mr. Rock for the best honey obtained without destroying the bees, was awarded to Gully of Tawton, and Mr. Bremridge's first and second prizes of 30s. & 10s for the best cultivated cottage garden in Barnstaple, went to Isaac Bennett and Wm. Crang.

Besides the prizes distributed by the society, John Guest, Esq., gave out his traditional donation of useful garden implements to the exhibitors who had most distinguished themselves.

There were 57 exhibitors, and the judges were named as: Mr. White, Mr. Seely, Mr. Gerry, Mr. Guest, Mr. Batten, Mr. Westacott, Capt. Williams, Capt. Davie, Mr. G.K. Cotton, Mr. Bale, of Westacott, and Mr. Pontey, of Plymouth.

After this, such a comprehensive report on this fair week event has not come to light again.

A heading in the *North Devon Journal Sept.* 1871 reads *"Exhibiting Fine Potatoes at Barnstaple Fair."* It gives an account of Mr. Henry Hodge of Witheridge, naming him *"The Devonshire Potato Fancier"* winning the highest prize of £3, which was being offered by Mr. Quick, manure merchant. However, no mention is made as to the the organisers of the exhibition itself.

It would seem that from around this period of time "The Cottage Garden Society" is no longer exhibiting in fair week, or perhaps it no longer existed in its original form? Local flower shows and festivals had probably taken over.

Bell Ringing:

The 19th century custom of bell ringing at fair week has now gone. Competition matches were arranged at various times, and the peals of bells could be heard all over the town. A good description of the atmosphere was given in <u>1836</u> when it was said - *"The continual ringing of the bells, the strains of music floating from the different booths, and the numerous itinerant musicians with barrel organs and other instruments, filled the air with harmony."*

It was usual for ringing matches to be arranged between Barnstaple and the village ringers from the neighbouring areas. We can see from the next two reports that the event was well thought about.

<u>1840</u> -*The **Ringing Match**, on Tuesday, went off remarkably well, so the judges tell us. Ten sets of ringers entered the lists, and rang a quarter of an hour each. The first prize was awarded to the Braunton ringers, having the least number of faults in their performance; the second to G eorgeham; the third to Goodleigh; the fourth to Bishop's Tawton; and the fifth to Westdown. The decisions of the umpires were satisfactory, and the music of the bells very well accorded with the harmony which prevailed among the competitors. At the close of the match, they all dined together at Sutton's King's Arms Hotel."* (High Street, Barnstaple)

<u>1844</u>- ***A Ringing Match*** *came off on Monday; and the town was kept alive all day by the musical tones of the church bells. The competitors were the ringers from Pilton, Landkey (two sets), Bishop's Tawton, Georgeham, Berrynarbor, Braunton (two sets), Marwood, and Goodleigh. The ringing was considered to be excellent and the triers had a difficult task to discriminate the respective merits of the competitors.*

The first prize (30s.) was awarded to Pilton; the second (25s.) to Landkey (young set); the third (20s.) to Bishop's Tawton; the fourth (15s.) Landkey (old set); and the fifth (10s.) to Georgeham."

Further mention of the bells was given in <u>1873</u> as *"The Bells gave out their merry notes of welcome to the teeming crowds of visitors at frequent intervals during the day."* And in <u>1875</u> the quote was — *"The day was beautiful as could be desired. The merry peals of the bells heralded the morning."*

There is no confirmation as to how many years the ringing matches were carried on as a special part of the fair week celebrations.

Fair Sunday and Blue Coat Charity Schools:

The Mayor and Corporation of Barnstaple — many years before the State took any active part in helping with education — showed their appreciation of the value of the work carried out by the town's old and long established Blue Coat School, by making their presence at Church each year on Fair Sunday, when a customary collection was made for the School's funds. This tradition was kept up until the end of the 19th century when it was felt that due to the voluntary system of education at that time, it would have been out of place for the Council to give its official patronage in aid of one particular school, and that one being the only school in the town possessing an endowment.

The school was founded in 1710, and was then located above the ancient North Gate until that was demolished in 1842. Initially it was a school for boys but when the new Blue Coat School was erected in 1844, on the site adjoining the North Walk, it became a school for girls as well. Prior to this date the girls had been located in a small school situated near the almshouses in Church Lane. Eventually the girls were transferred from the Blue Coat School to the National School, which had been erected around 1882 in North Walk.

41. Barnstaple Blue Coat and Charity School was erected in 1844,
designed by R.D.Gould.
(© North Devon Athenaeum/Museum of Barnstaple & North Devon)

Blue Coat Charity School.

THE Anniversary Sermon for the benefit of this Institution, will be preached in the Parish Church, on Sunday Morning, the 23rd of September instant, by the Rev. S. T. GULLY, A. M. Rector of Berrynarbor. Divine Service will commence at eleven o'clock.

Dated September 10th, 1832

In the course of research done on the Fair Sunday, one or two adverts have been found concerning the event and the usual North Devon Journal reports.

A much less sum was collected than was expected for the Blue Coat Charity in 1824. The donations made at the service in the Parish Church, only amounted to £26. This was said to be in consequence of the unfavourable state of the weather.

In 1835 the charity fared a little better with the liberal contribution of £40.5s.6d. being received at the door. The spacious church on this occasion was crowded to excess, and the children sweetly chanted a hymn prepared for the purpose. The full attendance was most likely due to the visit of the Lord Bishop of the diocese to the district. *"On Sunday last, our parish church was honoured with the presence and ministerial service of the Lord Bishop of the Diocese. In accordance with a custom that has for many years been observed here, on the Sunday in fair week, the interest of the Blue Coat School is advocated in a sermon, and a collection made of the congregation in support of its funds. His Lordship having fixed on this period for his official visit to this part of his diocese, kindly consented to perform this charitable service."* In 1844, the Rev. Samuel Thomas Gully, of Berrynarbour, preached the annual sermon. It was reported - *"The obnoxious novelty of making the collection during the reading of the offertory service was abandoned and made at the doors as formerly."* The newspaper took the opportunity of reminding readers, that the lately designed and partially erected new buildings for the Blue Coat Schools, had not been completed, the necessary funds not being forthcoming. Evidently, Messrs. Roberts and others of the friends of the charity had been liberal in aiding the good work, and needed to enlist co-operation to finish it.

"Fair Sunday", 1855, the Mayor and Corporation, with the borough officers, went to the parish church in state, preceded by the Blue Coat Schools, for the purpose, it was said, of

promoting the interests of that charity at the Annual Sermon. Two decades later all is not well with the Fair Sunday tradition.

At the opening of the Fair Ceremony in 1876, the Mayor announced to the Councillors present that he would have the honour of going to the church officially for the annual sermon on behalf of the Blue Coat Schools. He referred to the small attendance of the members of the Council for the last three or four years and hoped that there would be some improvement by having members of the Corporation join him. This admonishment seems to have worked for a while as the 1879 report in the newspaper reads — *"It is an ancient custom in this borough for the Mayor and Corporation to go in procession to church on the Sunday Morning in Fair week, on the occasion of the annual sermon on behalf of the funds of the Blue Coat*

Schools. In accordance with it the Mayor and several members of the Council met in the Council-room on Sunday morning last, where they were joined by the vicar of the parish (Rev. A.E. Seymour), the preacher for the day (Rev. William Francis, rector of Atherington), and some other gentlemen of the town, and from thence, preceded by the boys of the School, the police, beadles, and sergeants at mace, walked to the church."

However, in <u>1889</u> the Mayor and Corporation declined to attend, no doubt causing some consternation!

Nearing the end of the century it is clear the patronage of the Council is coming to an end, and so too is that particular custom. Very little is reported on the event –

The Mayor and Corporation were in attendance in 1897; the collection made being the small amount of £9.11s. and the Chairman of the Blue Coat Trustees at this time was stated as Mr. T. Wainwright.

Fair Sunday, 1883 —
Preacher, Rev. A.E. Seymour, Vicar of Barnstaple –

"In the course of his sermon he said it was a very common complaint now-a-days that children were not so obedient and dutiful to their parent as they used to be, and also that servants were not so trustworthy and devoted to their masters and mistresses as was once the case."

42. Boys from Barnstaple's Blue Coat School inspecting the memorial stone set up to commemorate the Millenary celebrations of 1930. (Photograph © R.L.Knight).

𝔄𝔡𝔳𝔢𝔯𝔱𝔦𝔰𝔦𝔫𝔤 𝔣𝔬𝔯 𝔉𝔞𝔦𝔯𝔱𝔦𝔪𝔢

For the best part of the 19th century adverts were placed in the North Devon Journal leading up to Barnstaple Fair. Wonderfully worded and tempting descriptions of the various commodities are a delight to read and savour. Ranging from clothing, novelties, gifts, food, fairing, refreshments, agricultural implements, cure-alls, perfumes, photographic likenesses, toys, watches, jewellery etc. to the enticement of all the 'fun of the fair,' nothing seems to be forgotten. Advertising for the event carried on into the 20th century, but after the First World War it wasn't quite so prolific, and by the 1960's it appears to have disappeared all together.

A few examples in their varying forms have been collected together to include in this book.

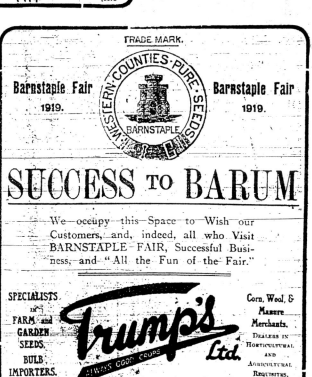

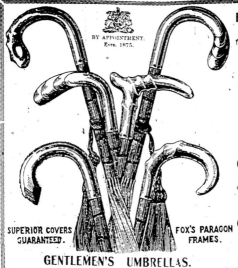

Barnstaple Ale & Fair Tippling Tales

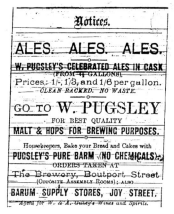

At Fair time the right to sell strong drink irrespective of justices and Excise was claimed — and freely exercised. The person who wished to sell liquor for the duration of the Fair simply stuck a bush in front of his house, and he thereby became a publican for the first time. In some years these "bush houses" were very numerous, and there was practically "free trade" in liquor in the very early years of the reign of Queen Victoria.

Up until 1869 the fully licensed public house could be kept open all night without hindrance, and ordinary beer-houses did not until that year require a magistrates' license, the necessary authority being granted by the Excise department on the payment of a stipulated fee. In the case of the beer-houses closing at 10 o'clock was insisted upon; and the owners of these "tiddlywink shops" (as they were commonly called) complained loudly at festive seasons of the injustice. Drunkenness was prevalent particularly at Fair time. Under the Licensing Act of 1869 the granting of beer-house licenses was transferred to the magistrates. Finally 11 o'clock was fixed as the closing hour for all licensed houses.

Barnstaple Ale was most certainly brewed by every innkeeper in the town during the early part of the 19th century, but gradually this was taken over by brewing companies. According to W.F. Gardiner, the first establishment of this kind was The Brewery in Taw Vale Parade, owned by a Mr. Kay, and later on in 1897 there were two breweries in operation — Petter's Anchor Brewery, and Mr. Pugsley's in Boutport Street.

In olden times it was customary for anyone caught breaking the law to be dealt with by the Mayor and one or two other officials, and at the end of the 19th century the Mayor is still performing his justice duties with the other magistrates.

During Fair time most charges of intoxication brought before the Mayor and the Magistrates were given some leniency owing to the festive occasion; some were not so lucky!

A few drink related cases have been noted out of interest:

1829 - "According to usual custom, some of our incautious farmers under the potency of "Barnstaple Fair Ale," and the vanity of displaying their hard-earned treasures, became the prey of a nefarious gang."

1836 - A number of innkeepers, whose licenses had been suspended during the fair, were admonished as to their future conduct, and their licenses granted with a few exceptions.

Before the Bench at the Guildhall on Saturday 22nd September, 1838

"A half-witted clown who had come from the wastes of Exmoor to see the wonders of Barnstaple Fair, was brought up from the constable's prison (where he had been accommodated with a nights lodging,) and fined 2s.6d. and expenses, on complaint of Mr. Blackmore, dentist, for drunkenness, and indecent behaviour to some respectable females in the Square the preceding evening."

155

1840 - A young woman of very suspicious appearance, who said she gained her livlihood by vending stationary at fairs, was seen following several farmers at night who were intoxicated. She was conducting herself in a disorderly manner, and was put out of harm's way for the rest of the fair, by a week's confinement in the prison.

1841 - Samuel Lander, of Yarnescombe, having been found drunk in the Square on Fair Monday night, was fined 1s. then discharged.

Mary Fogetty, superintendent of David Riddaway's notorious 'establishment' in Green Lane, was found drunk the same night and fined 1s.

John Parsley, shoemaker, of Tawstock, was charged with being drunk on the Tuesday night, and fined 5s. and expenses of 8s. and in default of payment, to sit in the stocks for six hours.

Thomas Phillips, horse-dealer, and Sally Pugsley, of Yelland, in Fremington, having been found lying under one of the stalls in Cross-street between three and four o'clock in the morning, were sentenced to be imprisoned in the borough gaol for one week.

1842 - Brought before the Mayor, Gilbert K. Cotton and Justices:
Ellen Webber, vendor of nuts in the fair, was charged with being drunk and disorderly in the streets at 2 o'clock in the morning. She was discharged by the bench, and "due to the considerable indulgence during fair week, on her promise to leave the town immediately.

William Williams and William Alto, two men from the company belonging to Cornwall's Equestrian Circus, were fined for being drunk and disorderly and disturbing the peace of the inhabitants of Back-lane, (Trinity Street) in the early hours of Sunday morning, and for resisting the officer — Policeman Snell — in the execution of his duty. The bench censored the defendants for disturbing the quiet of the borough. Mr. Law especially considered it a reflection on Mr. Cornwall and an abuse of the indulgence shewn him by the Mayor, to allow his men to disgrace themselves and him.

Mary Ann Waddison, an itinerant vendor of lace at the fair, was charged by John Geen, landlord of the 'Bear' in Green

Lane, with wilfully damaging his goods and assaulting him. The defendant had visited the 'Bear' with a couple of companions to partake of a glass at the close of the fair. Being well intoxicated and wanting further supplies of drink, the landlord refused to serve them without being paid first, whereupon the defendant vented her rage on the glasses and furniture, and by thrusting her fist into the landlord's face. The defendant refused to pay her fine of 5s.and 3s.expenses and was locked up. Eventually she was released when her friends paid the fine.

1844 - Shadrach Friend, a carpenter from Dolton, was found lying in the street near Pilton Bridge, with a severe cut to his forehead received from a fall while in a drunken state and incapable of looking after himself. He was taken to the station house for protection. The Mayor dismissed him with a caution extending to him the leniency of Fairtime.

Ellen Webber, the nut vendor, is in trouble again with her drunkenness! "She was picked up in a filthy state of intoxication between 11 and 12 o'clock the night before on the Quay, and was so completely overcome that the police were obliged to get a hand-cart to take her to the station-house. She is well known as a frequenter of this fair for many years, and never fails to record her name as a disorderly in the police-books — On her promise to leave the town, the Mayor dismissed her." (You can bet she took a flagon or two to help her on her way!)

The next year sees Ellen drunk and incapable yet again, and this time we know that she comes in all the way from Withypool. Although only admonished and sent on her way in previous years, on this occasion her luck had run out, and she was fined 5s.for being drunk. No further reference was found regarding Ellen's liking for Barnstaple Fair Ale after this time. I rather suspect she had passed on and had partaken of her last flagon of beer!

1850 - Report from the *North Devon Journal*, 26th September
"A desultory conversation took place between the magistrates as to the parish stocks, formerly occupying a prominent situation in the churchyard, which, it appeared, had been so long disused that someone had taken the liberty of burning them. As it appeared that this antiquated mode of punishment was the only one vested in the magistrates by certain old statutes that, for instance, which provides a punishment for drunkenness, and that the stocks had been a "rod of terror" if not actually brought into requisition, they expressed a wish that if the old pair could not be resuscitated new ones might be procured."

"Much to the credit of the townsfolk and visitors, no case of assault drunkenness, &c., was heard before the magistrates during the fair week. This is partly attributable, however, to the excellent steps adopted by the police under the superintendence of Mr. Aldham, and to the forbearance occasionally exercised by them."

1855 - In the new cattle market (later known as the Victoria Road site) a booth was erected in the meadow inside the wall by Mr. Kay for the sale of liquor. It was extensively patronized.

1862 - A one armed tramp by the name of Henry Clark, and his companion Thos. Jackson, were charged with being drunk and assaulting Mary Hambledon, the wife of one of the showmen, in the Fair. They had come on to the stage in front of her husband's booth, and began dancing. The complainant told them to go when they supposedly assaulted her. Two witnesses corroborated her statement, but Mr. Arthur Petter, postmaster, and Mr. Thomas Powning came forward voluntarily for the prisoners. They stated to the magistrates that the proprietor of the booth had first assaulted the tramps and then brutally ill-used them. The evidence was considered to be too conflicting, and the tramps were dismissed to dance another day!

1864 - Two prostitutes were charged with being drunk and disorderly. The first — a young girl, named Stanbury, (described as a dirty drab) was brought into custody by P.C. Gliddon for using "disgustingly obscene" language at 2 o'clock in the morning in Joy Street. The Mayor gave her a suitable admonition, and fined her 10s or a fortnight's imprisonment.

The second — Emma Gregory, of Green Lane, a juvenile prostitute of about fourteen years of age — was charged by P.C. Jones with being drunk and disorderly outside the 'Mermaid' public house, shortly after midnight. The prisoner was fined 5s.and costs or 7days.

Two men from different backgrounds were in trouble through drink in 1873.

Thomas Birchall, a stall-keeper in the fair, was charged not only with being drunk and disorderly in the Square, but also with assaulting his wife.Sergt. Eddy stated that on the previous afternoon, he saw a great crowd collected around the Albert Clock, and heard screams of "Murder!" Making enquiries he was told, "A man is murdering a woman." He then went to the West of England Bank, near where the assault was taking place, and found the prisoner very drunk and violent, being held by a man - the woman was standing close by. A witness by the name of Wm. Watts told the court that he saw the prisoner knock his wife down and heard from several people in the crowd, that it was in fact the wife that had started the affray by hitting the prisoner on the head with a stone, but had not witnessed it himself. Birchall was fined 5s.and expenses. (I think this is now termed as a "Domestic"!)

Thomas Hockins, who was described as a respectably dressed man, but with his collar stained and his necktie missing, was charged with being drunk and disorderly at the Fair. He was said to come from Exeter. He was found by,

Superintendent Songhurst in the early hours of that morning lying on the ground outside the Fortescue Hotel, surrounded by several men. He was drunk, but complained of being assaulted. The prisoner, in defence, said that he ought to have caught the excursion train, but having missed it went to three or four public houses in search of lodgings, and supposed he took a drop too much. He was sorry that he had been overcome by drink, and promised it should not occur again. He had been robbed of his watch and chain and all his money. — He was fined 5s. or in default seven days imprisonment; but the Mayor gave him a shilling to telegraph to his friends in Exeter.

Drunken disputes are often encountered whatever the century! At fair time in <u>1875</u>, Wm. Prust, a cattle-drover from Barnstaple, was charged by Richard Luxton, cattle-dealer and farmer from Black Torrington, with assaulting him in the 'Red Cow', Barnstaple. During their dispute the defendant struck the complainant a violent blow in the face, which blacked his eye. Prust said that Luxton began the assault by jumping at him and knocking his hat off, because he had lost at tossing, and had blacked his own eye by coming into contact with the edge of the door, and moreover assented that the complainant had bit him on the thumb! However, it was said that Prust had injured his own hand by thrusting it through a pane of glass. Having called no witnesses Prust was fined 10s.and expenses or in default of payment, 14 days imprisonment.

Removing the site of the fair in <u>1877</u> from the Square to Castle Street and the end of North Walk, did not affect the tippling public. James Wood, a hobbler, of Swansea, was found insensibly drunk in the middle of Trinity Street. P.C. Downing, who found him at half-past one in the morning, first feared that he was dead. With some assistance, Wood was conveyed to the station. He pleaded to be leniently dealt with, and said it was the first time in his life he had ever been brought before a magistrate. He was fined 5s.and costs, but being unable to pay was committed to gaol for seven days.

The fair-time drunkenness in <u>1879</u> was reported as being mostly of the good- tempered kind, and there was little or no occasion for the interference of the police. One amusing incident did occur however, and is herewith reported in full. –

"A Tippling Organ-Grinder. — A man named Wm. Gully, an organ-grinder hailing from Chittlehampton, was on Friday last brought by the police before the Mayor, charged with being incapably drunk on Landkey road at half-past two that morning. Information was given at the police-station concerning the prisoner, and P.C.s Thorne and Edwards went in search of him and found him lying helplessly drunk in the road near Newport, with his instrument in the hedge. They were provided with a hand cart, and on it they conveyed him to the station. — Prisoner was fined 5s. which was paid."

(I wonder what happened to the monkey!)

1880 - William Taylor, was found by P.C. Sargent, lying drunk and asleep outside the National School, Newport.

A like offence attracted the attention of the same Police Constable. A man named William Parker was found asleep at the High Street entrance gates to the parish churchyard. Fined 5s.and costs, or seven days.

(At the end of the 20th century, St. Peter's churchyard still attracted a few imbibers! – they are now prohibited.)

1890 - Arguments for and against the customary extension of time to the Licensed Victuallers during the Fair resulted in the magistrates declining to grant the application. Supt. Songhurst said that although there was no difficulty in clearing the houses at eleven o'clock on the first two days of the Fair, a lot of people came in from the country on Friday and it would be more difficult to do this as a large number did not leave until between eleven and twelve.

Backing the decision of the Bench it was stated that neither the pleasure of the visitors, nor the trade of the town would suffer, and that the comfort of the residents in the immediate neighbourhood of the Fair would be greatly enhanced.

Drunkenness against Frank James, in the employ of Shapland & Petter, was established at Barnstaple Police Court, during the fair in 1893. P.C. Tucker found the defendant lying in the footway in the Taw Vale Parade perfectly helpless, and had to be conveyed to the police station. James said he trusted the Bench would let him off lightly, as this was the first time he had been "run in" in his life. He could not account for the cut on his forehead he added, and caused much laughter in court when he said he had "lost" his legs on the previous night. He met the order to pay a fine of 2s.6d. with the remark "I must pay up and look big, I suppose."

1894 - "There was not so much drunkenness as has been seen in some recent years, and the Fair passed off on the whole in very orderly fashion."

Towards the end of the 19th century fair-time tippling is, as would be expected, still around but drunkenness doesn't appear to be quite so rife. The last tippling tale to be told happened in the Fair Week of 1898 and a heading in the *North Devon Journal* reads as follows:

"Disgraceful Scene in Churchyard"

According to the report, two men under the influence of drink were seen engaged in a mock burial service at St. Mary Magdalene churchyard. One lay prostrate on the ground while the other proceeded to conduct the service. They had also attempted to lock the verger, Mr. John Colwell, into the church thereby damaging the lock, and necessitating the services of a locksmith. Instead of being charged to appear before the magistrates, they both agreed to send a written letter of apology and the sum of one guinea to the church authorities as their punishment.

43. St. Mary Magdalene church and churchyard, scene of the drunks'
'funeral service' in 1898. (Photograph © R.L. Knight)

A Chapter of Accidents & Incidents

With any large gathering there is, on occasion, bound to be some form of accident. In the 19th century the horse was as familiar a form of transport as the motor vehicle is today, consequently, there were many accidents involving these animals and travelling to and from Barnstaple Fair has been no exception. The following references are a compilation of fair related incidents that occurred during that time.

The first report in the *North Devon Journal* for fair week accidents is given in 1829. A young man, servant to Mr. Lovering of Tawstock, was riding his master's horse to show his paces near the horse fair, when another rider came into contact with him quite violently, and knocked him off his horse. He was taken immediately to the Infirmary where he was first reported as dead. However, after the medical gentlemen had bled him, he made a good recovery.

The 1834 fairtime saw two accidents. Coincidentally, both casualties came from the same parish of Bratton Fleming. The first — a servant girl of Mr. Ridd — on going to the fair, was thrown from her horse and dislocated her shoulder.

The second — Farmer Pile — on returning from the fair on the Friday evening, and according to the report had indulged too freely with Sir John Barleycorn! And was thrown from his horse — "and received so violent a concussion as to deprive him of sensibility, and he lay speechless till the following Sunday; Mr. Ridd, surgeon of this town, was sent for, by whose judicious applications he had recovered his speech, but still suffers severely from the accident."

After a happy day at the fair in <u>1839</u>, a sad tale is told at the Inquest on a young woman —

Agnes Latham aged 24, servant to Mr. Richard Comer, in the parish of Loxhore, had been to the fair on the Friday, and in the evening had returned with a young man (a servant to Mr. Gill, of Bratton Fleming) whom she took into the kitchen. The following day her master expressed his displeasure at Agnes letting a stranger into the house so late at night; and was angry with her all day. On the Sunday morning she took a small quantity of a corrosive substance mixed with cold tea and was soon taken very ill. Mr. Torr, surgeon, was sent for who attended her until she died on the following Sunday. Her master gave Agnes an excellent character, but it appeared that the girl was rather nervous and of weak intellect. The Verdict of the Inquest was — Temporary derangement.

"<u>Melancholy and Fatal Accident</u>" is the headline in <u>1844</u>. William Lovering, of Combmartin, yeoman, had been at Barnstaple Fair, and in the company of three neighbours left around 8 o'clock. All were on horseback; - Lovering had been drinking freely and rode off from his companions at a furious gallop, down the hill toward Blatchford — His horse came into contact with the horse of a van driven by the son of the Ilfracombe carrier, John Pugsley. Lovering's horse sprang away, and in doing so the point of the shaft caught him in the leg, and he instantly fell under the horse in the van. Managing to get up he exclaimed "Oh my God! I am murdered!" By this time he was bleeding profusely. The surgeon, Mr. Torr was sent for, however, Lovering had expired before the surgeon's arrival. The wound was discovered to be 5inches long and the same in depth, which had divided the femoral artery, and extended into the abdomen.

It was noted that William Lovering had been born on the 19th of September - Barnstaple Fair Day - married on that day, and killed on the 45th anniversary of his birthday. (A disastrous celebration of events.)

In <u>1845</u>, Mr. Jacob Thorne, a farmer of Yard gate, in the parish of Northmolton, was returning from the cattle fair when his pony came into contact with a bullock being driven along the road. The rider thrown, landed on his head and was found to sustain a concussion of the brain. He lay in a condition that left little hope of his recovery.

An attempted suicide in 1849 by a desperate young woman named Prudence Coles of Morte was fortunately unsuccessful. It would appear that she had been keeping company with a young man, by whom she had become pregnant, On going to Barnstaple Fair she found the young man in the company of another female. He told Prudence he no longer wanted anything to do with her, whereupon she went directly to the shop of Mr. Weaver, druggist, and purchased a packet of Butler's Rat and Vermin Killer. Next morning she consumed the contents, but was saved by Mr. Pick, surgeon who applied the stomach pump to remove all of the poison.

The accident report in the year of 1852 reads:

"ACCIDENT IN THE FAIR. — *On Friday, a little deaf and dumb girl of the name of Burrington, was run over by a cart, and sustained a fracture of the thigh. The child was attended and the thigh re-set by Mr. Cooke, surgeon. She was at once conveyed to the Infirmary, and is doing well."*

Another accident described James Frayne, ostler at the 'Exeter Inn' receiving a kick in the abdomen from a horse, and was "dangerously hurt."

On the fair Friday of 1857 a boy named William Vicary, son of a currier, was driving a horse and cart from the 'Nag's Head' public house, along the North Walk. On his arrival at the entrance to Castle-house, the horse kicked causing the boy to fall from the cart and pitch on his head. The cart went over his bowels, and according to a witness cried out several times "Do save me." Blood was flowing from his ears as he was being taken to the Infirmary. The efforts of the house surgeon, Mr. Husband and visiting surgeon, Mr. Cooke were not enough to save him and the boy died on the Saturday morning, possibly from a fractured skull.

Condemnation was made of the common practice of ostlers, at the various inns of the town, in allowing young boys to drive horses and carts about the area. It was trusted that after such a sad accident, measures would be taken to put a stop to the dangerous practice.

In 1859 the fair was reported as passing off without serious casualties, except for one lamentable case of a violent collision between two horses on the Long Bridge, which resulted in the death of one of them.

The 1865 fair week resulted in three accidents, - A gipsy-woman named Henrietta Broadway, received a fracture of the thigh when she fell from her horse on the way from the fair to the encampment at Highbickington.

A man named Phillip Pugsley, of Lower Loxhore, received serious injuries returning from Barnstaple on fair Friday. He and four other men were riding in a large cart when he jumped off to walk up hill, and slipped and fell under the wheels, one ofwhich passed over his abdomen. He was in a critical condition at the Infirmary.

Lastly, a man named William Tucker, of Braunton, was admitted to the Infirmary suffering from concussion of the brain — the result of falling of his horse returning from the fair.

A man dying suddenly at the fair in 1868 was named as Sergeant Walsh, of the Devon Artillery Militia, Plymouth, who was on a visit to Barnstaple for recruiting purposes. Apparently, while standing between the West of England Bank and the railings of the Square, he complained to his companions of feeling unwell.

Mr.Charles Johnston, surgeon examined him and noticed a large quantity of arterial blood on the ground. He was found to be dead and in the opinion of Mr. Johnston the cause was a rupture of the aorta.

1871 *"Accident to a boy. — On Friday last, a boy about eight years of age, son of one of the showmen attending Barnstaple Fair, was sitting on the sea wall opposite the Square, when he fell over and pitched on the wall beneath thereby sustaining a slight concussion of the brain. The lad, who was named Henry Gest, was taken to the North Devon Infirmary, where his injuries were promptly attended to, and he had so far recovered in a day or two as to be able to leave the town with his parents."*

In 1874 A little girl three years of age, the daughter of Mr. J. Stevens, hatter, of Higher Maudlin Street, was knocked down by the Ilfracombe break of the Devon and Somerset Railway. As the

167

driver was proceeding at a slow trot through the Square, the little girl darted out of a confectionery stall belonging to her father close to Mr. Nicklin's shop. The driver was powerless to pull up in time and the child became entangled in the horse's feet. Although suffering from concussion and a bent arm, no bones were broken and within 48 hours she was well enough to go home.

A man who had been employed at the 1879 fair, was found lying insensible beside the stream, which ran at the foot of Pilton Lawn. Upon recovering consciousness at the Infirmary, he stated that he came from Milverton and was thrown bringing a horse into the fair.

An Amusing Incident in 1886:

Two young men, determined to blow away the effects of their merriment at the Fair Ball from the night before, decided to take an early morning row up the river. They eased their swollen feet by taking off their boots, puffed their "baccy" and kept their boat in mid-stream. When they reached Bishop's Tawton it was decided to change sides, and, in doing so they capsized the boat and became immersed in the flowing tide. Fortunately, they regained the boat and managed to right it; but alas, hats, boots, and pipes were gone. Mooring the boat, they decided to divest themselves of their sodden garments, made an awning with them, and took shelter beneath it while they waited for their wet garments to dry. Soon their late night and early morning exertions took their toll, and they both drifted off into the land of nod for a few hours. On emerging from their somnolent state, they found their clothes dry but could not ascertain the hour of the day. The tide by then had receded and the craving of empty stomachs added to their grief. There was nothing for them to do other than wait for the next tide. At the first possible moment they made their way towards Barum, which they reached about 8p.m. having been absent for about 14 hours! Fortunately it was dusk and some benevolent individuals seeing the forlorn young men, took pity on them and sped them on their way home by lending them hats, boots, etc. (I bet they never lived it down, and their escapade the cause of much merriment around the dinner tables!)

The next year of <u>1887</u> saw no amusing incident and involved a boat of a different kind. Enjoying a ride in one of the swing-boats at the fairground, a little lad of six years, named Charles Clement, fell out on to the ground. He was taken to the Infirmary where a severe cut to his forehead received attention.

<u>1889</u> — Three small accidents occurred this year — Mr. Powning, of High Street, was struck on the head by one of the competitors at a nearby booth, causing blood to flow freely. A visitor to the fair fell from the aerial railway, which caused the man to sustain slight injuries, and a lady fell from a whirligig and only suffered a sprained ankle.

At the Horse Fair in <u>1893</u> a horse ridden by a labourer named John Delbridge, of Newport, galloped away after a dealer struck the animal with a whip. People were scattered in all directions as the runaway went out of control, first knocking down a man, it then overturned a cart breaking the shafts, and eventually ended up outside the Guildhall were it threw its rider violently. Delbridge was conveyed to the Infirmary where attention was given to his severe cuts and bruising.

<u>1894</u> — A man received a nasty blow from a mallet being used in a strength testing experiment.

Barnstaple Fair in the last year of the 19th century proceeded without mishap until the Friday night when two accidents were reported.

The first involved a man named Phillips, of Barnstaple, who fell over a rope while carrying his child through the fair, which resulted in the child's thigh being broken.

The second casualty was a farm labourer by the name of Alfred Copp, of Westdown. On returning from the fair, he intended to go to Ilfracombe by train. At about 3.30p.m, groans were heard coming from the iron bridge that spanned the river Taw, and Copp was found with his head badly cut and bleeding profusely. It was surmised that the man had either fallen out of the train, or been struck by something whilst on the line. Apparently the railway authorities had seen nothing of Copp therefore some mystery surrounded the cause of the accident. Injuries sustained by him were found to be not so serious as first thought.

(Of the accidents during this time, many were the cause of quaffing too much liquor. Whether travelling by horseback or horsepower, the message is clear — "don't drink and drive!")

Pickpockets, Felonies & Misdemeanours

On such occasions as Barnstaple Fair the "light-fingered tribe" were diligent in their vocation, some even travelling great distances for their 'pickings.' One of the earliest cases researched is from:

> **"The Mayor's Court, in the 34th year of Edward the Third — (1361)**
> *John Coppe, a cut purse, was arrested on Thursday, the feast of the Nativity of the Blessed Virgin Mary, for stealing the purse of Walter le Knyth and twelve shillings and one penny in the same, against the peace, etc., and by sentence of the Court held on the Saturday following, his right ear was cut."*

Coming forward to the 19th century, many warnings are being given by the authorities, and the villains and their trade are well described in the *North Devon Journal.*

In the year of 1827 a man called William Wybron, of the parish of Marwood, was committed to the Borough gaol, to take his trial at the next quarter sessions for stealing an umbrella on the second day of Barnstaple Fair, from Betsey Nott, of West Buckland.

Following through to the October 1827 Quarter Sessions, the outcome was thus:

> *"The Petty Jury having been placed in the box of whom, Mr. Philip Hodge was foreman, and a true bill returned*

by the Grand Jury against William Wybourn, he was arraigned and charged with having on the 20th September last, stolen one cotton umbrella, of the value of 4s. the property of Betsey Nott. Another count charged the prisoner with having stolen the said umbrella from Mary Nott. To which he pleaded guilty, and in extenuation said he was in liquor at the time, and knew not but that it was his own umbrella till the following day.

In passing sentence the Deputy Recorder observed that he had been most mercifully dealt with; first by the Magistrates, who had permitted him to be at large to procure evidences to prove an alibi, which he must be conscious he could not do; and secondly, by the prosecutor, in not having charged him with stealing from the person, which would have subjected him, on conviction, to transportation for life, or a period of not less than seven years. He admonished him that should he ever be convicted on another indictment, he would most certainly be transported for life.

His sentence was to be imprisoned in the gaol of this borough for three calendar months, and during that time to be kept at hard labour."

Poor fellow! Another case of 'wit's out when the drink's in' I suspect. Not so the following cases of pick pockets —

1828 - Edward Pearse, a stranger from Liverpool, and one of a gang who came to the Fair to professionally appropriate whatever they could conveniently obtain, was charged with stealing a muslin handkerchief from the person of George Chidley. The offence was clearly proved on the evidence of three witnesses, and the Jury pronounced a verdict of *Guilty*. The prisoner was sentenced to six months in the Borough gaol, and to be kept at hard labour.

1830 - The Chief magistrate gave a public notice on both Sunday evening and Monday morning, that a number of suspicious characters were in the town and cautioned the public to be on their guard. Pick pockets robbed one young farmer of £57 as he was dining in a public house. Another farmer lost £27.

<u>1831</u> - Several pick- pockets were actively employed in the pursuit of their avocation. A party of three men were detected in robbing an individual of his watch, chain, and seals. The men were given into the care of the constable.

<u>1837</u> - George Warwick, alias Cockney George, was brought before the magistrates charged with picking the pocket of the wife of Mr. Land, hairdresser of Barnstaple. Mrs. Land was in the fair near the fish market, and detected the prisoner with his hand in her pocket. He was remanded for further examination. Sarah Putter, who obtained her livelihood by travelling about

the country selling needles, was indicted for stealing a silk handkerchief from the person of John Glandfield. He gave evidence that after walking through the fair until half past twelve at night; he went into a public house on the Quay with his brother George.

He left after half an hour a little ahead of his brother and stated that "*about five or six landyards from the house I saw the prisoner, and she said, "How d'ye do, sir," at the same time putting her arm around my waist; I said to her, "you had better be off, I want nothing of you," and she left; my brother came out just at the moment, and he and I went away together; about five minutes afterwards I missed my pocket handkerchief; I knew that I had it in the public house; it was in my left coat pocket; we went at once in search of the prisoner, and overtook her in the High Street. I said to her, "you have got my handkerchief," and she gave it to me, with a smile. She had it in her left hand under her shawl. I told my brother to go for a constable, and I held the prisoner some time until a great many persons came up, and as I did not know what gang she might have about her, I thought myself in danger, and let her go; but when the constable came up we followed her and took her into custody."*

The prosecutor's brother corroborated the evidence, and Samuel Rudd, the constable told of the apprehension of the prisoner and produced the handkerchief, which the prosecutor identified. The jury found the prisoner guilty, and the Recorder sentenced her to two months imprisonment.

<u>1838</u> - A farmer named Dart, of Parracombe, lost £22 to a pick-pocket, and another farmer, from Georgeham, was duped out of £50 by a trickster.

<u>1842</u> - Through the arrangements of the authorities, and the vigilance of the police, there were no serious instances of pickpocketing. It was said the police were too sharp for the sharpers!

<u>1845</u> - "Members of the light fingered tribe" were reported to be numerous -

One gentleman from Tawstock by the name of Symons, and being one of the overseers of his parish, had £50 stolen from his person. The money belonged to the parish and was brought in by him to pay into the bank.

Elizabeth Welch, from Plymouth, who stated herself to be an itinerant hawker, (but had no stock to trade) was charged with attempting to pick pockets in the fair.

<u>1850</u> - It was recorded — *"On Wednesday and Thursday, a considerable number of suspicious personages — consisting of the usual "rabble-rout" attending fairs throughout the country, sprinkled pretty freely with ladies and gentlemen of the swell-mob — were on the qui vive. The preponderance of these visitors caused the Superintendent on Wednesday to issue a notice cautioning the public. The usual number of special constables have been appointed by magisterial precept to assist the ordinary police force during the fair."*

1852 - *"John Hughes, a frequenter of fairs, was committed for one month as a rogue and a vagabond, for attempting to pick the pocket of Mrs. Lock, the wife of Mr. William Lock, boot and shoe maker of this town."*

1854 - James Pearce, *"a rather doughy looking youngster,"* about 17 years of age, was given into custody by Mr. T. Cann, as a suspicious character. Mr. Cann said that he had observed him at the fair on Wednesday, and, *"concluded him to be one of those light-fingered gentry who, like other birds of prey, always gather together wherever the carcass is."* He went on to state that he had seen Pearce again on Thursday, were he detected him attempting to pick the pockets of two young ladies in the Square. Mr. Cann very properly thought himself bound in duty to the public, to give such a customer in charge. On being brought before the magistrate (John Marshall, Esq.) Pearce *"pleaded his innocence of any such naughty tricks — said he belonged to Collumpton — was a shoemaker by trade — had been living for some while with his grandmother in Tiverton, and was now on his way to visit his uncle and aunt, at Torrington."*

He was remanded until the Saturday of fair week, when, not being able to give a better account of himself, he was committed for one month of hard labour.

Barnstaple Quarter Sessions, October 1855
It was stated that there were no prisoners for trial, and no indictments to be preferred.

The Recorder, William M. Praed, Esq., made the address — *"The absence of any case for trial was highly creditable to the town — the more so, as provisions were dear, and since the last sessions, they had held their annual fair. He believed that this state of things was mainly attributable to an efficient police."*

He went on to say that Barnstaple had greatly improved, and that the police deserved the good opinion of the inhabitants. (Praise indeed, but it appears the police had their charge books quite full with various entries, at fair time, in the following year.)
1856 - Robert Pidler, was brought before the magistrates and charged with assaulting Mr. John Smith, schoolmaster, of Marwood, and robbing him of his purse, money, and spectacles.

A tradesman of Boutport Street was reported to have lost his watch, and a Mr. Anderson, of Prospect-place, lost his purse, four sovereigns and ten shillings.

<u>1862</u> - Report from the *North Devon Journal* -

"The conduct of the police throughout the Fair has been most exemplary. By their zeal and efficiency good order has been maintained, and those who gain their living by dishonest practices have been disappointed of their prey. We congratulate the town on having a police force so well up to their important duties, and so apt in their performance."

<u>1864</u> - The only robbery during the Fair was stated to be against the Reverend T. Colling, of Buckland Brewer, who was eased of his watch while escorting Mrs. Colling to the theatre. (The watch was later discovered in an Exeter pawn shop!)

<u>1867</u> - A Pickpocket — Maria Bennett — was charged as a suspected person as being in the Square, with the intention to commit a felony. P.C. Molland took ther charge at the Station-house where the prisoner refused to give her name, and became very violent. In her bag the constable found £1 16s. 6d. a pair of earrings and a small knife which he said was such an instrument that would be used to cut off a woman's pocket. Mr. I. Bencraft (Solicitor) addressed the bench on behalf of the prisoner with a 'good' result for the defendant. The Mayor said the case was one of strong suspicion, but the evidence was insufficient. Consequently the charge against the prisoner was dismissed. It was reported that on leaving, she was joined by three suspicious looking persons — detected among them was a convicted Pickpocket. (Galling to say the least!)

<u>1870 - "A Pugilist and Vendor of Umbrellas in Trouble:"</u>

A description gives two pick pockets as "*a tall man named William Jones, hailing from Birmingham, and a wild-looking little man called George Curtis, an itinerant vendor of umbrellas, &c.*"

They were both charged with attempting to pick the pockets of Mrs. Hannah Stoyle, landlady of the 'Stafford Arms,' Trinity Street.

The story goes that a gang of rough characters including Jones and Curtis went to the house late on Fair night, and attempted to gain admittance. During that time a man known by the name of "Calfskin Jack" told one of the crowd to "touch the poshes." (Mrs. Stoyle supposed the meaning referred to pockets.) The prisoner Jones made a sudden grasp at her pocket with such violence it nearly pulled her to the ground. In order to prevent the men from forcibly making a way into the house, Mrs. Stoyle ran into the kitchen for a poker, which she gave to her husband, who threatened that if anyone came in, he would strike them with it.

Mr. Bencraft addressed the bench on behalf of the prisoners (who had been on remand for a week) and stated that the police had made strict inquiries on the prisoners and found nothing against them. He further remarked, "Jones was not one of the criminal class; he was a pugilist who had come to spar for the amusement of the British public, and the edification of those who were desirous of acquiring the principles of the 'noble art' of self-defence." Curtis, on being asked if he had anything to say in answer to the charge, indignantly denied it, and expressed sorrow for the loss of his umbrellas. He supposed he had thrown them away in a moment of ill humour when he had a "drop of drink." He went on to say that he had become a laughing stock for all the small boys of the town, who pushed him about because he had "indulged in intoxicating beverages to an extent which rendered him totally unconscious of what he was doing. Barnstaple was a town of he had never heard, but now to his sorrow he knew more about it than he desired. He said that if the magistrates would let him go he would take care to "skeddaddle" from Barnstaple in ten minutes."

Whether it was the fact they had Mr. Bencraft on their side, or the magistrates fell for the 'innocence' plea of George Curtis, we will never know! In any event, the Mayor felt they had been properly remanded for a week and hoped it would teach them both a lesson for the future. They were then discharged.

As he was leaving Court, the parting remark from Curtis was — *"You don't catch me in Barnstaple, never no more!"*

The first year of Castle Street and part of North Walk as a venue for the pleasure fair in <u>1877</u> hasn't deterred the "light fingered tribe."

George Reeves of Plymouth was charged with taking a purse of money from the pocket of Sarah the wife of Robert Cure, lace-twister, of Derby.

And, John Stanley, a tailor, of Gloucester, was charged with attempting to pick the pocket of Mr. John Dullam, farmer, of Higher Yelland, Fremington.

According to Mr. Dullam, he was in the yard of the 'Angel Inn' when he caught the wrist of the prisoner's hand as it was leaving his pocket and said to Stanley, "You have your hand in my pocket." The prisoner replied, "How could I?" To which Dullam responded, "It was so, because I caught you." Stanley then tried to make his escape through the archway into the road, but then bolted into the 'Angel'. The farmer followed him hooking the man's shoulder with his stick at the same time crying out, "Stop the rogue!" With some assistance, Stanley was boxed up in the bar until the police came. Upon the request of Supt. Songhurst, the prisoner, who said nothing, was remanded. (It was said that there was much interest in the case with many farmers and others being present at the investigation. Time hasn't allowed for following up the outcome of the case — Yet!)

<u>1885</u> - The Fair passed off in a most orderly manner and it was said to be the quietest for a number of years. There were no cases at the Police Court arising out of the fair, and it was quoted as being "a very unusual state of things, but none the less gratifying on that account."

The years of <u>1888</u> and <u>1889</u> were also free from serious crime with the former reported as *"The borough police force was considerably augmented during the Pleasure Fair. There was no serious disturbance in any part of the town, although there was a good deal of drunkenness."* And the latter as *"There were no "Fair" charges to come before the magistrates on Saturday — a fact which speaks for itself."*

<u>1890</u> - Out of several pick-pockets at Barnstaple Fair this year, one apparently possessed a high degree of daring and ingenuity, and according to the 'Journal' this is how he secured the sum of £5.

"Simulating intoxication, he rolled against a gentleman standing in his doorway and made a spasmodic clutch at his watch-chain. It was so clumsily done that the gentleman suspected nothing, but simply requested the drunken pedestrian to proceed quietly homewards. No sooner had the sharper rambled out of sight, however, than our townsman discovered with dismay and astonishment, that his purse, which contained over £5, had been abstracted from his pocket. It is needless to

say that the pick-pocket had sought "fresh woods and pastures new" with a celerity which rendered pursuit futile. The trick was very neatly executed; the victim will doubtless have scant sympathy for the eccentricities of drunkenness in future."

1895 - Elizabeth Kelly, an elderly woman, who said she came from Torquay, was charged with stealing 3s.2d from William Dymond, a labourer, of Yarnscombe. He said he had visited the Bell Hotel the previous evening, and on coming out saw the prisoner. She followed him, and when near Old Theatre Lane she spoke to him and put her hand into one of his pockets. Shortly afterwards he discovered his purse of money was missing. She was given into custody to P.C. Tucker and when he charged her with the theft, she said she was as innocent as a child!

The magistrates sent the prisoner to gaol for seven days with hard labour.

Throughout the 19th century many other charges were made relating to 'Fair-time' and a few of the issues recorded, are included here.

Assaults:

1827 - Richard Quick preferred a complaint against Richard Hodge, and stated that he (Quick) on the second day of the Fair was at the 'Green Dragon', in the capacity of waiter. Hodge it seems was dancing with a number of other young persons, when he overthrew a table, and broke some cups and glasses. Quick refused to let Hodge quit the room until he had paid for the damages, and Hodge was alleged to have struck him twice. Hodge produced two witnesses to prove that it was in fact Quick, who collared and kicked him before he struck back. (The case was dismissed!)

1849 - John Hocking, a groom to an equestrian troop at the fair, was charged with assaulting a police constable by the name of Chapple. The constable had been called in, by the landlord of the 'Ship' to quell a row, and during the course of this, John Hocking struck P.C. Chapple with a whip. Hocking was fined 10s.and costs.

1869 - David Stafford, an itinerant vendor of nuts, was charged with assaulting Mr. Henry Harper, of Newport. The complainant stated that he was standing in the Square when the prisoner, who is lame, took up his crutch, and without provocation knocked him down twice. The Mayor remarked the assault was one of the most unprovoked and ruffianly that he had ever heard of, and committed the prisoner for 14 days with hard labour.

1875 - Affray in the Fair — William Ford, an itinerant dealer in fruit, and Jane Harris, a rival in the same line of business, issued cross summonses against each other for assaults in the Square.

The dispute between them had originated with both of them claiming the same plot of ground on which to place their hampers. The woman had occupied the site on the day before; and Ford, seeing it was a better business spot, went early the next morning to appropriate it! When Jane Harris came a row naturally ensued, and having a stick she applied it about the man's shoulders. He then obtained possession of the stick and struck her in the mouth with it.

Ford was fined 5s. and expenses for the assault on the woman, and the counter-charge was dismissed!

<u>1895</u> - Wm. Franklin, travelling with a roundabout, was charged with assaulting Samuel James, ferryman, of Instow. According to James he went on the roundabout with his wife the previous evening, and paid the money charged him. A man in the employ of Messrs. Hancock came to him and again demanded payment. Declining to pay twice an altercation ensued and James left the roundabout with his wife. Franklin rushed at him, and gave him a severe blow in the eye with such force that it completely closed the complainant's eye. The magistrates considered that a gross assault had been committed, and it was their duty to protect the public by sending the prisoner to gaol for seven days, without the option of a fine.

<u>1897</u> - <u>Cattle Dealers' Squabble at Barnstaple Fair:</u>
"*At Barnstaple Guildhall on Thursday, Thomas Prust, and his uncle William Prust, cattle dealers of Bickington, were charged with having assaulted Nicholas J. Chamings, also a cattle dealer and farmer, at Barnstaple Fair on Sept. 15th. Thos. Prust pleaded guilty, and William Prust not guilty. Mr A.F. Seldon appeared for the prosecutor, and Mr. J. Bosson for the defendants,*"

In a nutshell, it would seem that Chamings had seen William Prust getting very excited with Wm Wilton, (nephew of Chamings) outside the Bell Hotel and hearing him say something about it "being a sheep-stealing job again and declaring that he would do for him if it cost him a thousand." Thomas Prust came down the yard of the Hotel shortly afterwards with his shirt-sleeves rolled up, and, incited by Wm. Prust, he struck Chamings in the eye twice, knocking him down. It was said that William Wilton made contact with Wm. Prust by rubbing against him and saying he would give him "rummage." He admitted that Prust had said, "You don't want to steal anybody's sheep dog and get locked up." John Manning, who was standing close by, recollected seeing Thomas Prust knock Chamings down, but did not see Wm. Prust touch him. Several other witnesses said they did not see him touch Chamings, and P.C. Pugsley informed the bench that no blows were struck after he arrived, but he should say that the Prusts had been drinking. The Bench dismissed the case against Wm. Prust, but said that on his own admission Thos. Prust had committed an assault. He was fined 10s. and expenses, with the alternative of fourteen days imprisonment. The Bench refused to order expenses for witnesses on either side.

1899 - The last fair of the 19th century bows out with the newspaper headlines - "**Free Fight at Barnstaple Fair.**" On the Fair Friday night there was a "disgraceful disturbance" which became the subject of much talk in the town and the neighbourhood. It arose out of an alleged attempt to make some young men unfairly pay a second time for patronising one particular roundabout. Their refusal to hand over more money, caused another attendant to come up to them which led to a young gentleman coming of a horse while a man tried to strike him with a mallet. He ducked, but another gentleman standing immediately behind received the blow in the head, which was so severe he had to be surgically treated. Shortly afterwards the proprietor of the roundabout had an altercation with a soldier who also refused to pay a second time. While they were talking, an attendant came up and aimed a blow at the soldier, who ended up with a badly scarred nose. Workmen employed in other parts of the fairground were summoned, and several disturbances within a small area arose simultaneously. P.C. Braund was present at a comparatively early stage and worked hard to separate the combatants, but as there were so many, there was little that he could do. A large crowd had collected by then, and not only persons who tried to smooth things, those who were simply looking on, were brutally assaulted. One young man who had said nothing received a severe blow behind the head, and was knocked down, whilst another received severe cuts from a ring worn by an attendant who struck him in the face. A third man was brutally kicked for doing nothing at all. For over half-an-hour there was a scene of great disorder, and no man who got near the roundabout in question could regard himself as safe.

Another police constable named, Drakc, tried to restore order, and P.C. Tucker remonstrated with some of the men who had been responsible for the disturbance, only to be met with abuse. Eventually things quietened down after other police were sent for, and the public boycotted the roundabout for the rest of the night.

It was said the whole affair was most disgraceful, and in the interests of the town it was hoped that things would be officially investigated, and steps taken to prevent such an abuse of the rights granted in respect of the Fair in future.

(The fair in the following year appears to be much quieter with little or no mention of the "pleasure" side of things. Perhaps diplomacy was the word!)

Trickery & Gambling:

<u>1844</u> - The newspaper was warning farmers of a gang of swindlers prowling about to trap the unwary — "*It is astonishing to find that the stalest tricks are practised with success on half-witted simpletons whom one hardly knows whether most to pity or blame.*"

<u>1845</u> - John Taylor, a seaman and native of Westminster, was charged with exposing a deformed hand for the purpose of exciting charity. He was committed for 7 days.

<u>1856</u> - William White, from Wedmore,Somerset, was charged by P.C. Gliddon with playing unlawful games in the Fair. The prisoner was seen engaged in the "garter" trick at which another man was playing with him and had apparently won two half-crowns. They were considered to be in league with each other to induce others to play. A country fellow had already been 'done' out of £1 by them. The prisoner was described as "*a poor, dirty sharp-nosed, vagabond with three small children born to vice and vagrancy.*" His wife, who had accompanied him, was recorded as "*quite his contrast in point of flesh, having a reddened face and looking fat, ragged, and sorry.*" He was found guilty of swindling, and after the magistrates admonished him to pursue a more honest way of making a living, they committed him to 14 days "*to aid him in his reflections and purposes of amendment.*"

<u>1862</u> - An impudent beggar — Joseph Jackson, was charged with begging in public houses and in the streets, and exhibiting a deformity in one of his arms to excite sympathy. It was said that several ladies had been greatly shocked by the "disgusting exhibition." Upon being apprehended, he struck the constable and used very abusive language. The prisoner was committed

to the borough gaol for 21 days hard labour, as a rogue and a vagabond.

1863 - Andrew Thomas was charged with in the fair. P.C. Cawsey, who had been on duty in the Square during the occurrence, saw the prisoner with a penny fixed on the top of an upright stick, and charging a penny for a throw at it to dislodge the penny. It was very rarely knocked off and the police constable remarked that he saw one child lose 1s.or 1s.2d.

Prisoner. - "*It was not exactly gambling; it is what we call 'cock shy.' *"

The Mayor (Michael Cooke). — "*Is this your sole employment?*"

Prisoner. — "*No sir; I am a ginger-bread maker.*"

Mr Gribble. — "*It's rather a strange thing for a ginger-bread seller to be going about fairs in this way.*"

The Bench decided that the prisoner was guilty of a systematic fleecing of children, and committed him for one week to the borough gaol as a rogue and a vagabond.

1865 — James Green, and Elizabeth Green, were charged by Sergeant Songhurst with gambling. The prisoners were seen at a table in the fair, where a game was being carried on known as "white or red cock," at which it was stated, "many fools were induced to part with their money." At one time the game was much indulged in at fairs, but had recently been suppressed as illegal.

The prisoners were each sent to gaol for 21 days with hard labour.

In consequence of many complaints having been made against indecent exhibitions in the Square that year, Sergt. Songhurst made it his duty to investigate. There he saw Walter French exposing several stereoscopic views of indecent character in a machine, and charging one penny to anyone wishing to look. On being charged with the offence, French denied exhibiting them, and challenged that a witness be found to confirm that he had shown them. Mr. Wills, of Cross Street, was sent for by the police, but he denied having seen the defendant or looking through his machine. (I wonder why!!) As no further evidence was forthcoming, Walter French was discharged and the views ordered to be destroyed. (A future "what the butler saw" do you think?)

<u>1873</u> - Matthew Fisher, who apparently was respectable dressed and displaying very little of the professional blackleg in his appearance, was charged with gambling at the fair. He was noticed in the Square, with two pins and a ball, and inciting the boys, who surrounded him, to play. Superintendent Songhurst stated that he saw one boy play and lose 4d at a penny a time. If the boy knocked both pins down he would win 2d.but from the way the pins were placed it was impossible to knock both of them down. The prisoner on being searched was found to have 6s. 10d.on him, and said it was not his ball and pins; he was only standing by in the absence of the proprietor. This gamble didn't work however, and Fisher was sentenced to seven days hard labour!

<u>1883</u> — The North Devon Journal reported — *"It is a noteworthy fact that none of the representatives of the Half-crown trick fraternity were at the Fair — doubtless owing to the fact that one of them was brought before the magistrates here last year for swindling."*

<u>1894</u> — Brought before the borough magistrates for gambling and inducing persons to participate in the game roulette, was a man by the name of Henry Fortescue, of Dublin. After P.C. McLeod had watched the proceedings for some time, he saw that almost invariably two confederates secured the money staked as the result of Fortescue manipulating the instrument used.

A caution was given initially, but as this was ignored, the constable, with assistance, captured the instrument, its accessories, and the remaining money. Fortescue pleaded guilty to using the instrument contrary to the Gaming Act. He was fined 5s.and costs and the equipment was confiscated.

<u>1898</u> — A further report from the *North Devon Journal* reads:
"They say — That the truism, "A fool and his money are soon parted," is nowhere better illustrated than at a popular Fair, like that held at Barnstaple; that the barefaced way in which some travelling hawkers take in credulous visitors is one of the sights of the Fair; that for example, many last week bought a worthless watch for half-a-sovereign in the belief that a gold piece was to be found inside the case, and that in another instance a

vendor, with brazen effrontery, offered a parcel of real silver spoons with each sixpenny lot and found a good number of purchasers; that one has to visit a Fair in order to realise the pitch to which the production of shoddy stuff has been carried, and that it is a pity that so many poor persons, whose money could be usefully expended in other directions, waste their shillings in acquiring showy worthless trash in the belief that they are making a bargain at the expense of itinerant vendors." (Even one hundred years later, similar sales pitches are being exposed!)

A few 'Horsy' Tales:

<u>1843</u> — An unwary countryman who had come to the Horse Fair with a pony belonging to his master, sold the horse for five guineas, and received in payment a £5 note and 5s.in silver, of which he returned a half-a-crown to the buyer for "luck". Later, the seller found the note was a bad one, as the Bridgewater bank who had issued it had failed many years past. Neither pony of purchaser was seen again!

<u>1855</u> — *Thursday, September 20th.* — *Before the Mayor and John Marshall, Esq.* The magistrates sat to hear a complaint arising from the Fair. Farmer William Thomas, of Bishopsnympton, made a complaint against the toll-taker at the Horse Fair — Charles Snow, of the 'White Lion'.
  It appeared that Farmer Thomas, having taken it in his head to ride from the 'Nag's Head' by way of North Walk to Bishopsnympton, was stopped by the toll-keeper, and required to pay toll. Farmer Thomas refused to do so declaring that he wasn't taking his horse to sell, and therefore didn't have to pay toll. He gave the reason for taking the round-a-bout way, as the High Street was so "vull o' vokes" that he rode into the Horse Fair for a quiet road. Mr. Snow remarked that when made aquainted with the case, he told the complainant to take the horse and go in peace; which Farmer Thomas resolutely refused to do. The Mayor then gave the complainant some good advice to take his horse now or he might find that the "farthest way round" was not the "nearest way home." The farmer refused to do this unless he was paid for expenses incurred! The magistrates declined to comply. The complainant then

expressed his determination to take it to the County Court! (I have no idea if he did in fact carry this out.)

1875 — George Lambert, a horse dealer, was charged by Grace Popham, wife of John Popham, scavenger, Barnstaple, with assaulting her on the previous evening. During the day the defendant had sold Mrs. Popham a horse for £18 on which she had left a £5 deposit. On hearing that Lambert was going away by train and in the process of removing his horses from where they were stabled at the 'Red Cow', Mrs. Popham went to see him and demanded the return of the £5 deposit. The defendant refused to it give her, she therefore got hold of him saying she would stick to him until the police came. When Lambert saw the policeman enter the house, he struck Mrs. Popham a violent blow on the cheekbone, which blacked her eye.

Lambert argued his case but the Bench considered that an aggravated assault had been committed, and he was fined £2 and costs.

The £5 had previously been returned to Mrs. Popham.

1897 — Travelling Menagerie Proprietor and his Servant Convicted:

At the County Police Court, Barnstaple, Joseph Crecraft, and his carman, Joseph Smith, (who worked as a dwarf) both of Trowbridge, Wiltshire, were charged with working two horses who were in an unfit state. Inspector Armstrong, of the Royal Society for the Prevention of Cruelty to Animals intercepted the menagerie at Swymbridge, whilst defendants were on their way to Southmolton. He informed the magistrates a roan mare attached to a van was suffering in its near fore leg from diseased fetlock and sprained tendons, and the same sprains in its off hind legs. He reported that the animal rested both legs in turn, and was unfit for work, and went on to tell of a black gelding who was lame in its off fore leg, sprained tendons and a suppurating corn. Upon removing the horse's shoe, matter oozed from the foot. Crecraft had informed him that the black horse had fallen lame at Dulverton, and then walked it to Barnstaple where he poulticed its foot. The inspector added that the animal was so bad that it had to be left at Swymbride. — Both defendants pleaded guilty, and expressed regret for their conduct.

One of the magistrates — Major Hogg — said the defendants did not care in which way they treated their horses as they travelled through the country, and the time had arrived when this sort of thing must have a stop put to it.

Crecraft was fined £1 and costs and Smith 2s.6d.and costs, or the alternative of a respective fourteen and seven days, imprisonment.

Miscellaneous:

1827 — Philip Gay, the farmer of the market tolls, preferred a complaint against Maria Rook, for refusing to pay for a stall that she had occupied in the fair. In reply, she stated that on the third day of the fair she found her stall removed, and felt that she had been deprived of the advantage of that day. The defendant was ordered to pay only for the time she had occupied it.

1848 - BARNSTAPLE POLICE, SEPTEMBER 20th.

"*Robert Saunders, a butcher's boy, was charged on the information of a gentleman named Earle, with cruelty to a sheep, the property of Mr. Copp, butcher. — The boy was driving the sheep through the Square during the fair, and the animal being frightened by the multitude of people congregated there, refused to move on, upon which he struck the poor creature a violent blow which brought it to the ground, where it lay for some time bleeding profusely and insensible. Mr. Earle of Glynn Cottage, happening to pass at the time, observed the boy's cruelty and gave information to the police. — The boy was severely reprimanded, and fined 5s.and expenses; and the Bench expressed their thanks to Mr. Earle for bringing the case before them.*"

1846 — "*Jane Skinner complained of Thomas Essery for negligently damaging her stall in the fair on Tuesday last. Complainant is an aged widow who earns her livelihood by attending the fairs and markets to sell sweetmeats.*"

Although his hand-fly came into contact with the stall and upset the show-glasses of comfits, the complaint was dismissed!

1848 — *"Richard Thorne, servant to Mr. Pomeroy, of Maidcuford farm, was charged with driving his horse and cart furiously through the streets on the 21st inst. — Defendant was employed for the day in discharging a load of coal from the Quay for the Derby factory; and it was proved that he drove through the streets at the rate of 10 or 12 miles an hour, and that by his carelessness and rapid driving he overturned the stall of an old woman named Nancy Hill, who was stationed during the fair at the bottom of Cross-street, and that when she approached him for it, he was very abusive, and threatened to do it again. — The offence was proved by the evidence of Mr. Lionel Bencraft and the Superintendent of Police; and the bench convicted defendant in the penalty of 2s.6d. and 4s.6d. expenses."*

1879 — Sydney Smith was summoned for having used bad language in the Fair, just after midnight. Sergeant Eddy, while on duty at the Fair with P.C. Pugsley, heard the defendant *"making use of the foulest language."* On being remonstrated with, the defendant only swore the more! He was fined 10s. and costs or 14 days, imprisonment.

The Pleasure Fair

Early records show the Pleasure Fair was no stranger to Barnstaple. Before 1591 in the reign of Queen Elizabeth, it was kept on the Quay where "The Corporation found standings."

From the Accounts of the Collectors & Receivers of Barnstaple an entry in 1586 reads — *"Paid to John Richards for 46 standings at the fair, 3s.10d."*

In 1622 — *"Paid for a paire of gloves at the faire, 4d."*

Gribble gives an account copied from the original of a brief held by a Defendants' Council.

"At our great Fair in September, which doth last four days, there would be 200 or 300 people all day playing at bowles, ninepins, wrestlers, and lookers on; and men, women, and children, continually walking up and down, sitting and lying on the Castle Hill, and rolling themselves down from the top to the bottom."

(In the olden days, soothsayers, strolling players, minstrels and ballad singers, jugglers and tumblers, mountebacks and dancing bears, were an expected part of the entertainment. As years flitted by on unfettered wings, other forms of amusement were added to the scene such as — Menageries of animals and birds, Circus performers, Freak shows, Fortune telling, Tests of strength for the lads to attract the admiring glances of the lasses, Swing-boats, Carousels, and the 'rides' which made the adrenaline flow as the 20th century took hold.)

Later on and up until 1876 the Fair was situated in the Square — a 19th century Guide Book quotes the Square as *"used as a public playground, and the scene of the Saturnalia during the annual fair."* (Saturnalia — scene or time of wild revelry!)

With the setting out of the Square as an ornamental enclosure in 1877 the pleasure fair made its appearance for the first time in Castle Street, and part of the North Walk. This continued as such until 1892 when none of the booths were fixed in Castle Street but confined together with the shows, "to the open space opposite the Castle Hotel and to the North Walk." The result of the new arrangements was said to be most satisfactory, and the change very popular as in former years the lack of space made a visit to the Fair, an unpleasant one. In 1896 the north end of the Island (sometime known as monkey island) was filled in to create even more space for the fair; the open area opposite the Castle Hotel was no longer being used for the accommodation of shows and booths. It was reported that there were more roundabouts than ever before seen at the fair.

The fair site from around the Town Station to the end of the North Walk continued into the 20th century.

1939 BLAME HITLER

For the Cancelling of the PLEASURE FAIR !
But DON'T FORGET our PLEASURE FARE—

The famous GINGERBREAD at 1/8 lb.

GET SOME NOW !

JOHN RICHARDS

THE CORNER CAKE SHOP, HIGH ST., BARNSTAPLE.

The pleasure fair was abandoned for the duration of the Second World War, but advantage was taken of some of that time to completely fill in the remainder of Monkey Island. (The Civic Centre now stands on the site.) This provided more room for the festivities, and so it stayed as it was until the plans for building the Civic Centre came to fruition and caused the fair to be re-located to the Seven Brethren Bank in 1967. It opened with some apprehensions, but on the whole the showmen seemed generally satisfied with the reasonable job done in preparing the layout of the riverside site by Barnstaple Town Council. However, all was not happy with the showmen's wives. Although the council had put down hardcore on the fair site (formerly the old rubbish dump) and covered it with chippings, no attention had been given to the area set-aside for the caravans. Consequently, when continuous rain set in during the setting up of the fair it turned the caravan site into a quagmire. Council workmen hastily moved in to cover the area in chippings, with a promise from the council's surveyor that everything would be done to make things more comfortable.

There were a few problems with the erection of the rides and sideshows with some showmen not too happy about their positions, and the site itself causing congestion. It was feared that Seven Brethren Bank might not be central enough, and that the fair would become largely an evening event with little business done in the afternoons.

As can be imagined, the public houses along the North Walk suffered greatly by the removal of the fair from their area.

In 1989 fears of methane gas building up from the former rubbish dump, caused the fair to be moved further along into the Leisure Centre car park and the surrounding area. At the end of the 20th century, the Seven Brethren Bank and the Leisure Centre car park is still used for the annual fair event.

AMUSEMENTS:

Back in the 19th century when the Pleasure Fair was held in the Square, the most popular forms of entertainment were the Circus, Menagerie, Equestrian, and Travelling Theatre Shows. An assortment of booths tempted the visitor to part with their 'fairing' money; boxing, dancing girls, penny peepshows, freaks of nature such as animals with two heads, "Infant Giants" and the curiosity to view the traditional "Fat Lady" were all part of the agenda.

Extract from "The Golden Bay"- By J. Weare-Gifford.
(A tale of piracy off the North Devon Coast —
Set in the 18th century.)

"And so it was that, in good time we entered Barnstaple town, and made straight for the Golden Lion Tavern. As it turned out, it was the day of the Midsummer Pleasure Fair, and the town was full of people. We crossed the bridge and passed a large booth in front of which was depicted a monstrous fat woman. 'Lucky we came this way, Silas! We shall have all the fun of the fair after dinner.'"

All was surrounded by a cacophony of noise emanating from itinerant musicians, good and bad, all playing differing forms of instruments; the fiddle, pipe and drum among them. Discordant barrel organs sent out their monotonous tunes into the crowd, and ballad-singers and storytellers vied with each other to attract the attention and sympathy of the public. Barkers touted for business, fruit and nut sellers side by side with cheapjacks, shouted their wares, and quack doctors enticed the gullible to part with their money in exchange for worthless cures.

1824 — EQUESTRIAN

CIRCUS.

MR. POWELL, has the pleasure of again paying his respects to his Friends and the Public in general of Barnstaple and the Neighbourhood, and begs leave to inform them, that in addition to his former Company, he has engaged several new and celebrated Performers, from Davis's Royal Circus; London, which with his beautiful and unrivalled Stud of Arabian and Hanoverian Horses, will perform at his Circus in the Square, for a short time only; in the fitting up of which, no expense has been spared to render it commodious for the Company who may honor his Performance with their presence.

BOXES 2s.—PITT 1s.—CIRCLE 6d.

☞ *For particulars see Handbills.*

One of the earliest reports, was given by the *North Devon Journal* in 1824 –

"We are in formed that Mr. Munn's exhibition, of his Foreign Dogs, has afforded high gratification to the great crowds of respectable individuals who have attended their performances. The sagacity they discover, and the extraordinary acts they are brought to perform, cannot but excite astonishment, and shew how near their instinct approaches to the operation of reason. Mrs. Munn's pleasing performances on the slack wire, and Mr. Munn's balancing feats, tend to vary and enliven the scene."

In 1828 it was said that from a Penny peep at Punch, to a striking Masquerade, Horsemanship, Fireworks etc., all tempted the light-hearted to disburden themselves of the small sums they had accumulated for the occasion. There were a few gratis exhibitions, such as a couple of blind female fiddlers, whose melancholy dirge added springs to the heels of the passers-by, to remove themselves out of earshot! Various groups of ballad singers tuned their pipes to playful notes, and collected a crowd around them who tried in vain to understand the words of the ditty being vocalised. Sympathies were excited by an alleged ship wrecked mariner, although, it was said, that in all probability he never been on board a ship in his life!

"The sun rises and sets, the years roll on, and they have enjoyed their holiday; tomorrow the plough and the harrow, the cattle and the poultry, will require their care, and they again return to their employments, indulging in the hope that they may another year again revisit the scene of bustle and hilarity."

This was not to be so, as in the following year many were employed in saving the outstanding corn in consequence of the fineness of the weather. They missed out on Southby's Exhibition of Fireworks, Miller's Equestrian Performances, and several Giantesses and Dwarfs to gawp at!

In 1831 an "Exhibition of Wax Figures" was attracting great attention in Boutport Street, near the Fortescue Arms. The Siamese Youths formed one of the most striking features, and a group of figures consisting of Burke and Hare, and the outstretched body of Mary Docherty which the murderers are selling to the surgeons, attracted considerable crowds. It was reported that the figure of Stacey (who was executed for the Portsmouth murders) impressed the onlooker at once with the idea of reality — Stacey being in the attitude of levelling at his victim the fatal blow with the hammer.

(Now that should give any crime buffs something interesting to research!)

In the Timber and Bark Yard near the North Walk, Mr. Blackmore's graceful performance on the Slack Rope, (the whole effect singularly heightened by means of chemical lights) was being advertised, and his "Grand Ascent on the Rope" upwards of 50 feet from the green, surrounded by "Fire Works of the most extraordinary description."

DURING THE FAIR. 1831
By Permission of the Right Worshipful the Mayor:
Grand Exhibition of Fire Works
And other Amusements,

IN the Timber and Bark Yard, near the North Walk, BARNSTAPLE.
At Seven o'clock, A FINE MILITARY BAND will be in attendance, and entertain the Company with a series of Favorite Airs, which will be followed, at half-past 7, by the admirable and graceful Performance of

Mr. Blackmore, on the Slack Rope,
The effect of which will be singularly heightened by means of Chemical Lights.
Mr. Blackmore will also make His
GRAND ASCENT ON THE ROPE,
Upwards of 50 feet from the Green, surrounded by Fire Works of the most extraordinary description and effect.
The ground will be illuminated in a splendid and novel manner, and the Chevalier SOUTHBY pledges himself that on this occasion the Fire Works which he will have the honour to produce, shall exceed, in variety and splendour, all other exhibitions.
Admission.—Seats, 2d. | Standing Places, 1s. Children, Half-price.—Tickets of Admission for the Seats to be had of Mr. DAVIS, Castle Inn, Barnstaple.
J. SOUTHBY, Artist in Fire Works,
No. 8, Saville Place, Lambeth Walk, London

The Pleasure Fair included the exhibition of a giant named Monsieur Louis; a well proportioned man standing seven and a half feet, and was said to have the fairest claim since the celebrated O'Brien. Mr. Batty's Circus was showing "The Sailor's Return" in which Mr. Hughes performed on a high pinnacle representing the Antipodes, and while standing on his head, he drank a glass of wine, and fired off a brace of pistols! Diminutive ponies only two foot high caused great interest, as did the Zoological Museum and Menagerie of Living Animals. The specimens were rare and beautiful, especially those relating to ornithology. The menagerie contained a good collection of the "wild inhabitants of the forest."

1832 — Due to an outbreak of Cholera, no public exhibitions or amusements were allowed.

Lack of fair business was made up for in 1833 with no instance of a greater number of people in the town being recollected. Harvesting had finished early due to the unusually fine weather, and in consequence the Pleasure Fair attracted multitudes from the surrounding neighbourhood. Numerous caravans occupied the Square, which denoted a supply of diversified amusements. Lawrence's Royal Pavilion formed the centre of attraction.

It was also in this year that crowds came from miles around to witness the novel spectacle of Mr. Graham, the Aeronaut, ascending in his balloon. However, after discovering that the gasometer, which contained 10,000 feet of gas, would not fill his balloon, Mr. Graham postponed his ascent until the next day. Many returned home annoyed but curiosity overcame resentment, and on the following day a crowd assembled for the appointed time. Again they were met with disappointment as they were told that from some imperfections in the air bag, a large portion of the gas had escaped making it impracticable for the aeronaut to ascend. Feeling that they had been the victims of some duplicity, the public initially wanted to inflict vengeance upon him, but as he had secretly withdrawn from the immediate area, they proceeded to demolish the aeronaut's packing cases etc., by way of retribution!

It would appear that before his disappearance, Mr. Graham had cut the cords confining the balloon and it had travelled some six or seven miles before descending in the parish of Chittlehampton. It was found to be in a far from perfect condition being punctured with holes, and incapable of retaining gas! After being deduced by many that Mr. Graham never intended to ascend, he had the temerity to publish another proposal to make the attempt. The public however, certainly had enough by this time and made it clear that nobody trifles with their confidence — especially at Barum Fair!

1835 — Mr. Bridges Junr., was advertising his Royal Arena, in the Square. The Grand Pageant included eight beautiful horses, followed by Firefly the pony performing his tricks. Seven year old, Master Bridges, was to ride a rapid courser as the 'Jolly God of Wine', and Mr. Thorpe to perform 'Daring Evolutions' on the flying rope. Mr. Bridges himself would be riding and managing "Four Rampant Steeds, as the Russian Courier." The arena in the evening was to be lit by gas.

In 1837 the fineness of the day attracted vast numbers to the Square, where Wombwell's Menagerie was contributing to the enjoyment. The splendid customary Equestrian Circus of Powells, Batty's and the Royal Arena, seem to have disappeared.

For the next few years the Pleasure Fair had "fallen off" with varying descriptions given as — "The respectable exhibitions which used, in olden times, to occupy the Square, have entirely disappeared," miserably deficient, ill-furnished, a second rate show of wild beasts, a meagre bill of fare — and so on.

The fair in <u>1844</u> boasted an exhibition of a "Gigantic Lancashire Fat Boy" who weighed 600 pounds. He also had the peculiarity of having five fingers and a thumb on each hand, and six toes on each foot. It was reported — "*His countenance is pleasing, and he tells the spectator, who is lost in wonder at the moving mountain of solid flesh, to move out of his way whilst he moves about to show his points.*" In contrast to this colossus, a diminutive specimen of humanity was shown. Reputed to have been born in Buckland Brewer, and although a man in years, he had only reached the stature of 36 inches, and boasted the weight of only 45 pounds. It was said at the time, "Such a grouping of nature's eccentricities is not often to be seen."

Things are looking up again in <u>1851</u>. The public were given a treat by the appearance for the fair, by Mr. Wm. Cooke. The report reads –

"The celebrated equestrian troop of Mr. Wm. Cooke, has just entered this town and made a circuit of the principal streets much to the gratification of the inhabitants, whose admiration was excited alike by the beauty of the horses, the splendour of their trappings, the gorgeousness of the carriages, and the skill of the horsemen and charioteers. There is to be a performance in a field on the other side of the bridge this afternoon and evening, and again tomorrow."

The Pleasure Fair on the Square was rich in itinerant exhibitions of all descriptions.

In <u>1853</u> there were two travelling theatres within the enclosure of the Square, and according to the North Devon Journal the managers were tempting customers to each by "bands of music and exhibitions of the bedizened actors in front — bells, drums, trombones, and bugles one trying to drown the other, from swingers, theatres, Great Goliaths, conjurers, and penny peeps, create such a babel of confused sounds which if they gave pleasure, it must be to very queerly constituted ears. "Cheap Jacks" "set the groundings" on a roar with their jibes elsewhere, and a bazaar where there are "no blanks and all prizes" is ready to take your shilling at the next stall. If none of these will do, you may see a donkey jump over a tub with a dog on his back."

Lawrence's Royal Pavilion,
1833 *On the Square, Barnstaple.*

MESSRS. LAWRENCE respectfully inform the Public, that they have opened the above commodious Theatre, which is furnished with splendid scenery and dresses, for the representation of the most popular dramatic pieces, by a company, whose exertions have been honored with the unqualified approbation of numerous and distinguished audiences in most of the towns of respectability in the kingdom.

The Act drop Scene is a magnificent representation of the late riot and conflagrations in the city of Bristol.

The Theatre will open on Thursday, and each succeeding day, of the Fair, with favorite entertainments as will be expressed in the bills of the day.

Price of Admission,—Pit, 1s.—Gallery, 6d.

September 18th, 1833.

BARNSTAPLE FAIR. 1844

TO BE SEEN ALIVE, in a commodious Caravan, for the first time in this town, and under the immediate patronage of royalty, the wonder of the age, Master DANIEL HARTLEY,

The Gigantic Lancashire Fat Boy,

A native of *Preston.* This phenomenon of nature is 16, years of age, stands 5 feet 9½ inches high, is of the astonishing weight of 600 lbs. measures round his body not less than seven feet, and round his thigh 39 inches. He has five fingers and a thumb on each hand, and six toes on each foot, is of excellent symmetry, pleasing features, with a beautifully fair skin, and is one of the most remarkable prodigies ever seen.

Also, in connexion with the above,

The Devonshire Dwarf,

a native of Buckland Brewer, in Devonshire, 33 years of age, only 43 lbs. in weight, and 36 inches in height; is perfectly proportioned, and, exhibited in contrast with the Giant Boy, presents a combination of natural curiosities never equalled!

☞ ADMISSION MODERATE.

Private parties admitted at an hour's notice.

BARNSTAPLE FAIR. 1844
GALAS EXTRAORDINARY.

MR. G. GYNGELL, whose former Exhibitions of Fireworks in Barnstaple and throughout the County of Devon have ever given the greatest satisfaction, has the honour to announce that he intends giving a brilliant and extensive Pyrotechnic Fête, in a spacious Yard, opposite Mr. PIDLER's, *Castle-street,* on Thursday, Friday, and Saturday Evenings; consisting of

A superb Display of Fireworks, Dissolving Views, &c.

An elegant Balloon will ascend each Evening, to announce the commencement of the Fireworks.

The yard will be decorated with evergreens, and illuminated with many hundreds of variegated lamps, tastefully arranged in festoons and other fanciful devices.

Admission to the Yard, 1s. each; to the Seats, 6d. extra—Doors open at 7, and the Dissolving Views to commence at 7½ o'clock precisely.

☞ Tickets to be had of Mr. CRIBBE, bookseller; and of Mr. GYNGELL, at Mr. SAUNDERS's, in the *Square.*

Dated September 19th, 1844.

Royal Arena, Square, Barnstaple.
1835 *On Monday, September 21st, 1835,*
GRAND CHANGE OF ENTERTAINMENTS.

MR. BRIDGES, JUN., begs most respectfully to inform the public of *Barnstaple* and its vicinity, that, for the gratification of country persons, his Equestrian Performances will open at an early hour on Monday.

TO COMMENCE WITH

A Grand Pageant in the Arena,

in which Eight of the Beautiful Horses will appear, representing themselves as Dying and Dead,—After which the admired Little Pony, FIRE FLY, will go through the whole of his Amusing Tricks.—To be followed by some pleasing attitudes

DE FEU FORCE,

BY MISS BRIDGES AND MR. BRIDGES, JUN.

Mr. THORPE will perform the whole of his DARING

Evolutions on the Flying Rope.

Master J. BRIDGES, (a child only seven years of age,) will ride on a rapid courser as the *Jolly God of Wine.*

STILL VAULTING,

By Messrs. Thorpe, Bridges, Field, Taylor, Seal, Bridges, jun., Cooper, Emily, Master Selino, and William, as Clown.

MR. FIELD WILL INTRODUCE THE WHOLE OF HIS

Equestrian Performances on the Single Horse.

MR. BRIDGES WILL RIDE AND MANAGE

Four Rampant Steeds, as the Russian Courier.

The whole of the Entertainments will conclude with a laughable Extravaganza, entitled *William Button, Esq. and the Kicking Horse.*

Boxes, 2s.—Pit, 1s.—Gallery, 6d.—Children under 12 years of age will be admitted at Half-price.

The Arena in the Evening will be lighted with Gas.

By Victorian times, many fairs had rides and merry-go-rounds;
people rode on wooden horses known as 'gallopers' and larger
roundabouts mostly had a mechanical turning device, operated
by a man with a handle. At Barnstaple Fair of 1853 it was
recorded that "*A boat swing, turned by machinery, carried those
who trusted their bones in its buckets, high into the air and down
and around again, according to pay — another rang his bell for
customers to a huge Whirlgig, upon the periphery of which stood
a number of wooden horses, saddled and stirruped, for juvenile
equestrians.*"

Showmen used teams of horses to pull their heavy vans from
town to town, but as the roundabouts became heavier and
steam power became available, the steam engine came into
being with the first showman's engine built by William Bray.
(The first steam-powered fairground ride was in 1865.)

Charles Burrell of Thetford, Norfolk, built his first showman's engine in 1889, and it was not long before the firm of Charles Burrell & Sons started to produce a long list of engines, which were embellished and ornately decorated to the showmen's own specifications. (Later on, electricity powered the rides and some of the magic had gone.) As for the gallopers, they became highly ornate and were painted in bright colours with a definite Italian influence behind the décor. (This made one elderly lady referring to a rather brightly painted altar screen in a local church, say that it was "like old Hancock's thing that comes to Barnstaple Fair!") Music was provided by a mechanical or steam powered organ in the centre of the roundabout, and before long no fair was complete without at least one set of 'steam gallopers'. William, Charles, and Sophia Hancock, bought a set of galloping horses from 'Savage's' in November 1878 and was the first machine they brought to Barnstaple Fair.

Returning to the year of <u>1854</u> the report mentions the arrival of sundry caravans and the setting of standings in the Square, Cross Street, and elsewhere.

"Towards evening, as business released the younger visitors from its yoke, the promenaders in the streets became more numerous, yet by no means crowded. The shops were set out in the "first style of the art," High-street making a very handsome appearance. The draper and the grocers, ironmongers and silversmiths, the chemist who tempt us with drugs, the booksellers who provide for our intellectual cravings, the saddlers who help us "to horse," and the confectioners who furnish the "fairings," all seem to vie with each other in winning public regard." In the Square was collected "The great "sleary" camp of wonder-makers, "wondering for their bread," travelling theatres, and Jack Puddings of many sorts. What with their cross-cries, clashing music, rumbling drums, tinkling bells, and flaring lights, (for many years the shows, stalls etc. were lit by naptha flares before the generators for electricity were introduced.) it appeared as if all the lunatics in England, had assembled there for a fete, rather than as the resort of rational beings."

1855 *"Barnstaple has seldom seen so many visitors present at one time within the borough as on Friday, the last day of the fair. High-street was filled from end to end, and from an elevation commanding almost its entire length a view of the moving multitude was an impressive sight. — The Square was densely crowded, as were the approaches from it to Boutport, High-street, and the quays."*

In 1859 the fair has been shorn of its former "ancient glory" with the shows in the Square having dwindled down to a few third-rate exhibitions. Among them were two Travelling Theatres, a collection of Waxwork Figures and Dioramas, a Photographic Gallery, a Penny Peep, Mechanical Figures, a Shooting Gallery, Swinging Boat, Merry-go-round, and (as the report says) "the inimitable Punch." It was also stated that there was a Boxing Booth, "where parties are initiated into the blackguard's art."

The exhibits and shows get progressively worse over the next few years, and the boxing is still not looked upon favourably and described as for those who have no self respect, or for "roughs." In the 1860's Jepson's Sparring Booth was one of the "contenders."

In 1864 Lawrence's Theatre is still showing, as too is Weight's Standard Theatre. The tragedy of William, Henry, Peter Weight occurred this year with his unexpected demise during the fair. He was buried in Barnstaple Holy Trinity Churchyard — as yet, I can find no trace of his grave.

The fair of 1864 was also remembered for a "disgusting exhibition" which horrified the onlookers.

A Negro known as "Allah" employed by Edward Elliot, was given a young living rabbit. Proceeding to bite it behind the head and suck its blood, the man then skinned it and ate part of its flesh. It was said - *"It was a most disgusting performance, which occupied an incredibly short time, and the savage devoured the flesh while quivering with life."* Having just witnessed Elliot's Show, both men were charged by a representative of the Society for the Prevention of Cruelty to Animals, with cruelly torturing the rabbit. As the perpetrators were being taken through the streets to the stationhouse, Master "Allah" appeared to be almost naked. A large brass ring "apparently" passed through his nose and it was remarked that it gave him a ferocious aspect!

The Bench considered the proprietor of the show was more to blame, and the Negro (who was discharged) to be scarcely accountable for his actions. Elliot was fined £2 and expenses, or imprisonment, (the money was paid) and the exhibition closed down. The parties were ordered to leave town, the following morning.

1866 — A sarcastic report was given regarding one of the theatre shows —

"on the outside of which, had a number of men in theatrical tawdry, and the same number of women in all the glory and majesty of threepenny muslin. One of the heroes, who sported a pair of Wellingtons, which once upon a time had gloried in red facings but the lustre of which had been dimmed very considerably, invited the audience to witness new plays never before performed in Barnstaple."

Tom Sayer's patent striking machine warranted to tell you the exact force that you could strike to an ounce, for the fee of a halfpenny. Many lads took the advantage of this to impress the lasses!

In addition there was said to be *"the familiar hobby-horses, the swinging boat, and the flying boxes in which young Barnstaple could go on an aerial voyage to inspect the house tops."* Plus, *"a cheap John, who on making a sale, vociferously exclaimed "sold again" but whether he alluded to having sold his wares or his customers we are not able to state."*

A repository for the sale of bibles and religious publications sold over £10 worth of bibles and testaments, and the public were given a selection of readings from the New Testament, by a number of gentlemen, under the superintendence of a Mr. Parry. (It was not unusual for religious societies to attend the pleasure fair at Barnstaple. It was probably thought good for one's soul among the vulgarities of the festivities. Gospel wagons frequented the fair throughout the 20th century and many people can still remember those evangelists who were full of character)

For the fair in 1868, Barnstaple was treated to a visit from 'Holbrook's Australian Circus' and if the advert (shown on page 199) is anything to go by, it must have been the highlight of the pleasure festivities. Exhibitions that embraced the fair that year were listed as — Lawrence's Models of Gold Diggings; worked by steam, Weight's Standard Theatre; Hurford's Temple of Amusements; shooting galleries, etc.

The confectionery stalls were said to be attractive; and among them were noticed Messrs. John Thornby's, T. Pedler's, T. Joint's, J. Dominicks's of Barnstaple; Mr. S. Fook, of Southmolton, and Mr. Newton, of Taunton. (The actual fair report was said to be — "Very brief doubtless due to the fact Barnstaple was in the throes of a fiercely contested Parliamentary election.")

The last year for the fair to be held at its customary site in the Square, was <u>1876</u>.

The band of the 1st. Devon Militia played a programme of music on Chanter's Green (the site inside the first entrance, to what is now known as 'Rock Park.')

The Square was said to be fuller than usual with exhibits of all kinds — Elijah Lightwood from Bath had brought his Boxing Booth, and a steam organ reportedly played, "Tommy make room for your uncle" all day long!

44. This photograph of the square was taken around 1870. The centre was enclosed by simple iron railings and bollards in 1715. With the removal of the the fair to North Walk after 1876, it was laid out as an ornamental garden. (Photograph © Knight's)

203

In the 19th century it was common practice for the Militia to attend fairs for recruitment purposes into the service of their country. Many a young man as a result of indulging too freely on ale, would be spurred on to take (in the case of Queen Victoria's reign) the "Queen's Shilling." Exciting tales from honey tongued recruiting sergeant, and the stirring accompaniment of trumpet, pipe, and drum helped with the encouragement. Barnstaple fair was no exception and some brief mention is given here:

1855 — "Of music in the street there was enough and to spare; every now and then one or other of the two sets of pipes engaged in the recruiting service made the tour of the town followed by a rabble rout, setting the country people agape."

1868 — Sergeant Walsh, of the Devon Artillery Militia, Plymouth, was on a visit to Barnstaple Fair for recruitment purposes. (The tragedy that befell him is mentioned in "A Chapter of Accidents.")

1872 — "The band of the First Devon Militia enlivened the streets with some capital music, with which, besides pleasing the public, a recruiting party sought to attract some business, but was only successful in a small degree, young men not appearing to be as susceptible as formerly to the charms of "the Shilling.""

Fair snippet: - The annual shooting of Barnstaple Companies of Volunteers, at Anchor Wood Range, was advertised for many years. It took place on Barnstaple Fair Saturday, from later in the 19th century.

Initially starting in 1859 as the Barnstaple Corps of Volunteers, it was described as having a uniform of drab grey with scarlet braiding, and a shako with a plume of cock's feathers. The motto of the movement being "Defence not defiance."

In 1876 the Volunteers were issued with a new scarlet uniform.

An example of a prize-winner in 1883, gives the first prize of a silver watch going to Colour-sergeant Roberts after a tie for first place with Bugler Berry resulted in the ensuing shoot off scoring a 3,4, win for Roberts.

In 1907 the annual shoot — Gold Medal series — Pte. Blackmore scored 95 and Pte. Challacombe 93. The — Drill Series — gave top scores to Sergt. Trapnell, Cpl. Vodden, and Pte. Blackmore - all with points of 37 each.

45. Brewer's Gallopers and Marshall Hill's Motors (early 1900s). In the foreground can be seen the large generating steam traction engine with extended chimney to ensure a clear and smoke-free ride on 'Brewer's Gallopers'. Note the railway track belonging to the Lynton to Barnstaple line which opened in 1898. (C.R.)

46. Barnstaple Fair, 1907. Showing the famous 'Hancock's living pictures'. (Photographer: W.S.Wood.((© The Medina Gallery)

47. Crowds at the Fair. Early 1900s. (© Beaford Archive)

48. 1914. Brewer's Gallopers, Marshall Hill's Scenic, Anderton & Rowland's Motors and Gondolas. (C.R.)

49. Roundabout Gondalas (from Venice) at Barnstaple Fair, 1925. Anderton and Rowland's Amusements. (© Beaford Archive)

50. 'Kewpie Doll' dealers and others at Barnstaple Fair in the 1920s. The large dolls stand in the middle of displays of very miniature 'kewpies' which could be viewed by enthusiasts through the portable telescope shown in the centre of the picture. (Photographer: R.L.Knight.) (© Tom Bartlett Postcard Collection EX34 9SE)

51. Golden Dragons at Barnstaple Fair, early 1900s. (C.R.)

52. 1923, Anderton & Rowland's Chairs and Gondolas. (C.R.)

53. Mr and Mrs Bruce Oliver taking a turn on the Gallopers at Barnstaple Fair in the early 1930s. Bruce Oliver became Mayor in 1932, and made an honorary Freeman of Barnstaple in 1974. It was Mr Oliver who thoughtfully restored the former Golden Lion Hotel in Boutport Street, and the Three Tuns in the High Street. He died in 1976 aged 93 years. (© North Devon Athenaeum)

54. c.1906.
Fair crowds at North
Walk, in front of the
Blue Coat School.
(Photographer:
W.S.Wood) (© Tom
Bartlett Postcard
Collection EX34 9SE)

Before we wander around Castle Street and the North Walk to take in all the 'fun of the fair', it would be quite delectable to taste a sample of -

FAIRING: (not to be confused with the other term of 'fairing' used for visiting the fair — children and adults alike saved their "fairing money.")

Traditionally a mixture of sugared comfits, sweets flavoured with cinnamon etc., and gingerbread shaped into figures and quite often wrapped in gilt paper. From time immemorial fairing has been a "sweet" part of Barnstaple Great Fair.

In the earlier part of the 19th century (and probably before that) Cross Street was the customary site at fair time for the selling of fairing. The whole of the street was lined with stalls all selling the toothsome confectionery.

To quote "Rambler" of the *North Devon Journal* (1886) from his article referring to Barnstaple Fair in the "olden days." –

"Cross-street was then the children's Paradise. Here the bees clustered around the lollipops and intoxicated themselves with a thousand precious sweets. The "fairing" was purchased for "the bairns," and lads treated the lasses to "whatever they liked best.""

When the Square was the venue for the Pleasure Fair, confectionery stalls would also be set up around the site and main streets of the area, especially by itinerant vendors. The most favoured stalls were those of local confectioners and one in particular appears to stand out from the rest.

John Thornby started to manufacture his confectionery for Barnstaple Fair around 1829 and gradually built up an established business at 66/67 Boutport Street, just off the

Square and next door to the then West of England Bank. In 1847 he was advertising his stalls at the fair as in his usual position opposite the 'Fortescue Hotel' and No.2 Cross Street. In 1851 the Census return gives the information that he is a confectioner aged 45 employing two apprentices. He has a wife Caroline aged 31. A few years later according to the Census, he has another young wife by the name of Susan. They eventually had a family of five daughters — Emily, Alice, Ellen, Elizabeth and Annie. A son (John) born to them, died in infancy at the age of nine months.

By 1866 John Thornby is a "*well-known and celebrated Sugar-Boiler & Lozenge manufacturer, and for the fair has "A Handsome Pavilion*" opposite the Fortescue which has now become the 'Royal Fortescue Hotel.'

A report in 1867 gives — "*Mr. Thornby's tempting display of sweets was never excelled even by himself.*"

In 1870 - the confectioners of Barnstaple and neighbouring towns had a tempting display of "fairing" conspicuous among the stalls those being of Mr. John Thornby, of Barnstaple, and Mr. Simon Fook, of South Molton, who had regularly attended the fair for 40 years. Mr. Fook kindly presented each of the girls belonging to the Union Workhouse with a small parcel of "fairing." Amongst the other stalls were those of Messrs. Pedler, Hooper, Dominick, Seyfert, Bowden and Palmer.

Sadly, a few years later John Thornby died on June 23rd 1873 aged 68 years. He is buried in the Holy Trinity churchyard at Barnstaple.

With five children to support Mrs. Thornby carried on in her husband's footsteps, and the report on the fair for that year refers to "The stalls of confectionery in the Square were largely patronised, especially Mrs. Thornby's whose late husband had pursued his vocation not only at Barnstaple Fair, but at all fairs in a wide district around for well over 40yrs."

When the pleasure fair moved to its new site in 1877 the confectionery stalls were lined on both sides of Castle Street. Mrs. Thornby has added "Tea Dealer" to her trade and "Wedding Cakes prepared at the shortest notice." A Handsome Pavilion for Barnstaple Fair has been included in her advertisement.

In 1881 it was noted that in contrast to the other sweet stalls the fresh looking appearance of stalls belonging to Barumites — Mr. T. Pedler, of Vicarage Street, Mrs. Dominick, of Boutport Street, and Mrs. Thornby, of the Square, was demonstrated by the amount of customers surrounding them to buy "Fairing." Mrs. Thornby had two stalls one of which was situated in front of the water company's office, and the other outside the Cattle Market.

Stalls extend from Castle Street in a line as far as the bottom of Cross Street in 1883, and Itinerant confectioners set up their stalls among the locals in Castle Street, and other parts of the town in 1884.

By 1888 Mrs. Thornby has become the less formal S. Thornby, and the Thornby's trade name has the addition of "Emporium of Confectionery" in its advertising.

The year of 1892 sees the death of Susan Thornby on July 27th at the age of 64. She is buried with her husband, John Thornby.

It is not clear if Thornby's stalls were still part of the fair scene after this time. What we do know is, the business carried on for many years in the same premises at the Square, and was still selling fairing well into the 20th century. Many of us can remember the wonderful homemade chocolates displayed in the shop beside the assortment of sweets. The business ceased to trade sometime in the 1970's and in 1999 the premises are an estate agents.

As for the other confectioners the well-known names have come and gone and so too have the adverts for fairing. The established firm of Youings, Tobacconist's that sold fairing once upon a time, appear to be the only local confectioner as such left in Barnstaple at the end of the 20th century. The itinerant vendor has been left to supply the public with modern day fairing.

55. Former residence and shop of John Thornby, confectioner. 66-67 Boutport Street, Barnstaple. (Photograph © Shane Woods).

56. Gravestone of John and Susan Thornby, confectioners. Holy Trinity churchyard, Barnstaple. Note other family names on the other headstone. (Photograph © Shane Woods).

1847

UNRIVALLED CONFECTIONERY!!

JOHN THORNBY, in returning his best thanks to his numerous Friends and 'Patrons in Barnstaple and the North of Devon, for the liberal support they have conferred on him for the last eighteen years, respectfully announces that his supply of CONFECTIONERY GOODS, MANUFACTURED FOR BARNSTAPLE FAIR, exceeds in quality everything he has yet had the honour of submitting for public approbation; and in consequence of the reduction in the price of sugar, he is not only enabled to make his Goods of a very SUPERIOR QUALITY, but he has the gratification of announcing that he has also determined on rendering them at the lowest possible remunerating prices.

☞ In addition to his resident establishment adjoining the West of England Bank, on the Square, J. T. will have the pleasure of waiting on his customers at his usual position opposite the 'Fortescue Hotel,' and at No. 2, Cross Street, during the Fair.

In brilliancy of effect and splendour of decoration, his stalls far exceed everything of the kind which has hitherto been witnessed in Barnstaple, or the neighbourhood. -

Dated Barnstaple, September 17th, 1847.

ALWAYS ON TOP **1926**

'THORNBY'S'

BARNSTAPLE

Fairing.

ONE QUALITY ONLY,

"THE BEST,"

2/- per lb.

SPECIALLY PACKED FOR
PARCEL POST IN

2/6 & 1/6 BOXES.

Send your Friends a BOX and include a Packet of our celebrated
GOLDEN

GINGER BREADS

2/- per lb.

AND HOME MADE

Sponge Candy.

NOTE THE ADDRESS :—

THORNBY'S,

THE SQUARE,

BARNSTAPLE.

1881

ESTABLISHED 48 YEARS.

SUGAR BOILER, LOZENGE MANUFACTURER,
AND TEA DEALER.

MRS. THORNBY,

BEGS to return her best thanks to the Inhabitants of Barnstaple and North Devon for their kind patronage ; and in soliciting a continuance of their favours, respectfully assures her friends and customers that she is prepared to supply them with Goods of Genuine Quality on the most Moderate Terms.

TWO STALLS, one Outside the WATER COMPANY'S OFFICES, and the other Outside the CATTLE MARKET, will be Opened, as usual, during the Barnstaple Fair.

WEDDING CAKES PREPARED ON THE SHORTEST NOTICE.

ALL GOODS SOLD AT THIS ESTABLISHMENT ARE WARRANTED PURE AND GENUINE.

[1382

Gingersnap Fairing

8 oz flour (sifted)
2 teaspoon baking powder
2 teaspoons bicarbonate of soda
4 tablespoons golden syrup
1 teaspoon ground ginger

half teaspoon of cinnamon
pinch of salt
2 oz brown sugar
4 oz butter
1 teaspoon mixed spice

Method;

Sift the flour, salt, spices and baking powder together.
Add bicarbonate of soda and mix well.
Rub in the butter and then add sugar (mixture should resemble shortcrust pastry mix)
Gently heat the syrup a little and pour into the paste.
Work well to a firm dough.
Flour your hands and roll the mixture into small balls.
Put onto a greased baking tray well spaced out, and flatten a little with your thumb.
Bake in a pre-heated oven at 400F (200C) or gas mark 6 for about 10 minutes near the
top of the oven, removing to lower shelf when they begin to brown (after around 8 minutes)
When cooked remove from tray to wire rack to cool.
Makes around 30. Store in an airtight container.

ENJOY!

NORTH WALK:

In <u>1877</u> the Pleasure Fair had moved to Castle Street and part of the North Walk. Train after train came in packed with people visiting the fair, and special excursion trains came up from Plymouth and down from Exeter. The annual rendezvous for many of the visitors was still being given its usual priority.

The principal shows were the well- known Weight's Brittania Theatre, Lawrence's Marionettes, and Johnson's Lilliputian Actors. Carl Devone the Man-serpent, twisted himself contortions of the body that made him seem without a backbone, and "General Toper's" special claim appeared to be, four feet instead of two feet and two hands! The new site was full of various shows and booths which all helped to make the 1877 fair a huge success.

Among the avenue of confectionery stalls were the local stands of Mrs. Thornby, and Mr. Pedler, and an appreciative public gave preference to them for their purchases of fairing.

It was also in 1877 that a great feature of the fair was the use of an abominable article called "the teaser" which some vendors interpreted as the "fun of the fair." *"It is a little metal phial containing perfumed water, which everyone you meet thinks he has the perfect right to discharge into your face or neck."*

According to the report many thousands were sold, and trade so extensive that they were being offered at the bargain price of seven for sixpence.

Much to the dismay of the majority of fair visitors, these offensive implements continued to be sold and used by the youth or immature of the town, into the 1880's. In the first year of that decade, Edward Bragg, a youth of Combmartin, was brought before the Mayor (W. Avery) by P.C. Edwards, and charged with assaulting Elizabeth Heddon, of Bradiford, with squirting at her. Not content with using the teaser on the lady as she came through the fair by the theatre, he followed her through Castle-street, continually squirting at his victim. Bragg said nothing in his defence, and was fined 5s.and costs. The following year tempers flared when James Quick, an old man living at Okeford, boxed the ears of Frederick McDermott, aged 14, when the lad used the teaser on Quick's son. McDermott allegedly retaliated by squirting liquid into the old man's eye whereupon the man knocked the youth down with a large stick. Events resulted in the cross-summons of each other, and after witness evidence was given, Quick was given a minimal fine of 5s.which took into account the provocation received. McDermott was admonished by the Mayor for using the teaser, who remarked that a number of complaints had been received by the magistrates of the conduct of boys like him using the instruments called "teasers" and demanded that some notice should be taken of it for the Fair which should be a place of enjoyment rather than annoyance. It was felt that as McDermott was but a boy, and had suffered too severe a punishment already, he should only be fined 6d.

Sighs of relief must have been heard aplenty in <u>1884</u> — On the first night of the fair teasers were freely used, but on the following day, the Superintendent of Police issued a notice forbidding their use. This seemed to have had the desired effect of almost entirely doing away with their use. The following year it was reported that the teasers were conspicuous by their absence.

(The modern day equivalent in terms of 'nuisance' is probably the cans of "silly string" that are used on festive occasions.)

North Devon Journal — September 26th 1878:

"A powerful organ connected with one of the roundabouts is playing a "marching" tune from a celebrated collection of hymns which has been imported from America. On the stage of a neighbouring show five different instruments are hard at work, consisting of a loud voiced organ, a gong, a wind instrument, a big drum, and a smaller one. Every other show makes its contribution to the general din in some form or another. There is the usual exhibition of vulgar buffoonery in front of the shows and elsewhere, and whilst witnessing it one wonders that those who flock into the town in such numbers on these occasions do not find some more rational mode of spending their money and leisure."

One can only imagine the jarring din of the discordant fairground!

In 1879 the babel of noise created by one of the organs in particular, was said to be heard a mile away, and that its restriction to two tunes, although comical at first, became distressing! (It must have driven the unfortunate people who lived in the vicinity, quite mad!)

This was the year that Hancock's, who after attending Barnstaple Fair for some years with their shows, brought their new acquisition in the shape of four-abreast Gallopers to the venue. The ride was built by the firm of Savage's and was steam driven.

1881 — A roundabout's horses and carriages had been replaced with bicycles. Reference was made to much amusement being given to the sight of some grown-up yokels trying to bring their feet in a proper relationship with the treadles of the machine that carried them round, "and still more ludicrous was it to watch the futile endeavours of some young "ladies" to look graceful while they took their circular ride." All went round accompanied by the organ tunes of "The cry of Maria," or "La di da."

The 1882 fair still had the reliable Weight's Theatre patronising it. Also in attendance was a miniature "Zoo" in which the lecturer informed his audience that the mongoose or ichneumon was an inhabitant of Ceylon, where it killed rattlesnakes and other poisonous "things." Another exhibition was that of the "celebrated Scotch giantess," of whom it was said "looking equal to something more substantial than a water-lily diet." There were two rival exhibitions of "Zulus," one of which "was so dreadfully wild that he was heavily manacled to prevent him tearing his visitors limb from limb." (A case of actor and showman up for an award!!)

"Cheap Jacks" then, as now, are a usual part of the fairground scene. In 1883 they were as always, plentiful, and the most popular one was undoubtedly Mr. George Lacy, whose long standing (and ready tongue) secured him many customers. Apparently he had for some time been associated with the Salvation Army and the Blue Ribbon movement, and during the fair he had to endure a lot of "chaff." However, his ready replies frequently turned the laughter against the wordy assailants.

In the same year there were two sparring pavilions; boxing now referred to as "the noble art of self defence." It was mentioned that the principle upholder was a Negro, and so-called outsiders hesitantly accepted the challenge to box the "champion" for a "bob and a glass of brandy."

There was no "wonderful fat woman" to be seen; but there was an individual termed the "lion-faced lady." On one side of her face she was said to have whiskers, like a man, while on the other was a peculiar tuft of hair. Her eyebrows were very prominent, but there was nothing remarkable about her face. — "If she does not resemble a lion she is a decided curiosity."

The "whirligig" was put in the shade by the novelty ride "sea and land." Patrons took their seats in boats (graced by sails), which were revolved by steam power. By means of a clever contrivance the boats were given a continuous up and down motion. The report in the 'Journal' gives the ride as not being exclusively for the juveniles. — "Indeed, more than one magistrate conferred a dignity upon the affair by patronising it!"

BARNSTAPLE FAIR. 1888

THE AUSTRALIAN JUVENILE

GIANT FAMILY

Will be on EXHIBITION at the OXFORD HALL, NORTH WALK, During the Fair,

CLARA, Victorian Giantess, 14 years of age. Weighs 28 Stone, 5 lbs.
TOM, the Juvenile Hercules, 10 years of age. Weighs 13 Stone, 2 lbs.
ANNA, the Baby Giantess, 8 years of age. Weighs 12 Stone, 2 lbs.

These remarkable Children have been visited by over 500,000 people in Melbourne, Sydney, Brisbane, and Adelaide, and also by large numbers at the Royal Aquarium, Westminster, London.

Mr. and Mrs. Snell, the Parents, are natives of Devonshire; and are always in attendance to answer any questions relative to their Wonderful Family.

OPEN DAILY.   ADMISSION 3d.

THE GIANT FAMILY
WILL ALSO
HOLD RECEPTIONS AT THE
ASSEMBLY ROOMS,
On Saturday & Monday, 22nd & 24th September,
From 3 until 10 p.m.   ADMISSION, 6d. [8217

In 1888 part of the fair exhibitions included a giant family from Australia, who were on show at the Oxford Hall, North Walk, and attracted many hundreds of spectators. A description is given in the accompanying advertisement. In the open space by the Quay Station, several itinerant "Cheap Jacks" held forth, while a clever conjurer, and Negro who gave a marvellous exhibition of strength, attracted large audiences.

The waxworks show's latest addition at the 1889 fair was a cast of Mrs Maybrick. (Florence Maybrick was accused and convicted of poisoning her husband, and became a subject of a television documentary over a hundred years later!)

At Hurford's boxing pavilion a match between William Samuels, of Swansea, and Tom Vincent, of Plymouth, took place on the Thursday night. Despite a charge of half-a-crown being made for admission, there was a crowded attendance. Samuels, who was 51 years of age and Welsh Champion for 31 years, went 14 rounds with the younger 25 year old, Vincent. Samuels, who had never been beaten before, laboured under the disadvantage of having a sprained hand. He finally gave out in the fourteenth round after failing to come up to time.

This year an "Aerial Railway" was introduced.

In 1891 the familiar Weight's Theatre returned after a few years absence, and by this time three steam roundabouts were attending the traditional gathering.

Owing to the holding of Fairs elsewhere the same week as Barnstaple in 1893 there were not so many shows as usual; but the smaller attractions were greater in number than in other years. Evidently there was great competition among the proprietors of phonographs, which seemed to "take" wonderfully.

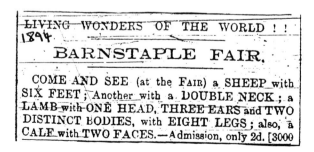

LIVING WONDERS OF THE WORLD ! !
1894

BARNSTAPLE FAIR.

COME AND SEE (at the Fair) a SHEEP with SIX FEET; Another with a DOUBLE NECK; a LAMB with ONE HEAD, THREE EARS and TWO DISTINCT BODIES, with EIGHT LEGS; also, a CALF with TWO FACES.—Admission, only 2d. [3000

Anderton & Haslam's exhibition was said to be "well worth seeing" in 1894 -

There was a magnificent collection of beasts with performances involving lions and tigers, the lion tamer being Captain Rowland. Professor Anderton went under the title of "King of the Wizards." Juggling, wire-walking, and other novelties were also part of the act. Thirty thousand people were alleged to have visited the performance in Plymouth. (Anderton was later to become the head of the famous West Country firm of Anderton & Rowland.)

The Circular Switchback Railway and roundabouts at the fair of 1895 exceeded £1,000 in takings alone.

W.F. Gardiner's book on Barnstaple
mentions the following in 1897 –

"In recent years the proprietor of a set of three "merry-go-rounds," gorgeously equipped arrangements, driven by steam and lighted at night by electricity — has taken £900 during the three days of the Fair. The Fair is supposed to bring between 18,000–20,000 visitors to the town."

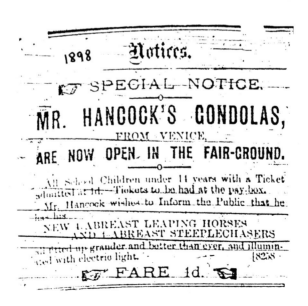

57. 'John Bull', 1906-14, Anderton & Rowlands. (C.R.)

58. 1938. 'William IV' ~ the last engine to come to Barum Fair (C.R.)

59. This photograph, taken at Barnstaple Fair in the early 1920s, shows the Peruvian Princess and Mystery Man sideshow! Entrance fee is 3d. A crowd of young chaps together are enjoying the entertainment – some more than others! (C.R.)

60. 1926. One of numerous side-shows at Barnstaple Fair. (C.R.)

61. Town Station (Castle Street) area of Barnstaple Fair in the 1920s. (© North Devon Athenaeum.)

62. 1927. The scene shows the fair side shows, with the living caravans on the left. To the right of the picture can be seen the Town Station, platform and railway track. In the distance, ships' masts can be detected from the ships moored by Queen Anne's Walk. The old bridge can also be seen. Umbrellas are the order of this fair day for the crowds making their way along from Castle Street. (C.R.)

63. 1954 — Wally and Cissy Shufflebottom's Western Show, Knife-throwing and Sharp Shooting. (C.R.)

64. 1954 — Shooting Range. Mrs Fay Clements and her son Tommy. (C.R.)

65. 1951 — Civic dignitories (Cllr. J.B.Sanders JP, Mayor) at Alf Whitelegg's Three Abreast Gallopers. (C.R.)

66. This wonderful photograph taken in the early 1960s shows a wealth of things that have since disappeared. The fair is being held on the North Walk site of the former "Monkey Island" (Cyprus Island) – pre-Civic Centre days! As can be seen, the trains are still running gfrom the Town Station to Ilfracombe. Castle House, on the right, is being used for council offices and behind it Potter's Lane is still intact, as is the Blue Coat School, shown a few yards away. Part of the VIctoria Flour Mills can be seen on the extreme left of the picture. (C.R.)

67. The Helter Skelter stands prominent in this 1960s view of the Fair at North Walk (Photograph © Dave Fry)

68. View of the 1966 Fair at North Walk.
(Photograph © Dave Fry)

69. 1966. Young Andrew and Martin
Fry enjoying some of the juvenile Fair
attractions. (His Dad, Dave Fry, was a
former Barnstaple policeman)
(Photograph © Dave Fry.)

70. This night-time picture of the Fair was taken in 1966 – the last
year of the North Walk site, before the Civic Centre was built. (C.R.)

Around 1898 W, C & S Hancock advertised the fact they were bringing their latest attraction of a set of Gondolas "direct from Venice," to Barnstaple Fair. Around this time they were the talk of the South West area for introducing a new form of entertainment, known as the "Living Picture Show." By then they had become known as the major amusement operators in the West Country.

The last Barnstaple Pleasure Fair of the 19th century had at least five roundabouts at the scene. A fight broke out at one of them, which put a damper on the Friday night's events. (Reference to this is given in the chapter of this book dealing with misdemeanours.)

From the days when the travelling showmen and their families arrived at the Square in wonderful horse-drawn, gaily painted and gilded caravans, and the Pleasure Fair was lighted by naptha flares, we now turn our footsteps toward, and tread happily into the 20th century fairground.

In the early part of the century people who had no access to any form of transport still walked miles into Barnstaple Fair. It has been recorded that one gentleman always walked in from Mariansleigh — many came in on foot from far beyond that.

It was a recognised practice on many farms for everyone to gather in the apple harvest during fair week, and then go the fair on the Friday. Making their journey in a long-tailed cart, they would return very late at night loaded with trinkets, and many stories to tell of all they had seen!

Unlike the 19th century, the Pleasure Fair is very rarely reported in any great detail throughout the 20th century, but what information has been gathered is mostly set out here.

It was the Fair that first brought the cinema to Barnstaple — at the turn of the century the 'Kinematograph was advertised as a sideshow. It stole most of the attention from the hitherto big spectacle of the showground, the Wild West Shows. It was said that it caused such excitement that even the country boys didn't gape quite so much in admiration of the dancing girl's free show outside their booths!

During the Boer War period (1899-1902) some of the galloping horses had their heads removed and replaced by those depicting famous generals and monarchs. The ornate scenic railway rides, having carved and gilded gondola cars riding around on undulating tracks, were changed from gondola seating to replicas of motorcars that were appearing on the roads. When motors became more and more common on the highways the cars of the roundabout were replaced by dragons.

The first Razzle-dazzle appeared in 1905 and the first appearance of the Helter-skelter at Barnstaple in 1907 was so successful at a penny a ride, that the proprietor was seen transporting his takings to the bank by the bucket load! It was also in 1907 that the cakewalk was seen. The first of Savage's electrically driven switchbacks made its presence known in 1910 but the marvellous Anderton & Rowland's Golden Dragons with its fantastic waterfall at the rear of the ride, and illuminated with many coloured lights, did not appear at Barnstaple Fair until 1922. Attracting the crowds at the top of the scenic railway steps, usually in full evening dress complete with top hat, could be seen the very well-known figures of either Sam Clements or Sol. Madden.

The Hancocks owned the largest showman's engine to come out of Burrell's works, and was known as the "Cornishman." In 1913 it fell through the road in the strand due to its heaviness.

71. 1913. Hancock's Cornishman, Barum Strand. Oops! the incredible weight was just too much for the road surface to withstand. (C.R.)

Much later Mr. Alf Whitelegg became the new owner of a three-abreast galloping horses roundabout. Although previously steam-driven it eventually became electrically operated.

(In 1927 the "Dodgems" were invented, and was soon to became part of the Barnstaple Fair scene.)

For some time no showmen were allowed into the North Walk with their equipment until 7am on the Monday morning of Fair week. This meant that any spare piece of ground would be utilised, and back lanes, alleys and yards hired and occupied. The owners of the big rides would usually park up in the railway yards, and it was a customary thing for members of the public to take a stroll around the town on the Sunday afternoon to look at all the engines, caravans etc. that had arrived. The women seated outside their living vans could be seen wrapping pieces of brightly coloured paper around bits of card that would be used in the lucky dip. Barnstaple wives would be in awe at the fairyland appearance of the caravan interiors, and their husbands probably longed to sneak a look at the magnificent engines that were still under wraps. Monday morning was the time for the Clerk of Works and his assistant to show the travellers were to set up their roundabouts, swings and shows. The smaller stalls and sideshows were erected on the Tuesday afternoon after all else had been completed, and the Clerk of works had allocated the individual pitches. Tests would be made; organs started to play; whistles blew; lights came on and roundabouts gave a free ride to anyone around at the time.

It was traditional for a showmen's ball to be held on the Tuesday evening for the showmen and their families. The venue was usually the Assembly Rooms, or on occasion, the Forester's Hall.

September 1931 "SHOWMEN'S BALL — Attended by a huge number, the annual showmen's ball was held in the Assembly Rooms, on Tuesday evening when music was discoursed by the Avalon Dance Band, with Mr. Chichester Ridd as M.C. — Refreshments were provided by Mesdames Baker, Holloway, Yeo, Jarman, Mock and Misses Bowden and Jarman."

72. The Showman's Ball held at the Assembly Rooms, Barnstaple, in 1933. Shows a happy gathering of Fair families (C.R.)

Wednesday morning would see a final polishing of brass, and baskets of flowers hung from the larger shows and roundabouts. The proclamation of the opening of the Fair at noon from the Guildhall was followed by the fairground organs playing; whistles blowing; and flags of all nations fluttering from the tops of revolving roundabouts. The Pleasure Fair was about to begin.

It was probably at its best in the <u>1920s</u>. Approaching the fair from the Strand involved having to push a way through an avenue of cheapjacks, illusionists, photographers with a cup of developing solution on a pole, and an assortment of escapologists, contortionists, pedlars and beggars, all lining Castle Street. At the entrance to the Fair 'proper' confectionery stalls selling their mixture of sweets, comfits and gingersnaps, known as "fairing," lined the way along with the fortune-tellers. Coconut shies, skittles, and Aunt Sallies came next followed by the shooting galleries. To the rear of these, parked caravans and trucks were separated by smaller steam engines that puffed away as they drove dynamos to produce light for the amusements. At the end of an avenue of small entertaining games, people entered the main part of the Fair.

On the left was the helter-skelter (a tale is told of a local Doctor losing his mat and reaching the bottom of the tower minus the seat of his trousers, which caused him to hurry home with a newspaper covering his embarrassment!) Next to it stood a set of steam driven galloping horses, ostriches, and cockerels, with a huge generating engine at its side sizzling; the smell of hot oil mixing with the aroma of fresh sawdust that was scattered around the carousel. The fair spread out from there with the big rides overshadowing the hoopla stalls and juvenile rides. A chair-o-plane stood near the famous gondola switchback, whose beautifully carved and gilded passenger cars were upholstered in red plush. After 1922 the bigger and heavier new ride, the Golden Dragons (which was electrically driven) stood next to the older, ornate ride. This was owned by Anderton & Rowland who were justifiably proud of their acquisition that had dragons with illuminated eyes and smoke belching from their mouths. Every Fair Friday a barker in a top hat and opera cloak, and holding a golden walking stick, would stand on the steps of the ride. The scenic set of a woodland glade with an illuminated waterfall, was described as "The most wonderful in the country."

(Some years there would be six or seven large rides. and other well-known names attending Barnstaple Fair at that time included — Brewer. Clements. Cribb. Conelly. DeVey. Gratton. Hancock. Harrison. Lock. Stiles. Smith. and Whitelegg.)

73. W.J. Nott's interpretation on a latterday Barnstaple Fair setting. around the Town Station (© W.J. Nott)

The shows came next with the larger ones. such as Hancock's. having an organ at the top of the steps. Performers came out and did a "turn" which drew crowds to the front of the show. Following this display a gentleman with long flowing hair. sporting a Stetson hat and carrying a gun. would persuade the crowds to "come inside." The smaller shows exhibited people of huge dimensions or dwarfs and grossly deformed human beings; animals with more legs or heads than was normal. and a self conscious young girl sitting among a display of immature pythons. Another show had a man throwing knives all around his wife — (Oops! Sorry dear!)

Billy Butlin (before he became Sir Billy of holiday camp fame) ran a "spider's web" side show. Competitors turned handles and the one who managed to get the spider into the centre. won a prize. His other side show attractions were Kentucky Derby. and Monkey-up-a-stick.

The well-known Chipperfields of Circus fame was a regular feature. and according to a spokesman the families had been visiting Barnstaple Fair for around 300 years. The proprietor of the circus once took his lion cubs to the children's ward of the North Devon Infirmary to be formally named. giving the sick children much pleasure.

Boxing Booths, offering local would-be fighters to "have a go" were supplied by Sam McKeowen, Jack Lemm, and Alf Wright. Freddie Mills, who became British Middleweight Boxing Champion, was part of the McKeowen team.

Notable characters were an accustomed part of the fair then, especially the Negro, Prince Samuda, who was an illusionist. Wearing a top hat he would be seen galloping in along North Walk with a four-horse team to get a good pitch. There he would get a member of the audience to place his fair-haired wife in a sack and securely tie it. After being placed in a trunk which was bound up, a curtain was drawn around, a pistol shot heard, then before the public's eyes Madame Samuda appeared on stage, her costume completely changed into that of a sailor.

Another Negro, with his oft-repeated phrase of "Buller, not a word" as he rolled his large eyes, balanced a cartwheel on his head and "broke copper wire on the muscle." His son, who had accompanied him, would proceed to lift 56lb weights above his head "as easily as though it were a cricket bat."

Johnny the Magician, dressed as a Turk, was another character known to the fair; his sleight of hand tricks forever deceiving the naked eye.

Mr. Tucker of Barnstaple came with his swing-boats. An artist sat in the fairground opposite the Blue Coat School and sketched portraits in charcoal for 6d. Evangelists came to preach the Gospel at the fair with unabated fervour and zeal. A German Band performed, dressed in blue uniforms and peaked caps, and a dancing bear, chained and muzzled, made its appearance at the fair; its sojourn being with its master in Green Lane.

A budgerigar in a golden cage assisted its traditionally dressed Italian girl with "fortune telling," and Welsh cockle women dressed too in their national costume, came to sell the cockles that they carried effortlessly around in hefty tubs. Grape sellers sold large almenas for 4d.and6d.a bunch. Nougat sellers sold their wares for 2d.a half bar, and Barnstaple Fairing sold at 1s.per pound; ginger snaps at four for a penny. (At this time switchback and roundabouts were a penny a ride!) The mixture of smells emanating from engines, sawdust, animals, ripe fruit, and exotic perfumes added to the fairground atmosphere.

From the screams of laughter brought forth by the effects of the tent of distorted mirrors, and the delighted excitement of small children on the juvenile rides, to the noise of the steam engines, organs, whistles, bells, and the raucous shouts of the showmen, Barnstaple Fair was apparently in its heyday.

In 1930 Barnstaple celebrated its Millenary, and the Pleasure Fair that year had some notable attractions. The big feature was described as the "Wall of Death" and was provided by Anderton & Rowland. It was said that the arena was one of the largest in the country being 41ft.in diameter. Motor cyclists (one of them a young lady) rode round and round a perpendicular wall, 17ft.high and cylindrical in shape, at amazing speeds of 50 miles an hour, that left the spectators aghast at their daring! Steel-nerved riders on Indian Scout machines performed the so- called "Death Ride."

Chipperfield's were showing their first live baby elephant ever seen at Barnstaple Fair.

Billy Lennard brought something entirely new to the Fair termed as "Britain's greatest novelty show." It was said to be full of high-class entertainment and entirely free from any suggestiveness or vulgarity, and the show was found to be entertaining and wholesome! The cabaret girls on the outside did their utmost to remain cheerful in the depressing state of the weather. (Nearly an inch and a half of rain fell during the three days of the fair, and was reported as the worst fair weather seen for many years past.)

Prince Zulamkah was present with his "Ashanti Village" and evidently the fire eating performances alone, were worth the admission fee.

Apart from the obvious attendance of the traditional fair folks and their rides, other amusements mentioned included: John Lock's animal freaks; John Anderton's mirrors; Ernest Hill's four-abreast and dodgems; Lock's three-abreast gallopers; W.Jones' chairs; Harry Coneley's slip; Cribb's and J. Cadmore's juveniles. Shooters included: J. Gratton, W. Cribb, A. Lock, and J. Whitelegg. Among the "Darts" was T. Clements. (Suffice to say the list is endless!)

Sam McKeowen's, boxing booth was advertising — Matthews, the welterweight champion, Halliday, the ex-navy jaw smasher, and Dixie Brown.

Palmists were represented by — Madam Smith and Florrie (with their brand new reception parlour), Madam Olga and Madam Myra who were described as "the posh pair from Paignton. " Madam Morffyd the "Welsh Witch", Madam Lorenzo, Madam Lylla, Madam Linton, Madam Janetta, Madam Cornelia, Gypsy Lee, the Royal Gypsy, and Abaydos, the spirit worker from the land of "Brum."

The "run-outs" (cheap-jacks) popping out in between the showers included "Flash Harry," Speedy Shelton and his Rick, Curly Brennan, Frenchy Joe, Slock, Ginger, and the "Two Mushrooms." Others who peopled the pitching colony were the "Two B.'s" (Bernard and Bert) with their cargo of yellow songbirds, "G.G." the strop selling genius and his helpmate Len, "Psycho," the pill-pushing philosopher, Stanley and Sammy, the prize "jerry-mongers" together with Percy, Arthur Roberts, the sharp sharpener-seller, Leslie Hall, the "bob-a-time" draper, and Charlie Cusworth, the clobber dealer from Oldbury.

The Barnstaple Branch of the National British Women's Total Abstinence Union, made their appearance at the fair in 1930 (this was their second year of attendance) and supplied a temperance refreshments buffet. Innumerable visitors were served with hot drinks and wholesome food, and so pressing was the need on the Friday, that closure was not possible until after midnight. (A far cry from the drunken debauchery in the Alehouses of the 19th century!)

From a Gospel wagon, in accordance with a custom observed for many years, open-air meetings were addressed at the fair. The principal speakers being from the London Open-air Mission and help being given by members of Barnstaple Rackfield Mission, and others.

It is not possible to mention all the things relating to the fair in Millenary Year, but a little snippet about a dog will make a nice ending. –

A Borzois breed of dog belonging to Mrs. Lennard, wife of one of the amusement caterers, was reported to be appearing in the film "The Devil's Maze" which had recently been released. The dog, known as Beauty, appeared as the companion of a well-known film star of the day, Miss Trilby Clarke.

The Barnstaple St. John Ambulance Association's services were demonstrated at the fair of 1931 when no fewer than thirty-two cases were dealt with! These included concussion, cuts and bruises, and cases of fainting and sickness. The Brigade, under the supervision of Supt. E. Butcher, was on duty all three days of the Pleasure Fair, and with the help of Barnstaple Nursing Division (under Supt. Mrs. Knott) fitted up a casualty ward at the Castle.

Three persons fell from the "Noah's Ark" ride at the Fair — Mrs. C. Vicary, of Barnstaple, was removed to her home. Mr. T. Stapleton, who sustained nasty wounds, and Mr. F. Dymond, a Braunton farm labourer, who sustained concussion were both conveyed by ambulance to the North Devon Infirmary.

On the Saturday morning the Brigade were summoned to the Great Western Railway yard. Evidently two employees of Messrs. Anderton and Rowland, entertainment caterers, had been engaged in getting one of the wagons on a truck; the wagon slipped and as a result both men fell heavily in the roadway. The employees named as Nat Gould, and Carlo Marino, sustained concussion and were speedily conveyed to the Infirmary.

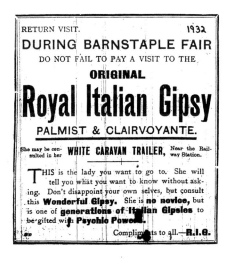

In <u>1933</u> one of the boxing tournaments featured Bert Tubbs who was a well-known Barnstaple exponent.

Great fun was provided by the clever displays of Mr. Will Golding, the conjurer. It was his first visit to the fair, and the report gave him appearing at several Royal Command Performances.

The roundabouts were said to have taken a new form with one of the most notable being the "Lightening Swirl" with cars revolving at an amazing turn of speed, and the "Ghost Train" was seen as a novel form of entertainment which proved a great draw. The "Theatre of Varieties" was distinctly meritorious by reason of the exceptionally clever performances. There were also many new attractions one of which was the "Banks" where pennies were inserted to hopefully win several more. The "Noah's Ark" proved a great venue especially to the young, and the "Golden Dragons" were said to seem more golden than ever. Another hugely popular feature was the "Dodgem Speedway" together with the familiar Eiffel Tower, coconut shies, and shooting galleries.

The remark was made that it was refreshing for many (on both entering and leaving the fairground) to hear the uplifting messages relayed by the Rackfield Mission and the local corps of the Salvation Army.

The next milestone on our Fair travels takes us to the years of the "Second World War" which greatly altered its aspect. Although the proclamation ceremonies were not allowed to lapse in order to prevent a break in tradition, the Pleasure Fair side was abandoned from <u>1939</u> until "lights went up again" in <u>1945</u>. The sweet stalls, the Chocolate Kid, and the Nougat Queen were conspicuous by their absence (due to rationing) and the grape vendors and the like were missing. However, the amusement section made up for it, the Moon Rocket being the latest novelty. One itinerant vendor had his car ticketed for sale at £2,500 — it was a Rolls Royce!

The following year the fair was "Washed Out" when a freak gale swept North Devon. On Fair Friday Barnstaple's fairground was reduced to little more than a shambles in just half an hour with winds reaching 100mph. A large part of a tree fell on the circus "big top" and wrecked all but the front of the structure — fortunately no one was inside at the time. Stalls and small sideshows suffered heavy damage with some of those around the Town Station area being blown into the road. A few of the larger amusements re-opened later, but the spirit of Barnstaple Fair was completely absent.

Mr. Heal, proprietor of the Moon Rocket, said it was the worst he had witnessed in 40yrs. And it was a bitter blow for the showmen especially the small businesses. Mr. Thomas Whitelegg, the biggest proprietor of rolling stock at the fair, agreed that it had completely knocked them all and everyone would be out of pocket.

BARNSTAPLE FAIR - - - 1945
LOOK OUT FOR THE NAME :
T. WHITELEGG,
who this year is presenting the
FOUR MOST UP-TO-DATE SUPER RIDES
ever seen at Barnstaple Fair :
1 — Dodgems Superb. 2 — Ben Hur Cycle Speedway (50 miles an hour; 'fastest ride in the Fair). 3 — The Double Thriller, the Waltzer. 4 — Electric Speedway (with 20 Sports Cars).
1,000 SMILES AN HOUR
on
WHITELEGG'S RIDES.

One of the major attractions at the Festival of Britain in London — the "Rotor" — made its debut at Barnstaple Fair in 1951, having been brought by Mr. Jimmy Hill. The price of fuel had risen putting a strain on the profits of some of the showmen. One firm alone had eight generators each using 30 gallons of oil per night! Also, it was feared that many of the country visitors would not be in attendance at the Fair due to the harvest still to be gathered in.

For the first time since the 1860s Mrs. Annie Lock (Granny to generations of show people) was not at the Fair. A few months previous, the grand old lady of the fairground had passed away at Bristol. She was in her 98th year.

In 1953 showmen were blaming reduced profits on television competition, and people spending their money on trips to London for the Coronation. Mr. Tom Whitelegg, who was attending his 69th fair at Barnstaple believed the public were getting more "choosey" and Mr. DeVey put forward the opinion that there wasn't much glamour in the modern day rides; the old gondolas had gone. The magnificent 98-key golden organ that had always accompanied the old rides was still there at that time for the Barnstaple Fair visitors. The new ride site for that year was occupied by the "Swoosh." The place was formerly the home to the "Octopus" and the "Rotor."

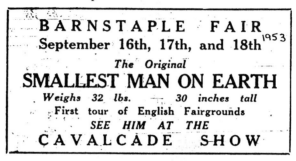

BARNSTAPLE FAIR
September 16th, 17th, and 18th 1953
The Original
SMALLEST MAN ON EARTH
Weighs 32 *lbs.* — 30 *inches tall*
First tour of English Fairgrounds
SEE HIM AT THE
CAVALCADE SHOW

1955 — "There are no nude shows at this year's Barnstaple Fair," said one of the amusement caterers. It would appear that in the previous year, some strip-tease shows and "art studies" had come to Barnstaple, which resulted in a number of complaints, particularly from the local authorities and church officials. The Showmen's Guild and the majority of the showmen were against the shows making a return visit.

The newest and fastest ride in the fair was the "Jet Ride" which was driven by compressed air, and carried thirty-six people in twelve "rockets." Another new attraction, a mechanical greyhound, racing stadium, was said to be the only one of its kind travelling on the road. The West of England Boxing Academy was making its first appearance at Barnstaple Fair, and included the "villain of the mat world" known throughout the country as Charlie Northy, "The Golden Terror."

Gaily painted caravans were reported as parked tightly together along North Walk, having come as far away as Oxford and Weymouth, for the second largest fair in the West. The oldest traveller was 86 year-old Mrs. Clara Hurrell, who had been making the annual visit to Barnstaple all her life. "I shall be at my Coconut-shy all the time," she was reported as saying.

It was also in 1955 that three well-known personalities were missing from the fair. Fifty-six year old Mr. Henry Charles, died suddenly on the Monday as everyone was ready to pull their waggons into place. Known as "Pyjama Johnny" he had been an attraction at Barnstaple Fair for a good many years, and was chairman of the West of England section of the Showmen's Guild.

1953

HERE AGAIN
at Your Fair

PYJAMA
JOHNNY
with

BIGGER AND BETTER
PRIZES THAN EVER

Consisting of Morphy-Richards pop-up TOASTERS; Prestige PRESSURE COOKERS; Premier ELECTRIC KETTLES; Pifco HAIR DRYERS; PRAMS; PUSH CHAIRS; Chilten TEDDY BEARS; BONE CHINA; decorated TEA SERVICES; 8-day CLOCKS, EIDERDOWNS; BLANKETS; BEDSPREADS; 33-piece CANTEENS OF CUTLERY; DOLLS; coloured SHEETS and PILLOW CASE SETS; etc., etc., etc.

Barny and Joy Worth, both weighing well over 20 stones, had died during the year. Joy passed away first, then Barny followed not long after from a broken heart.

In 1956 leading showmen confirmed that Rock 'n' Roll music would not be played at the fair. "We do not believe in the rubbish," said Mr. T. Whitelegg. The comment from Mr. J. Gratton was - "We are hear to keep the peace; not to make strife."

Supplies of coconuts for one of the oldest sideshows — the coconut shy - was seriously delayed by the Suez Canal crisis.

Three Africans and a Londoner were among the newcomers at Sam McKeowen's boxing booth, together with a troupe of all-in wrestlers.

The sideshows included, Miranda the Mermaid; La Belle Mimi; The Jungle Girl; The Palace of Varieties; and the Paris Revue.

The fair scene went on much as usual during the 1960s until 1967 when its removal to the site on Seven Brethren Bank, saw the crowds crossing Barnstaple Long Bridge eager as ever to join in 'all the fun of the fair.' There were the usual number of attractions, which included the waltzers; four rinks of dodgems; the big wheel and the helter-skelter.

Skipping along to the 1980s we find the charges for the roundabouts are 25p.and the dodgems 40p.

In 1989 it was said - "Much of the 'fun of the fair' has disappeared from the town since its removal from the centre to the Seven Brethren Bank."

Into the 1990s and nearing the end of the 20th century, bigger and faster rides have taken the place of some of the older familiar attractions, but the Gallopers, Helter-skelter, Big Wheel, Noah's Ark, Waltzers, Dodgems and even the Ghost Train are still holding their own. The traditional Shooting Galleries, Darts and Hoopla stalls, stand cheek by jowl with the newer innovations. "Cheap Jacks" are still to be found, but somehow lack the eccentricities and character of yesteryear. Fairing as usual is purchased in abundance, although some would say that it isn't a patch on the locally made toothsome quality from the old days!

The smell of the Fish & Chip van that was always parked outside the Police Station in Castle Street, has now been overtaken by the pungent odours from the modern day hotdog, hamburger and onion stands, which waft across the river from the fairground.

The 'nice to know' bit is that many of the familiar showmen and their families are still attending Barnstaple Pleasure Fair. It's just another generation of them that are now entertaining us, and we trust, will long continue to do so!

74. Dr Martin Fry, a guest at the 1996 fair opening ceremony, accompanies
Carnival Queen, Melanie Down, on one of the fairground rides
(Photograph © Dave Fry)

74A. (Photograph © Dave Fry)

75. Rowlands Groove Rider in 1996 attracts the attention of Barnstaple Fair Guests (Photograph © Dave Fry)

76. 1996, Seven Brethren fair site, (taken from the roof of the Leisure Centre.) (Photograph © M. Burridge)

The Showmen's Guild & A Few 'Fair Folk' Facts

In 1889 Parliament planned to restrict and licence all caravans. The travelling showmen were most affected and consequently this would have made the lives of the fairground families almost impossible. A group of showmen formed a Van Dweller's Association to defend their interests and were successful in defeating the legislation. Later, the Association became known as the Showmen's Guild.

The Guild's rulebook ensures that all members have equal status within the Guild, and the rules cover such matters as the orderly running of fairs and the conduct of members, both on and off the fairgrounds.

The Guild is accepted at both national and local levels as the negotiating body for travelling showmen, the administration and operation being democratically determined by its members. Forming the base of the Guild's structure is a system of ten regional sections covering the whole of Great Britain. The South West area is covered by section 7 — Western.

The organisation of a fair such as Barnstaple's is mainly in the hands of the Guild. Since Barnstaple Fair moved to the Seven Brethren Bank site in 1967, the allocation of positions on the fairground have been undertaken by the Showmen's Guild. With the aid of a tape measure and pegs, individual plots are marked out for occupancy of the various amusements. (Previously this job had been the responsibility of a borough council official.) In Barnstaple's case the ground rental (or toll) is eventually paid to the Town Council.

Today, advertising for fair events is made in 'The World's Fair,' which is a weekly trade paper published by the Guild. Prospective tenants learn of any relevant details in this way, and it is also a means of helping fairground families to keep in touch with each other. The newspaper is commonly known as the 'Showmen's Bible.'

The Showman's Life:

Life has always been a hard one for fairground workers. Most of the work involves forever erecting, dismantling and repairing equipment, and is not often seen by the public. Fairground families are constantly on the move from one event to another, and whatever the weather — foul or fair — 'the show must go on!'

One of the important elements of a showman's life is his caravan or living-wagon, being both his home and business headquarters. In the olden days his wagon was a horse-drawn wooden one, picturesquely painted, and quite often cramped. The modern day caravan couldn't be more different: economic and imaginative planning creating a well fitted kitchen, bathroom etc. They have comfortable and airy living areas, many having under-floor heating.

The most important thing to a showman is his family; divorce is virtually unknown, and the support of the closely-knit travelling community is paramount. Fairground families usually know each other very well, and most can claim a family history in the business, which goes back several generations or even centuries!

Barnstaple Fair:

One of the most famous names that came to Barnstaple Fair was that of the Hancock Family who were Plymouth Show-folk in the 1890's, consisting of two brothers — William and Charles — and their sister, Sophie. Charles had a wooden leg and was known by the familiar name of "Peggy" and Sophie adopted no less than sixteen children — many of whom travelled from fair to fair with the family. It was Sophie, dressed in a jersey, short skirt, and wearing men's boots, who was the prominent figure that directed the erection of the famous "Hancock's Galloping Horses."

SHOWLAND FAMILIES assembled outsid W.C & S Hancocks "LIVING PICTURES AND MENAGERIE SHOW" Barnstaple Fair 1900. Showman's Engine "Lord Roberts" extreme left of picture. Note the large number of boys in front row many of whom were adopted by the Hancock family.

77. This wonderful photograph of showmen's families was taken at Barnstaple Fair in 1900. The caption gives some interesting information, particularly that many of the boys in the front row were adopted by the Hancock family (C.R.)

78. Hancock's show at Barnstaple Fair in 1908 (C.R.)

Another showman was Henry Haslam, who out of respect for the man who taught him the business changed his own Christian name to Anderton, and eventually, together with his son, Rowland, traded under their Christian names founding the now familiar firm of "Anderton and Rowland's." (In 1954 the business celebrated its show business centenary.) Rowland's sister Martha married George DeVey, who was a descendant of a French Revolution refugee family — he became one of the most famous showmen ever to come to Barnstaple Fair at the North Walk site. Anderton and Rowland's amusements are still part of our local fair scene, and at the end of the 20th century are now being managed by the DeVey family.

79. 1911. Mr T Rowland & family ~
Mrs Rowland is the lady with the eyepatch. (C.R.)

The 'Whitelegg' showmen started in the business slightly later than Anderton and Rowland's. Mr. Tom Whitelegg (his wife's name was Rosie) was reported in 1955 as having been a showman for 70 years. In 1945 he advertised his rides for Barnstaple Fair as "1,000 smiles an hour" and the Ben Hur Cycle Speedway as being "the fastest ride in the fair." The Whitelegg name is still a familiar one at our fair event, especially with Billy Whitelegg's ride — 'The Twister.'

Many memories regarding the McKeowen family of boxing booth fame are still related. Sam McKeowen was the famous promoter, but it is Esther McKeowen that former Mayor William (Bill) Forward remembers so well. The following information was given to me by Bill with his permission to quote him for inclusion in this chapter.

Left to right..Jimmy Jury..Battling Jojo..Albert Cann..Bob Turner..
Reg Ballinger..Joe Underwood..Pat McKowen..Freddie Mills..Esther McKowen

80. Barnstaple Fair sometime in the 1930s shows the contestants fronting Sam McKeowen's Boxing Booth. Freddie Mills (future British Middleweight Champion) is on the right of the group. Taking the entrance money on the far right is Esther McKeowen (C.R.)

"The McKeowens were part of Barnstaple Fair right through the 20th century and may well have been attending for many years before that. For most of the time they ran a boxing booth. There were demonstration bouts by the professionals and then young local men were challenged to go three rounds with one of the boxers. If they lasted they won a sum of money. I remember in the 1930s it was £3. They rarely lasted three rounds.

Mrs. McKeowen was 90 years old in 1987. We presented her with a town plaque. She told me then that she had come to every Barnstaple Fair since her birth in 1897. She said she even came before she was born during her mother's pregnancy!

When I gave her the plaque she was still very active and taking money at the pay desk of one of the shows, although the boxing booth has long since disappeared. She said that she enjoyed a cigar and a drop of whisky and added with a twinkle that other pleasures were now more limited!

The incredible climax to this story is that ten years later in 1997 she was still attending the Fair and of course we made a big occasion of her hundredth year of attendance. Although now needing a wheelchair she was still as bright and humorous as ever. She has now passed away but her family are still prominent members of the showmen's community."

Some of the other families who came to Barnstaple Fair in the earlier part of the 20th century and are still attending are — the Clements who now include members of the Gratton family, (Mr. Tommy Gratton liked to buy his shirts in Barnstaple) Cribb, Smith, and Hurrell. The 'Gallopers' brought along by David Rowland is always a welcome sight as are all the other familiar amusements, and of course, the 'Fair Folk' themselves.

Snippets:
A travelling caravan is always placed on site during Barnstaple Fair for the educational needs of the showmen's children.

On Barnstaple Fair Thursday, the showmen entertain local disadvantaged children.

81. 1932. Annie (Granny) Lock and Mrs Tommy (Rosie) Whitelegg. Annie died in 1951 in her 98th year. (C.R.)

82. Barnstaple Fair in the 1930s. The photo shows a gathering of 'Fair folk'. Left to right: Mr Tommy Gratton, Lizzie Cribb, Mr Bill Cribb, George Stubbs, Ernie DeVey, Sarah Cribb, Tom Cribb, Fay Cribb, Tommy Clements and Nellie Cribb (C.R.)

83. The 1930s photo, taken at Barnstaple Fair, shows, left to right, Tom Clements, Fay Clements, Henry Jones, Mrs W Cribb and Mr W Cribb (C.R.)

84. 1936. Rev. H.Muller with Irene McKeowen and some of the Gratton family. Young J.Gratton stands in front of Irene and the young man with the dog is most likely one of the Lock family. (Irene McKeowen was the second eldest of the family and used to wrestle in the show. She was the mother of a very prominent Hampshire showlady, Bernice Wall.) (C.R.)

85. 1922. Alf wright with walking stick points out the attractions for entering the exhibition. A notice announces that it is the show's first visit to Barnstaple Fair, entrance fee is: adults 2d., children 1d. It is not clear what the entertainment is ... (C.R.)

86. 1934. Miss Grace Paulo, Miss H. Paulo, sister Clara and family, Albert Flexmore. Madame Clara & her two sons. (C.R.)

𝔄 "𝔉air" 𝔚eather 𝔯eport

"We all do pray the weather be fine
'til it be past old Barum's Fair-time"

Oh the vagaries of the weather! And none can be more relevant than those of Barnstaple's Great Fair. Invariably the remark for that occasion is, "you can tell it's Barnstaple Fair week — it's raining!" It does appear to be the accustomed view, however, upon reflection all is not as it seems. Take heart all you fair visitors — fine weather has honoured the event more than we know!

The Fineness of the Fair in the 19th century:

1829 In consequence of the fine weather the country neighbours were better employed in saving the outstanding corn.

1833 Favoured with unusually fine weather.

1836 Promoted by the fineness of the weather the fair "drew a large and motely group from the surrounding country."

1838 The weather was very propitious.

1840 ⎫
1841 ⎬ All fine
1843 ⎭

1844 Both the business and the pleasures of the fair were facilitated due to a welcome succession of bright and dry days — "The weather throughout the week has been the finest that could be desired. It is an old remark the Barnstaple Fair is always rainy; but this year has proved to be a most Agreeable exception to it."

1846 "Favoured by the most delightful weather."
1849 "Delightfully fine."
1850 No finer September.
1851 Favouring influence of very beautiful weather.
1855 ⎱ Both fine
1857 ⎰
1866 Very favourable.
1870 Unusually fine weather.
1871 Glorious days.
1875 ⎫
1876 ⎪
1877 ⎬ All fine
1879 ⎭
1881 Beautiful weather throughout.
1882 ⎫
1883 ⎪
1884 ⎬ All fine
1885 ⎭
1886 Magnificent weather.
1888 Delightfully fine.
1897 Delightfully fine.
1898 Brilliantly fine weather and completion of harvesting
     work combined to produce a record attendance at the fair.
1899 Long drought conditions are mentioned.

The Foul of the Fair in the 19th century:
1839 Tolerable but heavy rains retarded the harvest.
1842 Tremendous showers accompanied by cold winds
     throughout the week.
1848 A tremendous storm occurred on the Friday of Fair Week
     much to the consternation of the revellers, and a report
     was given by the *North Devon Journal* - "*On Friday evening
     last, we were visited by a tremendous storm of thunder
     and lightning, accompanied by a heavy rain. The day had
     been very sultry. The storm commenced about half-past six
     o'clock, and continued, with transient intermission, until
     two the next morning. The thunder resembled a continuous
     charge of distant artillery. The lightning was extremely
     vivid: and so frequent were the flashes that they kept the
     horizon in a state of illumination for hours. It is many years*

since we have seen so much lightning in these parts. We have heard of many cases of fright from it, and some of injury, but none, we are happy to say, to human life. A bullock was killed by it at Bishop's Tawton, the property of Mr. Humphrey Ghent; another at Chittlehampton, belonging to Mr. Joce; and Another, we have heard, in the same parish belonging to Mr. Facey."

1859 Disagreeable, with much rain early on.

1864 Cold with rain heavily descending in incessant showers. (This is the subject of "A Young Lady's Lament for the Wet Fair" in the 'Fair Poems' section.)

1868 Twenty years later Barnstaple was the victim of another thunderstorm on fair Friday, and again we have the 'North Devon Journal' to thank for the intelligence report. — *"On Friday last, at about four p.m. the town of Barnstaple was visited with a terrific thunderstorm, which lasted for nearly an hour. Rain descended in torrents, flooding numerous houses and sending a deluge of water through the various streets, to the great inconvenience of the thousands of visitors to the Annual Fair. We regret that considerable injury was also done to property, especially in the vicinity of the Square. The basement of Mr. Thornby's premises was flooded and flour and other articles in stock either destroyed or greatly damaged; the shop was also covered with water to the depth of six inches; and the consequence will be a loss of several pounds to an industrious tradesman. The state of the stalls and exhibitions in the Square, where a great concourse had gathered, may be imagined — it beggars description; everywhere there was a waste of waters which accumulated until it became truly alarming. Happily the subsidence of the rain and the ebbing of the tide so as to open the outfalls of the sewers prevented any further damage. The rain was accompanied by thunder and vivid flashes of lightning, which increased the alarm of the timid and hastened their departure to their homes."* (During the storm, two bullocks were struck by lightning whilst grazing in a field at Pilton, and died instantaneously. They were the property of Mr. John Sanders, wool merchant.)

1872 } Unfavourable - lowering and cold.
1873 }

1880 Constant drizzle varied by sharp showers ensured the "Fair umbrellas were as much in requisition as the drover's stick."

1887 }
1889 }
1890 } These years varied from unfavourable conditions to heavy rain.
1891 }
1896 }

All the in-between years not mentioned from the 1830s to end of the century, appear to have had mixed weather conditions for Barnstaple Fair.

It is interesting to find that during 70 years of Barnstaple Fair in the 19th century 31 enjoyed beautiful weather; 17 had a mixed bag; and only 14 appears to have had a rainy event!

Up to the first half of the 20th century the wettest fair was in 1920, although the millenary year of 1930 took some beating with one and a half inches of rain recorded over the Wednesday and Friday.

The following year "faired" much better as it was reported as being fine, and in 1932 it was "The most brilliant weather remembered for many years."

1928, 1938, and 1948 were all completely dry. (Eight is the showmen's lucky no.)

1946 is remembered for the freak gale that swept North Devon making the Fair a washout in scarcely 30 minutes! Very early in the afternoon, winds reaching 100 m.p.h. on "Fair Friday" wreaked total havoc in the fairground and the surrounding areas. The small stall-holders and sideshows were put completely out of business; the boxing booth received a "knock-out" early in the storm, and the circus next door was completely wrecked apart from the front of the structure, when part of a tree landed on its "big top." Hundreds of pounds worth of broken glass and crockery littered the North Walk, and thousands of pounds in business was lost from the fair as a whole. Apparently the 'Big Wheel' stood the ordeal well but the 'Auto Cars' were quickly flooded out along with many other amusements. Although the roundabouts swiftly organised themselves for business again after the freak conditions had passed, it was said that the spirit of Barnstaple Fair was completely absent.

At the height of the storm a wooden shed from the roof garden of the Bell Hotel landed on the roof of the Regal Cinema. During the removal of the shed the film programme was temporarily halted. On the river Taw nearly all the small rowing boats around the Rock Park boathouse were either driven into the bank or thrown on to land; several were sunk. Women who had set out from the Sticklepath district to visit the Fair were forced to turn back at the bottom of the hill. Roads throughout the district were knee deep in branches and frequently blocked by fallen trees. Many farmers returning to outlying areas from Barnstaple Fair met with precarious conditions on the roads. Large estate gardens such as Youlstone Park suffered heavy damage, and houses in Shirwell village suffered some loss. At Ilfracombe mountainous seas swept across the sea front washing away scores of deckchairs; a glass covering over the pavement at Belgrave Promenade was completely wrecked; and a tree fell across the road in front of the Ilfracombe Hotel causing the omnibus service to be held up for an hour while the trunk was sawn through in order to remove it. Mr. A. Pugsley, landlord of the Dolphin Hotel, Combe Martin, had a narrow escape when a glass roof under which he was standing collapsed. Combe Martin beach was littered with apples that had been washed downstream by the floodwater, and small boys were evidently very active in "salvage" work! (The War had been over for a year but it must have looked like a battle zone, not only at the Fair, but the whole of North Devon!)

In 1956 The North Devon Athenaeum investigated the theory that it always rained during Barnstaple Fair, and surprisingly found that of 123 consecutive fair days taken over a period of 40 years, rain fell on only 69 of them.

Time has not allowed for any assessment on the same theory for the following years up until 1999. What will be remembered however, is that the last Barnstaple Fair Saturday of the last year of the 20th century was plagued with gale force winds and torrential rain for part of the day, but it did clear away before all events were over.

To quote an old saying, "every cloud has a silver lining" and whether we remember sunshine or showers, it seems that Barnstaple Fair has seen more bright days than it has been given credit for!

The Carnival

On relating the history of Barnstaple Fair we cannot miss out the Saturday Carnival of Fair Week. This subject would make a book in itself, but that will have to remain for someone else to take up the challenge! However, a brief history of Barnstaple's Carnival is included here.

Although carnivals were held in Barnstaple from the late 19th century in aid of hospital funds, it wasn't until <u>1931</u> that they were held in their present form and became a recognised Fair Saturday feature.

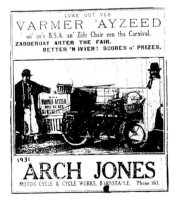

On a beautifully warm, rain free day, on <u>Saturday September 19th 1931</u> — the judging having taken place in the Cattle Market, the procession started around 5.30pm to wend its way through the thoroughfare of the town. It was well over a mile in length with 400 entrants — 300 of which were schoolchildren of the borough. The route taken started by way of North Walk (Cattle Market) along the Strand to the Square, along the full length of High Street, into Boutport Street and back to the Square, Taw Vale, Newport Road, Victoria Street, BarbicanRoad, Summerland Street, Alexandra Road, Bear Street, Joy Street and back into High Street, Pilton Road, Yeo Vale Road, Kingsley Avenue, St. George's Road, Pilton Road again, Boutport Street, finishing at the Corn Market. (What a marathon — no wonder some of the little ones dropped out along the way!)

87. Early 1930s Carnival. Parading back through the square. Behind the crowds the old and new stand together in the form of horse & carriage, and the motor car! (Thornby confectioner's shop can be seen to the right of the procession, in the centre of the picture. (© Beaford Archive)

The head of the Carnival was lead by the Marshal — Mr. A. Pleavin, followed by KING CARNIVAL — Mr. W. Lee, who was seated in a Victorian coach and pair. The 6th Devon's Band played during the procession, and a selection of the winning entrants are as follows:

Trade Section
First — Raleigh Steam Laundry tableaux depicting a miniature laundry.

Tableaux Ordinary
First — Barnstaple Branch of the British Legion portraying a concert party in a 1914 dug-out.

Original
First — Mr. W.J. Squires' three little girls, in a pretty setting of "A Christmas Eve Scene."

Mounted
Ladies:
First — Huntsman (Miss L. Penhale)
Second — Cavalier (Miss Doreen Jones)
Third — Lock's Circus (Miss Betty Lock)
Gentlemen:
First — Mexican (Mr. J. Perryman)
Second — Cowboy (Mr. A.J. Symons)
Third — Things of the Past (Mr. W.J. Squire)

Fancy Dress Pedestrian
Ladies — Twin Golliwogs (Miss Betty Stevens and Paul Stevens) First.
Gentlemen — On the Dole (A.G. Simmons and J. Littlejohns) Third.

Children's Classes
Fancy - Spanish Dancers (Joan and Enid Copp)
Comic — Capt. Slatter's Housing Scheme (Geo. Hill)
Original — Traffic Signals (Madge Hardy)
(Sydney Burrington had 6th place with "Ancient Barumite.")

It was reported that thousands of townspeople and visitors were delighted by the spectacle, and £280 was raised in aid of the North Devon Infirmary and the North Devon Children's Convalescent Home at Lynton.

(The Baby Show was won by 9 month old, Derrick Hiscock from Combe Martin.)

Afterwards, the Market Confetti Carnival took place and was attended by a huge crowd. Sideshows and competitions were well patronised, and several Fair Showmen assisted by lending their stalls and sideshows on an equal sharing basis.

The following year Miss Jean Burroughs, a pupil at Ashleigh Road School, was invited to be Barnstaple's first Carnival Queen. Her attendants were — Grace Roach, Betty England, and Flo Bond. Mr. A.C. Kempe, took the part of Carnival King.

This time the procession was a mammoth two miles in length of which, Lee's Pilton Circus was a feature — there were nearly 100 performers; including two elephants, a wild animal show, and several clowns. (It must have been a spectacular sight!) The event ended with a Carnival Dance in the Pannier Market in the evening.

Mrs Norman, a seventy eight year old lady, residing in Green Lane, was the winner of the carnival draw for a £45 motorcycle! Fortunately for the elderly lady the auctioneer, Mr. Chas.Webber, consented to dispose of the machine by auction, free of charge.

Daily Mirror,
September 18th 1933.

The 1934 Queen was Irene Perryman, (she later became Irene Kingdon) who went on to become the carnival committee's wardrobe mistress for the following 52 years. Irene, from Braunton, retired from the post at the age of 83, in 1987. (The vacancy was filled by, Mrs Vera Ackland.)

There have been many changes in the carnival over the years:

The 1939 Queen — Iris Williams — was never crowned due to the Second World War breaking out before carnival day. The annual event went on hold until 1945 when a hurriedly arranged parade took place to carry on the celebrations of the ending of the war.

In 1946 the Queen was chosen as 16yr.old Betty West, of Braunton. The crowning took place in Rock Park by the Mayoress, Mrs Romeo Berry. The carnival was arranged by the Hospital Week Committee in aid of the North Devon Infirmary, and was a huge success. Half the Pannier Market was reserved for dancing, with stalls (many from the fair) in the remainder.

A 'Mystery Man' was advertised as — spending the afternoon in Rock Park and along the route of the procession. If anyone had a Carnival Programme, they could challenge him with "You are Bobby Budd! I claim my prize." Which was one guinea.

Barnstaple Fair Carnival
1946

FRIDAY, SEPT. 13th - GAUMONT CINEMA
Final Selection of CARNIVAL QUEEN
and ATTENDANTS.

SATURDAY, SEPT. 21st.
CARNIVAL AND PROCESSION

Judging in ROCK PARK at 4 p.m.

Prizes Valued £50.

THREE BANDS IN PROCESSION.

Full details can be obtained from, and Entries should be sent (BEFORE SEPTEMBER 16th) to:—Hon. Secretary, Carnival Committee, North Devon Infirmary, Barnstaple.

Eighteen year-old Pat Hardman was the first Queen to be invited to the Fair Luncheon in <u>1949</u>, and was also the first Barnstaple Girl to be chosen as Queen for many years.

After the war, the Queen was chosen by popular vote and in the <u>1950s</u> it was not unusual for a crowd of 2,000 people to pack the Pannier Market for the occasion. With as many as 24 entrants it was run on proper election lines, with a returning officer, lieutenants and official voting papers.

In 1963 the contest was moved into the Queen's Hall. After a brief spell of ticket selling — whoever sold the most tickets became Queen — it reverted back to the 'vote.' With the Queen's Hall changing to a theatre, by the end of the 20th century voting is taking place at the Barnstaple Hotel.

It became traditional for the Mayoress to crown the Queen, and in <u>1961</u>, Mrs Betty Woolaway — who herself had been crowned in <u>1946</u> — crowned Miss Marilyn Shapland. (In 1981 it was recorded that Mrs Woolaway was the only Queen to become Mayoress of Barnstaple.)

88. 1952. Carnival Queen, Beryl Montague, after the crowning ceremony performed by the Mayoress, Mrs Cruse. (Note the prettily decorated Bandstand in Rock Park.) (C.R.)

89. 1954. Carnival Queen, Daphne Meredith, with Mayoress Mrs Clarke. (C.R.)

90. September 1962. Carnival Queen, Patricia Fry, with attendants and Guard of Honour. (C.R.)

91. Mayoress Mrs Rosie Potter crowning the Carnival Queen, Jean Pugsley, in 1973. (C.R.)

92. Barnstaple Carnival crowning ceremony of 1980. The Queen, Sue Robb, kneels before the Mayor (Ian Scott) and Mayoress. To the far left of the picture is Mrs Irene Kingdon, wardrobe mistress, and former Carnival Queen in 1934. Standing beside her is Mrs Laurie Roberts, carnival committee secretary (later chairman) - now retired. (C.R.)

The 1986 Queen's Float made by Friends of West Buckland and Filleigh P.T.A. and F.D.S. of West Buckland. Carnival Queen, Nicky Spain-Gower.

93. 1986 (from the carnival programme). (C.R.)

94. (C.R.)

In 1968 Lorna Forrester, aged 21, was the first married woman to become Queen for 33yrs.

The 1951 "Festival of Britain" inspired one entry into the carnival.

Bertie Hill, the Olympic Rider, lead the Carnival procession as Marshall in 1953. A deluge of blinding rain ruined all the efforts of the entrants and caused tableaux to be abandoned and the saturated participants to flee homewards.

By 1953, although the traditional fun fair was still being held in the market, the dance had been transferred to the 'Queen's Hall' and was advertised as a "Grand Carnival Dance." (These dances were very popular and continued up until the beginning of the 1970s.)

In 1954 Mr. Billy Lee, dressed as John Bull, acted as Marshall, and an entry from Ilfracombe arrived too late to be judged having taken six hours to make the journey!

The 1957 Carnival had a fifteen year-old schoolgirl — Miss Tonia Anderson — leading the procession. It was customary to have a man to marshal the event, but owing to sickness, Mr. William Lee had to fall out.

Torrential rain interfered with the 1958 Carnival. Lorries filled with water and entrants tried to cover up as best they could in the face of the relentless downpour. The Queen, Ellen Hill, and her attendants, braved the elements under umbrellas. The "coach" that year was covered with a thousand lemon-coloured marigolds; it had been designed in secret, and carried out by the Borough Council Parks Superintendent, Mr. R. Pelch, and his staff.

A new route starting at Pilton Park was tried out in 1959, but was reverted back to Rock Park the following year.

Around this time, R.A.F. Chivenor were holding its flying display to commemorate the "Battle of Britain" on the same day as the Carnival. The spectators wishing to see a bit of both events blocked the roads and brought North Devon to a standstill!

Mr. Francis Chichester (later to become 'Sir') was Guest of Honour in 1965, but it wasn't until 1968 that the Carnival exhibits showed mainly nautical themes with 'Noah's Ark' from Fremington Methodist Church, stealing the headlines.

In 1975 Massed Pipe Bands lead the Carnival, which was reported as being one of the most impressive and largest in post-war history.

Everything seemed to be going wrong in 1978. The popular static helicopter display was abandoned to attend a genuine rescue mission. The 5,000 people that went into the Sports Ground to see the 'Red Devils' Parachute Team perform were disappointed to find, that because of the blustery wind the event had to be called off. Floats for the procession jammed up due to late arrivals. A lady fell and broke her ankle; two people fainted; and Naomi Sykes fell off her horse!

An estimated 15,000 people watched the procession — proceeds raised, amounted to £1,300.

The Carnival held its 50th Anniversary in 1981; souvenir programmes were printed which included a full list of entrants, and a brief history of the Carnival.

In 1991 it celebrated its Diamond Jubilee with a special programme produced by the *North Devon Journal*.

The last Carnival of the 20th century — *1999* — was a potential washout with gale force winds and torrential rain forecast. The initial downpour occurred at 2.30 in the afternoon, but gradually cleared up for a, thankfully dry, procession!

The Mayor and Mayoress that year were John and Jane Wilsher. The Carnival Queen was Fiona Piper, and her attendants, Tanya Woodbridge and Sarah Friel. The Prince was

7 year old Thomas Hill, and the Princess, 6 year old Sammi Wooldridge.

95. The 1999 Carnival 'Royal Family' with the Mayor & Mayoress. (© North Devon Journal)

The Carnival Queen's gondola shaped float, was designed by Adrienne Thompson, of Saunton Sands Hotel, and was sponsored by the Brend's Hotel Group.

The top entrants' award of Supreme Champions went to the 'Sarah Anne Westcott School of Dance,' for their colourful "Barnum Bonanza," which involved teeny clowns and trapeze artists.

Among the floats, - and first in their class — was the 'Chichester Arms' with "70's Explosion;" the 'Braunton Belles' came second with "War Years," and third place went to 'Lucky's Nightclub' with, "Clowning around with Abba."

96. 1999 Carnival. Pirates, of course! The Berriman Family
(© North Devon Journal)

97. 1999 Carnvial. Braunton Belles with "Bulldog Spirit through
World War Two".
(© North Devon Journal)

Members of the Carnival Committee in its present form have changed through the decades, but lack of space prevents the mention of everyone since its inception. However, it would seem appropriate to mention the Chairman, Secretary and Treasurer, of the first and last events of the 20th century.

1931
Chairman: Mr. Fred Northcote (apparently known as Uncle Fred)
Joint Hon. Secretaries: Miss. M.J. Abbott and Mr. Reg. E. Watts.
Treasurer: Councillor G.F. Jewell.

1999
Chairman: Mrs. L.B. Roberts.
Secretary: Ms. J. Thompson.
Treasurer: Mr. R. Bliss.
(Mrs Laurie Roberts joined the committee in 1972 becoming Secretary in 1973 and Chairman in 1986.)

Every Barnstaple Carnival has raised funds for local charities, and in the past the hospitals have been one of the main beneficiaries.

In 1931 the amount raised was £280.

Between the years of 1972 and 1999, nearly £60,000 has been raised.

In recent years many small local charities and organisations have benefited from these funds.

Past and present committee members and others have put in a lot of time and much hard work to make the Carnivals a success. Appreciation of all that they do behind the scenes is not always forthcoming, but the end result of the enjoyment given and the benefits received by so many, does not go un-noticed.

The face of the Carnival has changed over the years, but one thing we can be sure of — it will continue to be part of the Barnstaple Fair scene for many "processions" to come!

Crowds watching tradesmen's tableaux passing through the Square during the great carnival procession at Barnstaple.

The Children's Favourites, a nursery rhyme group including Jack Horner, Boy Blue, Dick Whittington, and many others.

Wurzel Farm, or how to make farming pay.

A selection of scenes from Barnstaple Carnival, September 18th 1933.
(*Daily Mirror*)

Japanese Tea Garden in the class for original tableaux.

Uncle Tom Cobley and All from Combe Martin.

This charming floral tableau was entitled " A Basket of Flowers."

A selection of scenes from Barnstaple Carnival, September 18th 1933.
(*Daily Mirror*)

98. 1960s Barnstaple Carnival scene. (C.R.)

99. Bickington Youth Club float for Barnstaple Carnival, 1980.
(C.R.)

Concluding Address

And so this has been a glimpse into the history of Barnstaple Great Fair. So many changes have occurred over the centuries; hordes of fair-goers have come and gone; a great diversity of humanity have pedalled their wares; the entertainers and showmen have thrilled and delighted down through the ages. Many people have left their mark in time, from the high born down to the lowly. Some Fair traditions have been cast aside along the way — others have been protected and passed down for unending generations to enjoy. How privileged we are in this modern age to see, and be a part of this legacy.

When scarf-like wisps of mist begin to lie in little hollows, and hedgerows are laden with blackberries and the red fruit of the dog rose, we know that summer has blushed into autumn and it is time for our annual Barnstaple Fair.

The River Taw has flowed down through the centuries, and has witnessed the Fair on each side of her banks. Oh what a tale she could tell if she were able to give up her secrets!

Maybe on a fine Fair night from a retreat somewhere along the riverbank, it might be worthwhile to leave the clamour of the modern day fair behind and close our eyes for a few minutes. If we are lucky, we just might hear the rumble of a cart's wheels as it passes over the Long Bridge, and the peals of laughter of the occupants as they approach the Square. The clatter of hooves from the horse fair and the hallooing cries of the riders as they put the horses through their paces, would certainly be part of our thoughts. Listen carefully, and we will hear the joyous peals of the church bells, the high-pitched sound of voices and cacophony of noise and music drifting across the water from the 19th century fairground!

All too soon our little dream will fade away, and so too will our modern day fair. The showmen, their families with all paraphernalia, will once more head their caravans out into the highways; Barnstaple's saturnalia has ended for another year.

Generations of "Fair Folk" have visited Barnstaple Great Fair for hundreds of years, and it is to be hoped that the tradition will be kept alive for centuries to come.

Bibliography and Sources

Town Council Archive
North Devon Athenaeum
Barnstaple Record Office
North Devon Journal (1824-1999)
North Devon Herald (1913)
The Cave and Lundy Review (1824)

Tom Bartlett — *Postcard Views of North Devon* Vol.IV

R.D.Blackmore — *Lorna Doone* (1869) & *The Maid of Sker* (1872)

J.R.Chanter & Thomas Wainright — (reprint of) *Barnstaple Town Records* Vols 1-2 (1900)

W.F.Gardiner — *Barnstaple 1837-1897* (1897)

Joseph Besly Gribble — *Memorials of Barnstaple* (1830)
(reprint: Edward Gaskell, Lazarus Press, 1994)

Lois Lamplugh — *Barnstaple Town on the Taw* (Phillimore, 1983)

W.J. Nott — *Amusements at Barnstaple Fair. 1875 -1925* (unpublished)

Showmen's Guild of Great Britain — *All the Fun of the Fair* (Showmen's Guild, 1987)

Barnstaple Town Council — *Barnstaple Guildhall* (1986)

J. Weare-Gifford — *The Golden Bay*

Richard Wood — *History of Markets and Fairs* (Wayland, 1996)

Printed and Bound by Lazarus Press
Bideford Devon